IMAGES
of America

THE VILLAGE OF GROSSE POINTE SHORES

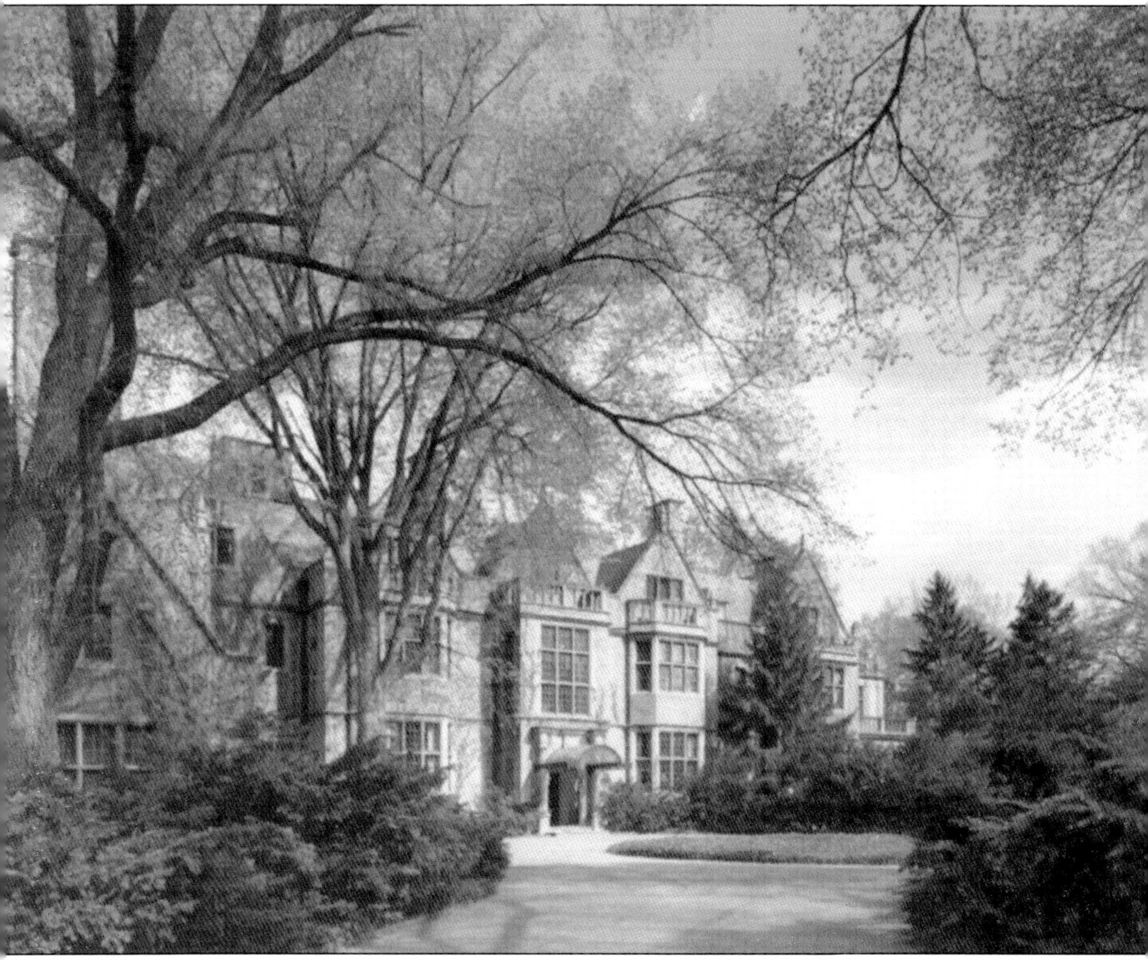

THE SCHLOTMAN HOUSE. This was one of the grandest of the great mansions that once lined Lake Shore Road in the Village of Grosse Pointe Shores. In 1914, Joseph and Stella Schlotman commissioned Albert Spahr of Pittsburgh to design their new home, which they named Stonehurst. Completed in 1917 at a cost estimated at $2 million, this 40-room manor with its beautiful gardens occupied 30 acres fronting on Lake St. Clair. (Courtesy of the Balathazar Korab Collection, Grosse Pointe Historical Society.)

ON THE COVER: ENTRANCE TO THE CLAIREVIEW FARM. This is the entrance to the Claireview Jersey Stock Farm with its long driveway leading to the two-story house and grounds. The shape of the farm was patterned after the early French ribbon farms. The Claireview Farm measured two miles deep with 1,400 feet of lake frontage. Today, Claireview Road in the Village of Grosse Pointe Shores marks the location of the farm. (Courtesy of the Burton Historical Collection, Detroit Public Library.)

IMAGES
of America

THE VILLAGE OF GROSSE POINTE SHORES

Arthur M. Woodford

ARCADIA
PUBLISHING

ISBN 978-1-4671-1299-4

Published by Arcadia Publishing
Charleston, South Carolina

Printed in the United States of America

Library of Congress Control Number: 2014940528

For all general information, please contact Arcadia Publishing:
Telephone 843-853-2070
Fax 843-853-0044
E-mail sales@arcadiapublishing.com
For customer service and orders:
Toll-Free 1-888-313-2665

Visit us on the Internet at www.arcadiapublishing.com

Grateful acknowledgements are made to
the Victoria and Robert G. Liggett Jr. family
and
John Armaly
for their generous support of the publication of this book.

Contents

ACKNOWLEDGMENTS

As with any book of this type, the author usually needs to thank a number of people for their assistance. It seems to me that this phrase is particularly true for this particular book. For I, indeed, had the help of many people in the selection and preparation of the photos and the manuscript for this book. To all the archivists, museum curators, librarians, historical society staffs, village staff, local residents, colleagues, new friends and old—thank you. Here is my list: Grosse Pointe Historical Society, Izzy Donnelly, Helga Liedtke, and Pam Scanlon; St. Clair Shores Historical Commission, Cynthia Bieniek; Monroe County Historical Museum, Christine Kull; Burton Historical Collection, Mark Bowden, Ronnie Minor, Dawn Eurich, and James Evenhius; National Automotive History Collection, Paige Plant; The Henry Ford, James Orr; Albert Kahn Associates, Donald Bauman and Robert Sharrow; Bentley Historical Collections, Malgosia Myc; Manning Brothers Historic Photograph Collections, Alyn Thomas; Reuther Archives, Elizabeth Clemens; the staffs at First English Lutheran Church, Grosse Pointe Woods Presbyterian Church, and Grosse Pointe Memorial Church; Grosse Pointe Public Library, Vickey Bloom and Kim Hart; Grosse Pointe Yacht Club, Larry Stephenson; Edsel & Eleanor Ford House, Cindy Olsen; Detroit Historical Society, Joel Stone; Web Litho Inc., Bob Murphy and Jim Ryniak; the Osius family; Thomas W. Brunk; Thomas P. Kliber; Lynn Kurtz; and Kenneth Schramm. In addition, I must thank Village of Grosse Pointe Shores Mayor Ted J. Kedzierski, Mayor Pro Tem Bruce Bisballe, and Council Members Alexander Ajlouni, Robert Barrette, Kay Felt, Robert Gesell, and Daniel Schulte; Ambassador Committee chairperson D.J. Boehm and members Gloria Anton, Alex Lucido, Madeline Phillips, and Chase Wakefield; Village of Grosse Pointe Shores Council Liaison Kay Felt; Village of Grosse Pointe Shores administrative staff City Manager Mark Wollenweber, Laurie Duncan, Tom Krolczyk, and Lynn Michaux; and Chief of the Department of Public Safety John J. Schulte. And finally, a special thank-you to my wife, Mary Rose, for her support and her understanding.

INTRODUCTION

Nestled along the shore of Lake St. Clair, just to the north and east of the city of Detroit, is the Village of Grosse Pointe Shores. At 1.1 square miles, 18.1 square miles of Lake St. Clair waters, and a population of only 3,000, the Village of Grosse Pointe Shores is the smallest of the five Grosse Pointe communities but has the longest shoreline. Yet, the community is the most unique. This residential community has no business district and only one commercial property, the Grosse Pointe Yacht Club, and one not-for-profit property, the Edsel & Eleanor Ford House.

Although small in size, the Village of Grosse Pointe Shores has a long and fascinating history. Like the other Grosse Pointe communities, the area was a stopping off point for Native Americans traveling the waterways of the Great Lakes. During stormy weather that turned the normally calm lake dangerous, these early travelers would often use the Milk River, located at the northern edge of what is now Grosse Pointe Shores, travel through the Black Marsh, and along the Fox Creek as a shortcut to reenter the Detroit River.

After the settlement of Detroit in 1701, the area that would one day become Grosse Pointe Shores saw the arrival of French settlers, or habitants. Their early homes and farms were built with lake frontage of 200 to 800 feet. These farms extended back in some cases two to three miles. In this fashion, each family had access to the water. Because of their distinctive long and narrow shape, these properties became known as "ribbon farms."

During the first decades of settlement, the region was a quiet French farming community. Then, beginning in the 1850s, the area began to change as Detroit industrial leaders and wealthy families began building summer homes along the shore of Lake St. Clair. These "cottages" were usually built on several acres of property, where some of their owners even maintained small farms. This little community soon became a most desirable place to live. It was not long before some of these homes became year-round residences.

The next major change to the area came in the 1880s with the development of the interurban railway system. The Shore Line Division of the interurban started in downtown Detroit and traveled through the Grosse Pointes, St. Clair Shores, and on to Mount Clemens. This new form of rapid transit enabled residents to easily commute between their homes and jobs in the city of Detroit. It was not long thereafter that another new form of transportation appeared—the motorcar, and it too would usher in a new era of change.

By the end of the 19th century, more substantial homes were being built all along Lake Shore Road. In 1911, the residents of the community, under the leadership of successful Detroit businessman George Osius, voted to establish a more manageable form of local government, the Village of Grosse Pointe Shores. George Osius built his new home on Lake Shore Road and was instrumental in local affairs for more than 30 years.

The breathtaking views of the lake are a focal point for the community. Drawn by the inviting waters, avid sailors and owners of fine sailing yachts and powerboats migrated to Grosse Pointe Shores. In the winter months, many of the younger men joined in the sport of iceboating. It was this interest in sailing, both in the warmer days of summer and the coldest days of winter, that inspired a group of village residents to found the Grosse Pointe Yacht Club in 1914. Originally open only to residents of the village, the club members first met in each other's homes. This soon changed. In 1929, a grand clubhouse and harbor were constructed on the lake at the foot of Vernier Road. The club prospered and grew and is today one of the most prestigious yacht clubs in the country.

It was also at this time, when the Village of Grosse Pointe Shores was formally established, that the first of the great mansions were built along Lake Shore Road as year-round estates for some of Detroit's most important industrial leaders and wealthiest families. These grand homes, many designed by world-renowned architects, were built to last, but in reality, most survived for only a relatively short period of time. With the passing of the original patriarchs and matriarchs, family members subdivided the grand estates and rebuilt the land with luxurious homes.

One of the largest of these estates that did survive was that of Edsel and Eleanor Ford. Located on the site known as Gaukler Point where the Milk River flows into Lake St. Clair, this grand estate became the new residence of the Edsel Ford family in 1929. Edsel, at the time president of the Ford Motor Company, was the only son of Henry Ford. The estate continued to serve as the family's home until Eleanor Ford's death in 1976. Today, following her wishes, this beautiful estate is open to the public and is one of Michigan's premier cultural attractions.

Many of the cosmopolitan residents of the Village of Grosse Pointe Shores traveled widely. Closer to home, nearby downtown Detroit was the location for many career and professional endeavors, upscale shopping, professional sporting events, arts, and world-class cultural events. Residents also enjoyed the convenience of nearby amenities in the other Grosse Pointes, including golf, private clubs, shopping, churches, libraries, schools, and hospitals.

By the end of the 20th century, the Village of Grosse Pointe Shores had grown into an impeccable, established community of beautiful homes, fine landscaping, and stunning lake views. On February 24, 2009, the residents of Grosse Pointe Shores, looking to enhance their local form of government, voted to incorporate as a city with the name the Village of Grosse Pointe Shores, A Michigan City. Two years later, during the summer of 2011, these residents celebrated the 100th anniversary of this special community.

The citizens are proud of their heritage and their history, and it is this story that will be told on the pages of this book.

One

The Early Years

The first visitors to what is now Grosse Pointe Shores were Native Americans traveling the waterways of the Great Lakes. They had no known permanent settlement here but undoubtedly stopped here on their journeys on the lakes. Detroit was founded in 1701 by the French to control the lucrative fur trade of the Great Lakes. Before long, French families began establishing farms along the Detroit River and along Lake St. Clair. These farms consisted of river frontage of 200 to 800 feet, and in many cases extended back two to three miles. In this manner, each farm had access to clear, clean lake water. Because of this distinctive long and narrow shape, these eventually became known as ribbon farms. Although Detroit came under control of the British in 1760 and then the Americans in 1796, the region now known as Grosse Pointe Shores remained a quiet French farming community. That changed around the time of the American Civil War when well-to-do Detroit families and industrial leaders began building summer cottages along the picturesque shores of Lake St. Clair. Before long, permanent, sometimes spectacular, year-round homes and estates replaced the cottages. During these years, a trip to Detroit by horse and buggy or boat was a long journey. The principal route was along the river road, which was known as Jefferson Avenue in Detroit and Lake Shore Road by the time it reached present-day Grosse Pointe Shores. All this changed in the 1880s with the construction of the Detroit United Railway interurban system. Beginning in Detroit, the interurban lines stretched out north, west, and east. The Shore Line Division, built along Lake St. Clair, passed through the Grosse Pointes on its way to Mount Clemens. Although the interurban drastically reduced travel time to and from the city, the horse and buggy was still the principal mode of transportation along Lake Shore Road. Then, in the first decade of the 20th century, a new form of transportation, the automobile, arrived, and life along Lake Shore Road changed yet again.

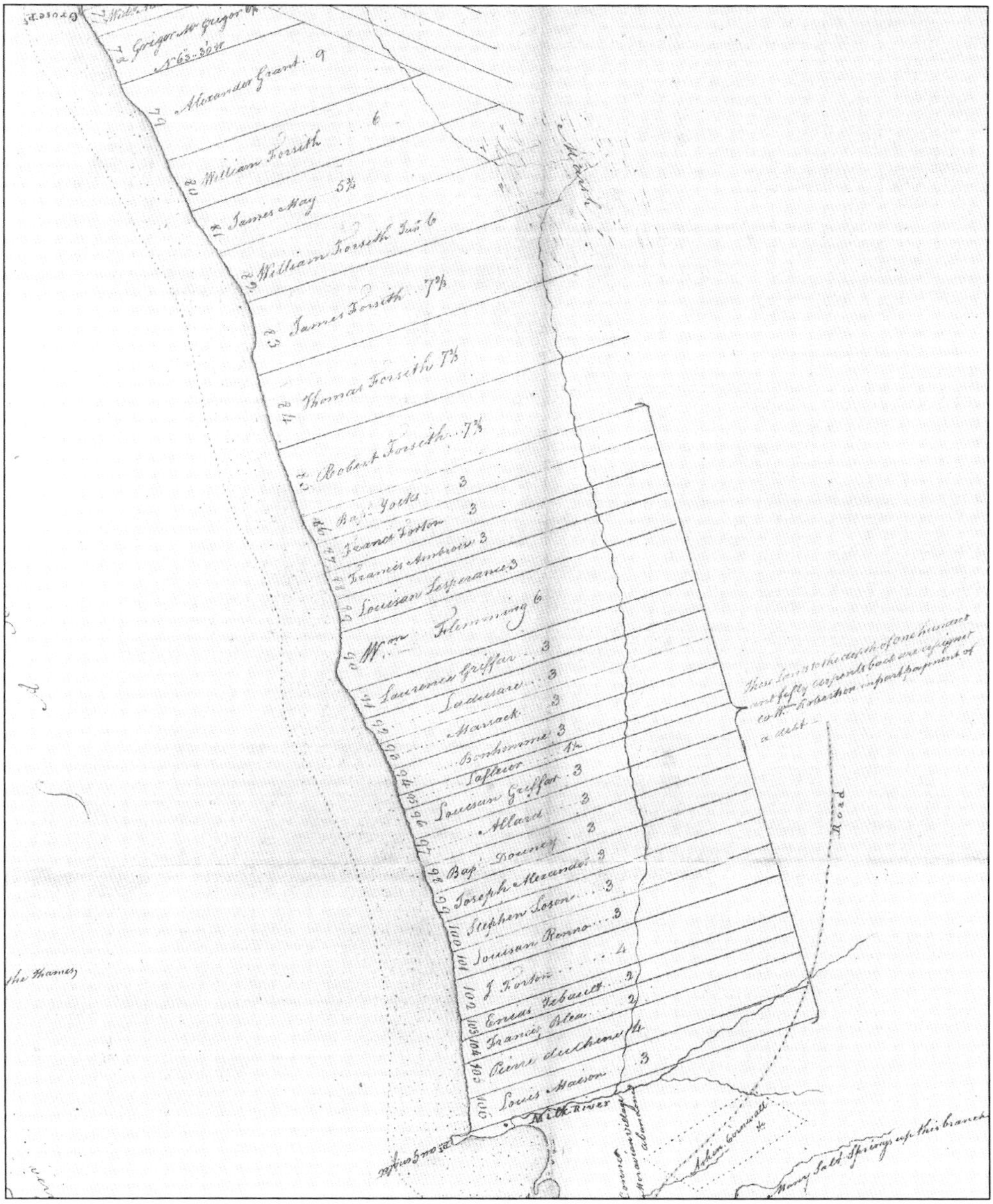

McNiff's Map of 1796. When the Americans finally took control of Detroit from the British in 1796, one of their first tasks was a survey of property up and down the river from the fort. The surveyor hired for this project was Patrick McNiff. Pictured here is the section of McNiff's map covering present-day Grosse Pointe Shores. Of particular interest is the recording of the original French ribbon farms with the names of the owners. Clearly noted at the bottom are Point à Guignolet, present-day Gaukler Point, and the Milk River leading up to the Black Marsh. Note the point of land at the top, which McNiff labeled "Grose Pt." (Author's collection.)

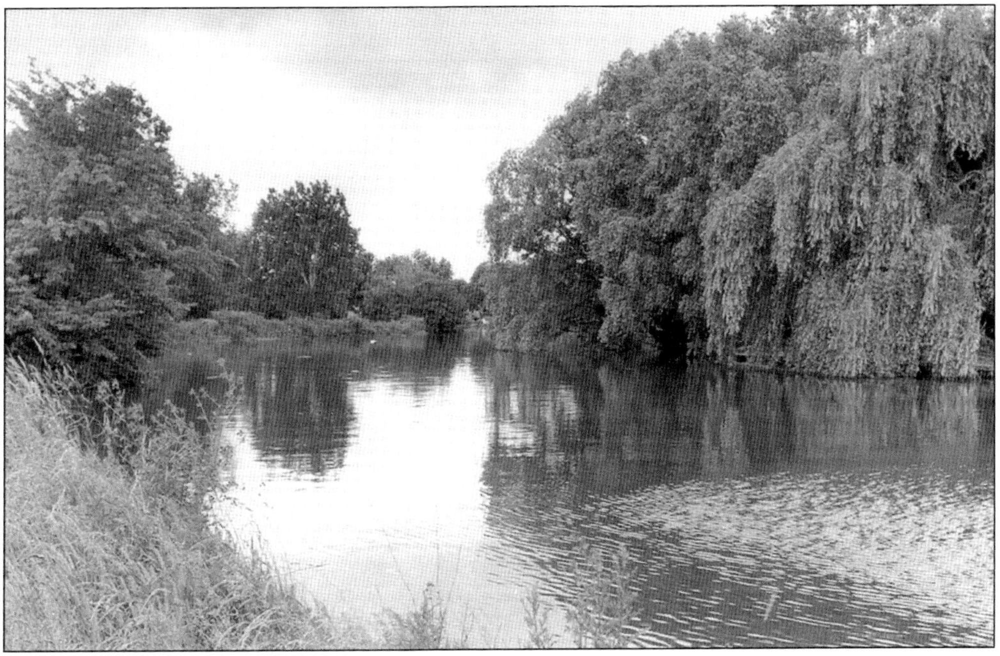

The Milk River. Located at the northern edge of present-day Grosse Pointe Shores, the Milk River once drained a swampy area so thick with vegetation that it was called the Black Marsh. The river was always muddy and slow and was, at times, whitish-brown in color. To the early French habitants, it was as thick as milk. (Courtesy of the St. Clair Shores Historical Commission.)

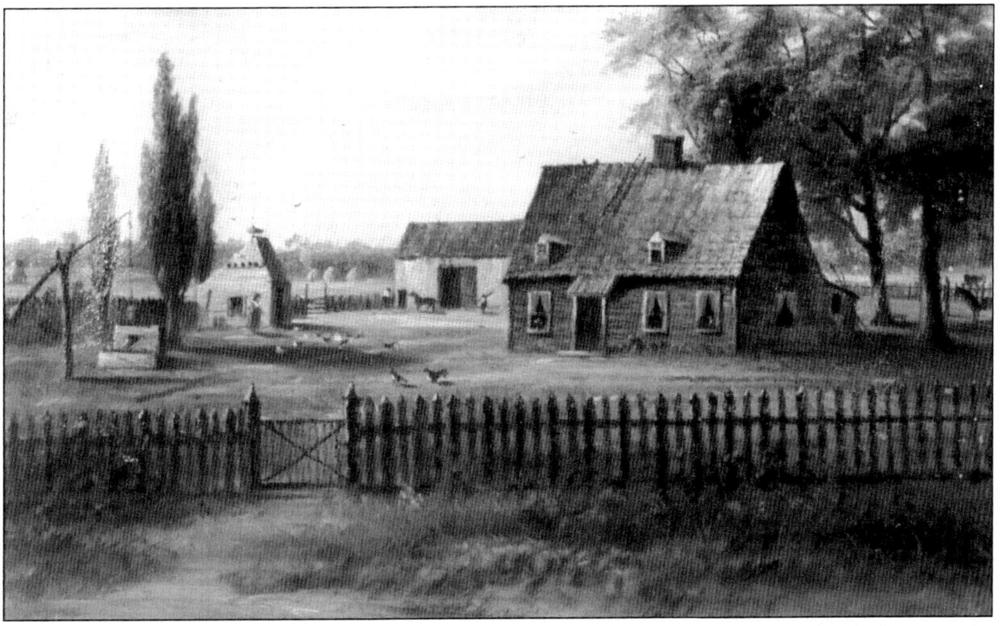

The Farm of a French Habitant. The homes of the French habitants were built facing Lake St. Clair so that each property owner had easy access to the water. The fertile soil of these ribbon farms yielded good crops of wheat, oats, and corn. Almost all of the farms had cattle, pigs, and chickens. Each farm also had its orchards of apple, peach, and pear trees. (Courtesy of the Monroe County Historical Commission.)

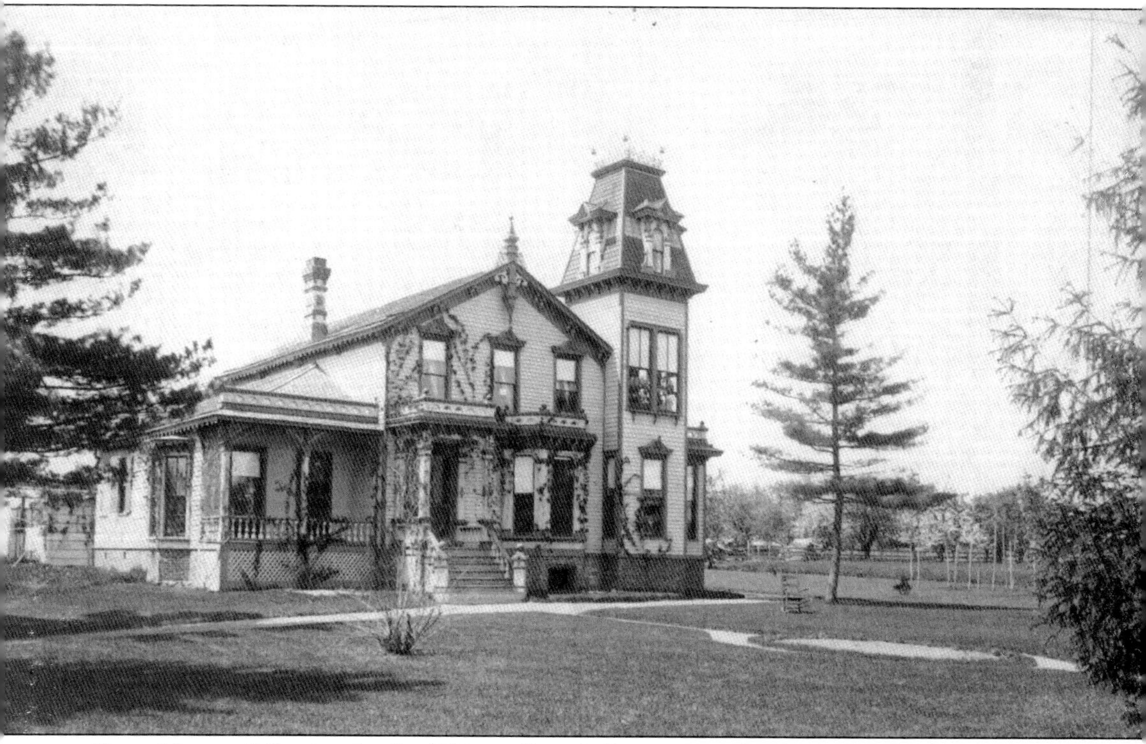

Belle Meade. Following the Civil War, well-to-do Detroiters and industrial leaders began building summer homes along the shore of Lake St. Clair in what is now the Village of Grosse Pointe Shores. Built in 1866, Belle Meade was the summer house of the Dudley B. Woodbridge family. This view of Belle Meade, dated 1886, clearly shows the style of a typical Victorian cottage with its gingerbread trim and porches where the family would gather to enjoy a warm summer evening by the lake. By this time, an addition to the house had been added to the left and a distinctive tower to the right. (Courtesy of the Burton Historical Collection, Detroit Public Library.)

Dudley B. Woodbridge. Dudley B. Woodbridge built Belle Meade in 1866, and with his wife and four daughters, spent several enjoyable summers here. This soon became their year-round home, and thus, the Woodbridges became one of the first full-time residents of what would become the Village of Grosse Pointe Shores. Woodbridge maintained a large working farm here. Active in community affairs, he was instrumental in the formation of the first Protestant church in Grosse Pointe. (Courtesy of the Burton Historical Collection, Detroit Public Library.)

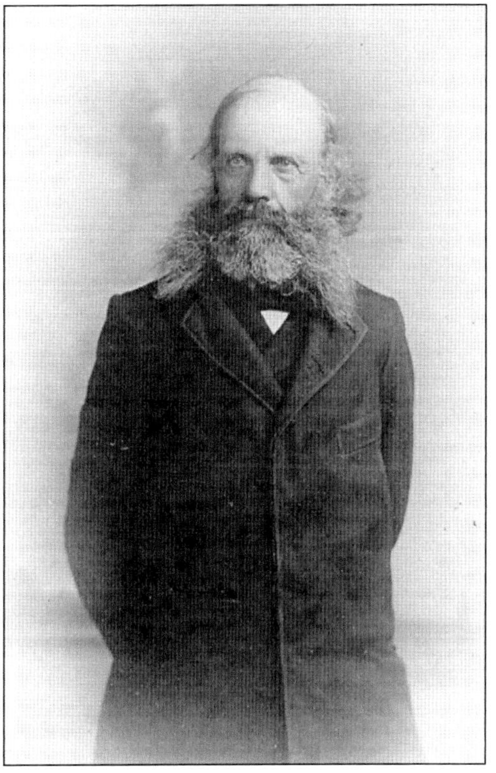

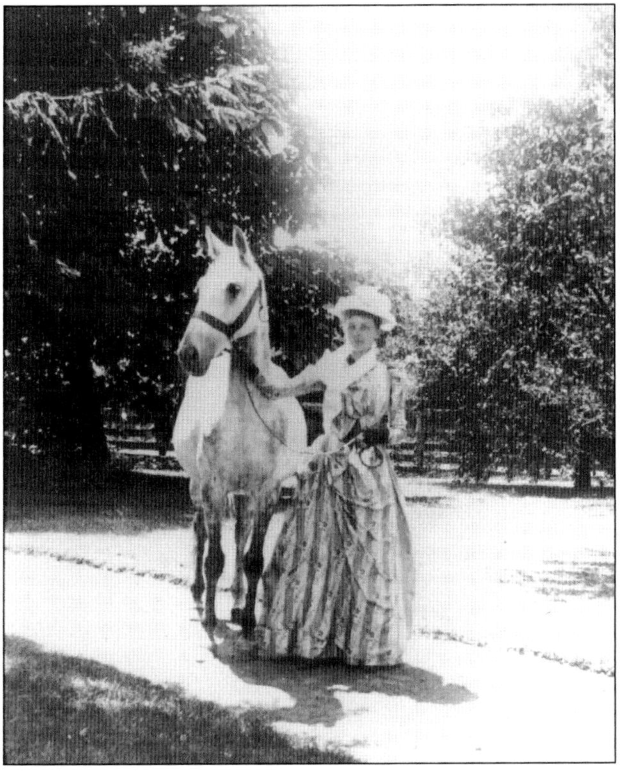

A Girl and Her Horse. At Belle Meade, Dudley Woodbridge, who had an interest in horticulture, had a substantial working farm and a stable of thoroughbred horses. Local part-time residents boarded their horses here. This young lady brought her beautiful Arabian stallion from the stable to show her fiancé from Boston, who was visiting in 1890. (Courtesy of the Grosse Pointe Historical Society.)

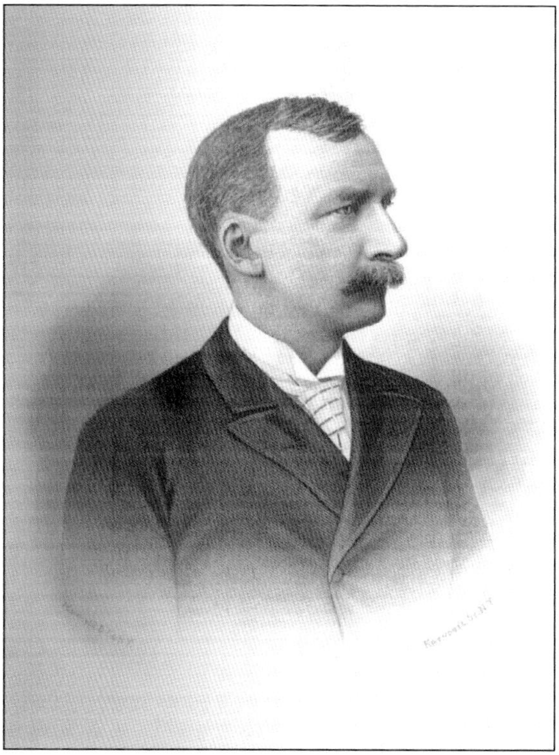

George S. Davis. George S. Davis was a partner in Parke, Davis & Company, once America's oldest and the world's largest pharmaceutical company. Founded in 1867, the firm was located on the Detroit River near the foot of Joseph Campeau Street. Davis owned a summer home and farm of 281 acres in what later became the Village of Grosse Pointe Shores. Davis's farm was known as the Claireview Jersey Stock Farm. (Courtesy of the Grosse Pointe Historical Society.)

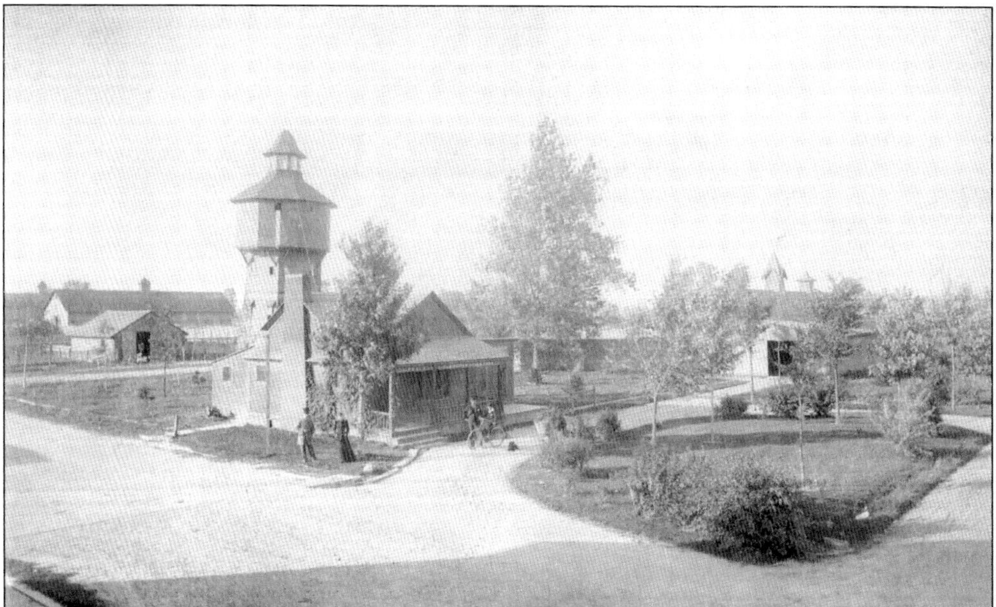

Claireview Farm Buildings. The farm measured two miles deep with 1,400 feet of lake frontage. It had 28 buildings, a blacksmith shop, 60 horses, 30 brood mares boarding there, and a herd of Jersey cows, all tended by 25 employees. The farm's cow barn was later moved to the nearby Hunt Club, where it stood until it was destroyed by fire in 2001. (Courtesy of the Burton Historical Collection, Detroit Public Library.)

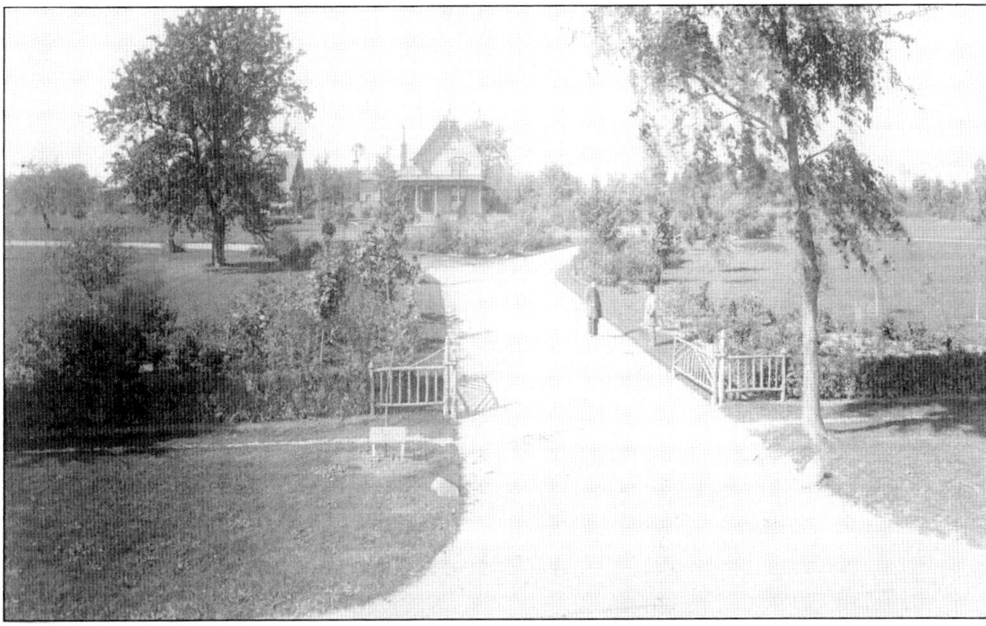

Entrance to the Claireview Farm. This is the main entrance to the Claireview Farm, sometimes spelled "Clairevue," with a long driveway leading to the two-story home. The property ran back from the lake to present-day Mack Avenue and included property where the Sheldens, Torreys, and Specks would later build their homes. (Courtesy of the Burton Historical Collection, Detroit Public Library.)

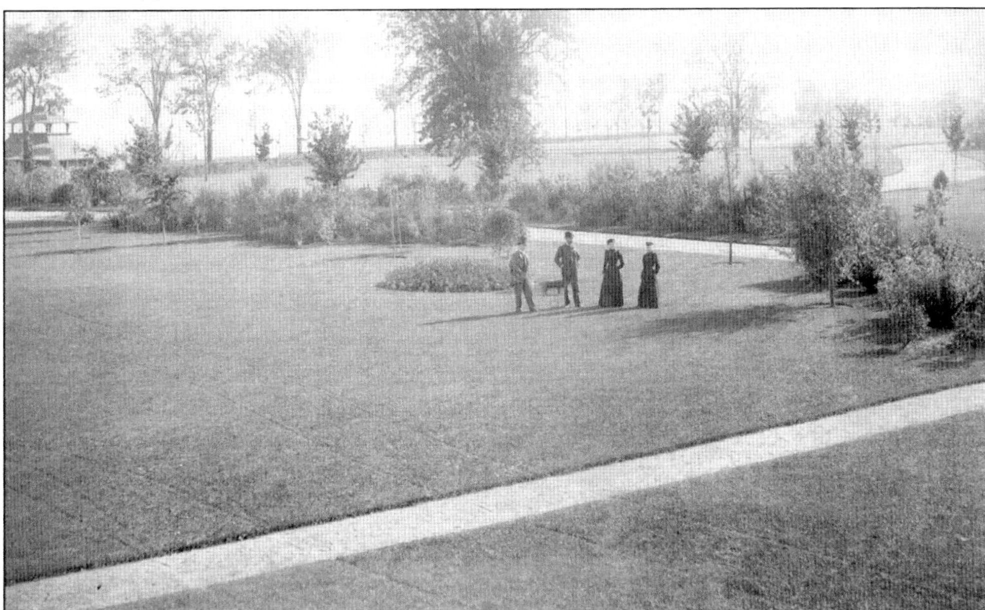

Lawn of the Claireview Farm. The two couples seen here around 1890 are enjoying a walk on the lawn of the Claireview Farm, fronting Lake St. Clair. Summer residents were welcome to visit the farm's docile Jersey cows. On the eastern part of the farm was an orchard, including two large French pear trees. Today, Claireview Road in the Village of Grosse Pointe Shores marks the location of the original farm. (Courtesy of the Burton Historical Collection, Detroit Public Library.)

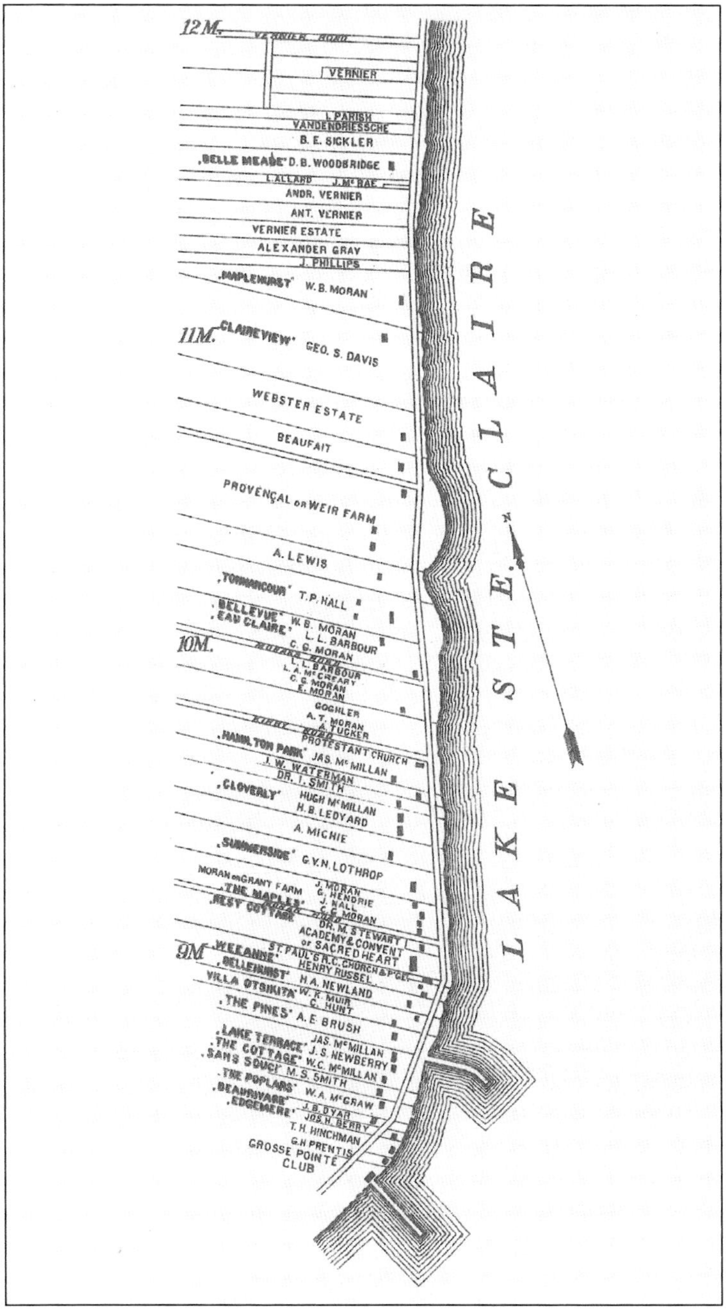

Map of Lake Shore Road. This map, dated 1886, shows the residences lining Lake Shore Road in what would one day be the Village of Grosse Pointe Shores. Seen here are the Woodbridge home Belle Meade and the Claireview Farm. Note Vernier, Moross, Kerby, and Moran Roads. The mile notations mark the distance from downtown Detroit. These properties clearly follow the shape of the ribbon farms of the original French habitants. At the bottom is the Grosse Pointe Club, later the Country Club of Detroit. Today, this site at the foot of Fisher Road is home to the Grosse Pointe War Memorial, Grosse Pointe Memorial Church, and the Grosse Pointe Club. (Author's collection.)

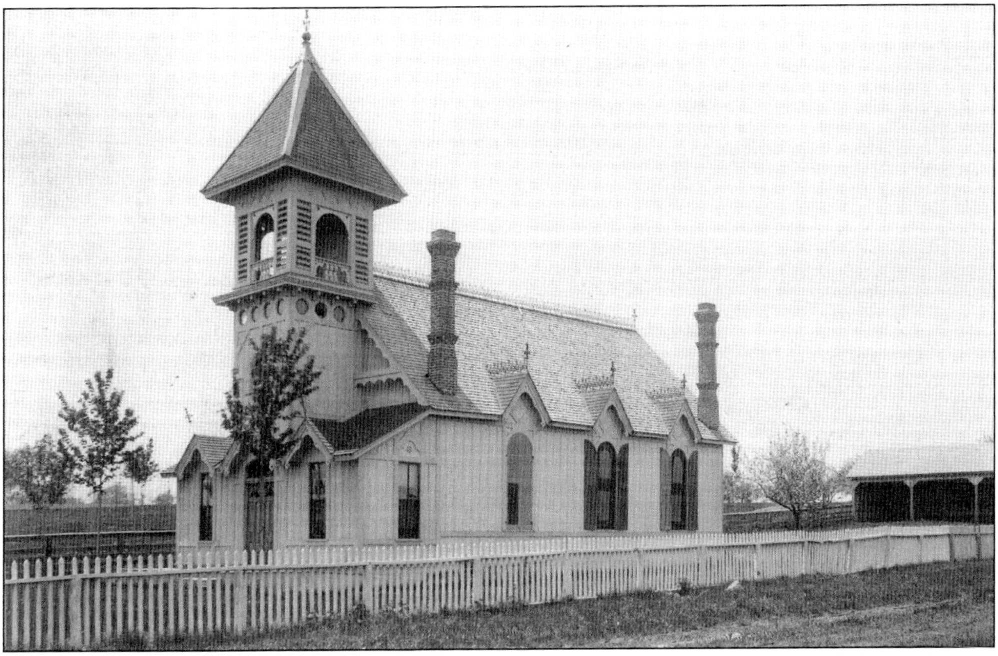

The Protestant Church. Having no Protestant church to attend, a group of Grosse Pointe residents including Dudley B. Woodbridge met and began plans for constructing a church building. This first church, known as the Grosse Pointe Protestant Church, was built in 1867 at the corner of Kerby and Lake Shore Roads. With its elaborate belfry tower and decorated gables, the church continued to serve the community until 1894, when the congregation moved to its new church at Lake Shore and Fisher Road. (Courtesy of the Burton Historical Collection, Detroit Public Library.)

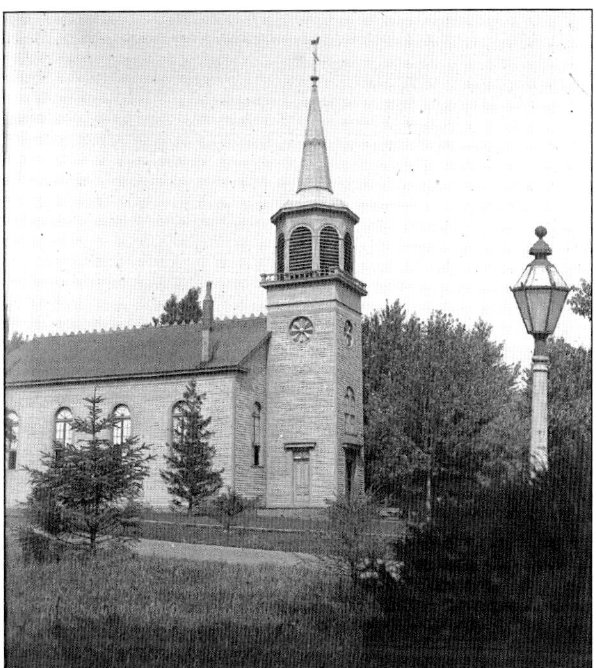

The Catholic Church. Services were first offered in French at this chapel constructed in 1848 on Lake Shore Road near Lewiston. It was the second home of St. Paul's Roman Catholic Church, replacing the original log chapel built in 1825 on the Reno Farm just north of Vernier Road in Grosse Pointe Shores. The church, seen here around 1880, later served as a parish hall until dismantled in 1914. (Courtesy of the Burton Historical Collection, Detroit Public Library.)

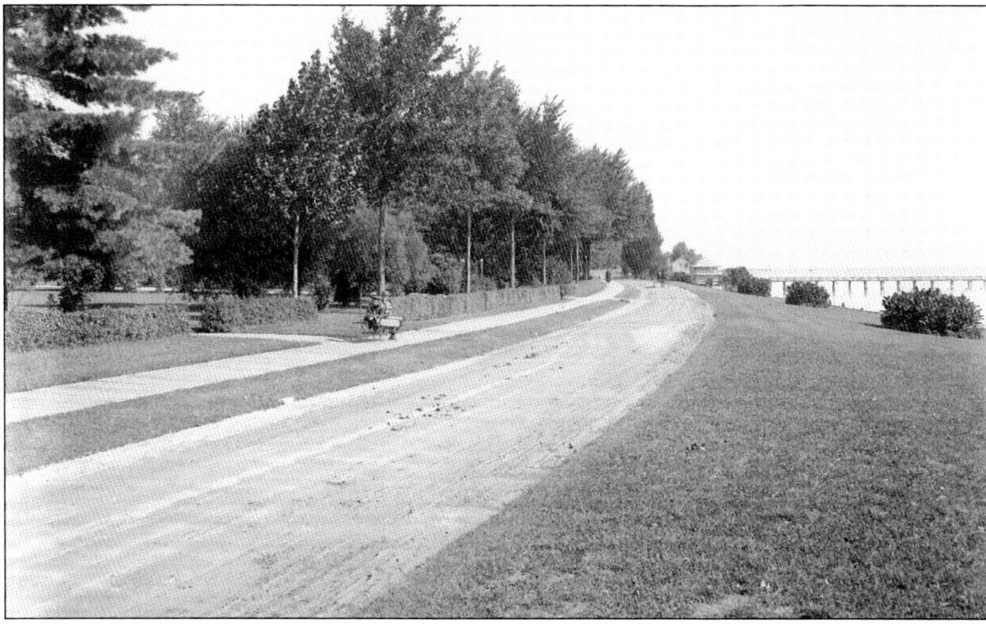

LAKE SHORES ROAD, 1891. This was the road residents and visitors used when traveling from Detroit and along the shore of Lake St. Clair. Originally known as the Shore Road, or the Grosse Pointe Road, the name was officially changed to Lake Shore Road in 1913, though in Grosse Pointe Park and the City of Grosse Pointe, the road retains the name Jefferson Avenue, its name in Detroit. (Courtesy of the Detroit Publishing Company, Library of Congress.)

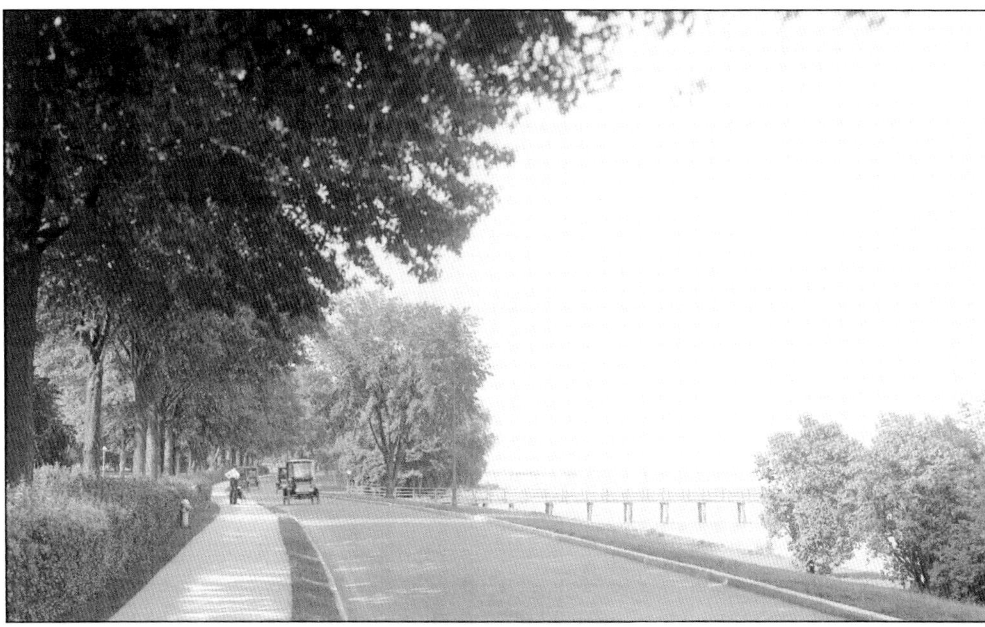

LAKE SHORE ROAD, 1911. By 1911, the year the Village of Grosse Pointe Shores was established, the view along Lake Shore Road had changed. Although manicured lawns and neatly trimmed hedges remained, gone were the horse and buggy (and that which the horse left behind on the roadway). Now, only 20 years later, the motorcars seen coming down the road were the principal mode of transportation. (Courtesy of the Detroit Publishing Company, Library of Congress.)

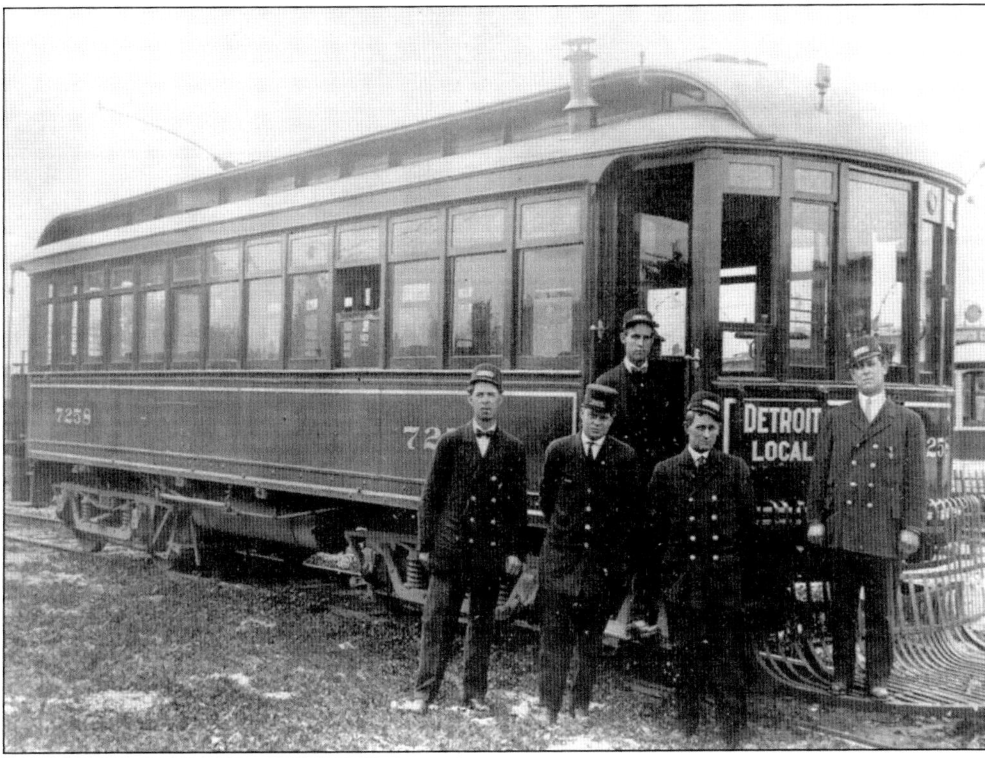

The Interurban. Transportation from Detroit to Grosse Pointe changed dramatically in the 1880s with the construction of the interurban railway system. By the 1890s, the Shore Line Division reached Grosse Pointe Shores on its way to St. Clair Shores and Mount Clemens. Here is Shore Line Car No. 7258 heading out to Grosse Pointe Shores in 1898. (Courtesy of Kenneth Schramm.)

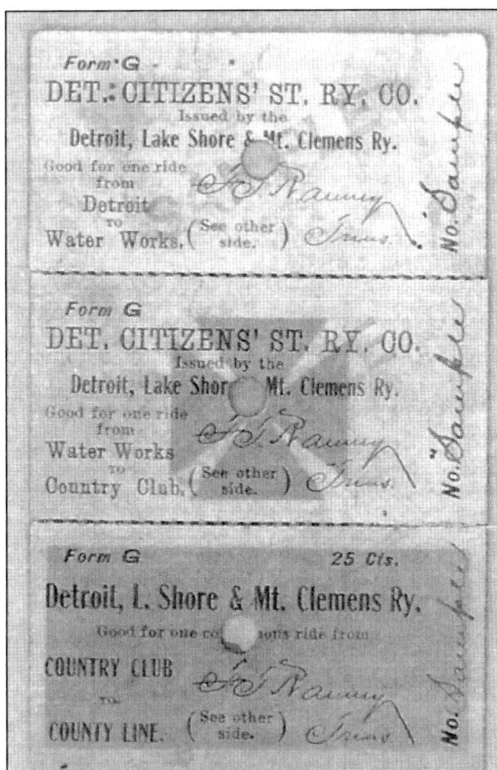

Form G
DET. CITIZENS' ST. RY. CO.
Issued by the
Detroit, Lake Shore & Mt. Clemens Ry.
Good for one ride from
Detroit
TO
Water Works. (See other side.)
No. Sample

Form G
DET. CITIZENS' ST. RY. CO.
Issued by the
Detroit, Lake Shor[illegible] Mt. Clemens Ry.
Good for one ride from
Water Works
TO
Country Club. (See other side.)
No. Sample

Form G 25 Cts.
Detroit, L. Shore & Mt. Clemens Ry.
Good for one co[illegible]ous ride from
COUNTRY CLUB
TO
COUNTY LINE. (See other side.)
No. Sample

A Ticket to Grosse Pointe Shores. A resident traveling the interurban from Detroit to Grosse Pointe Shores on the Detroit Citizens Street Railway (as the Shore Line was later named) had to purchase a three-part ticket: first, from downtown Detroit to Waterworks Park; then, Waterworks Park to the Grosse Pointe Country Club, which was then on the water; and finally, from the Country Club into Grosse Pointe Shores to the Macomb County line. (Courtesy of Kenneth Schramm.)

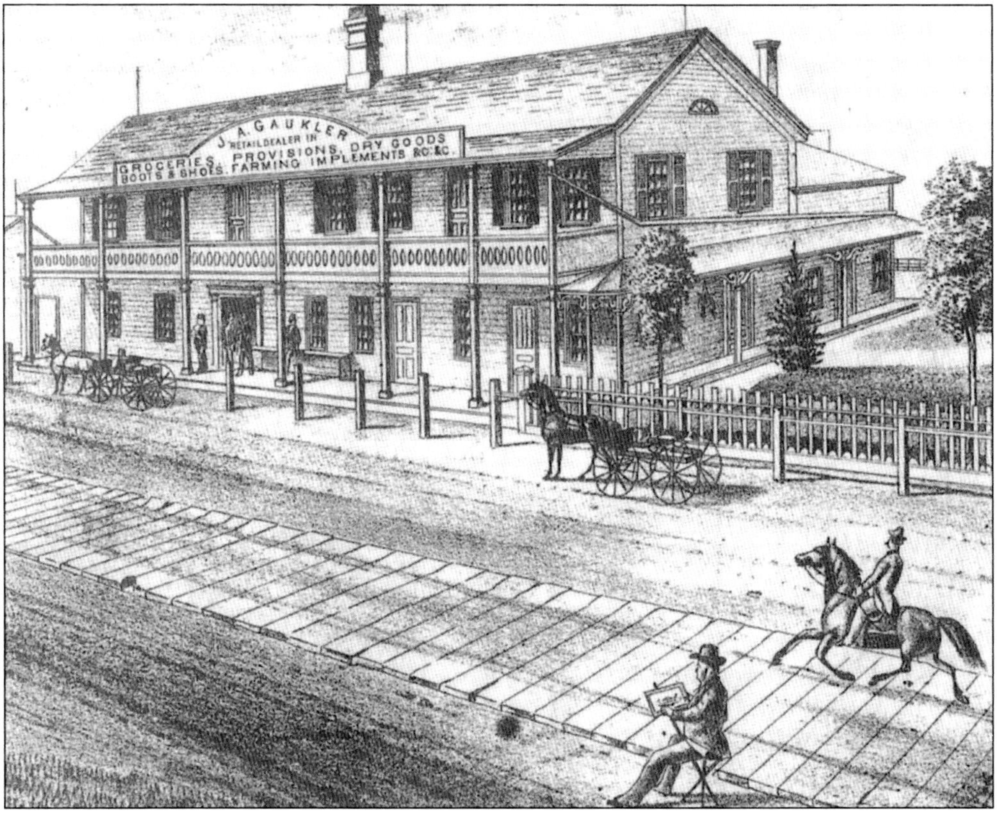

GAUKLER STORE. The point of land jutting into Lake St. Clair at the northern boundary of Grosse Pointe Shores is today known as Gaukler Point. It has been called that since about 1876, when Jacob Gaukler, a prosperous merchant who owned this store on Gratiot Avenue in the village of nearby Roseville, built a lakeside summer home on the point of land that soon gained his name. (Author's collection.)

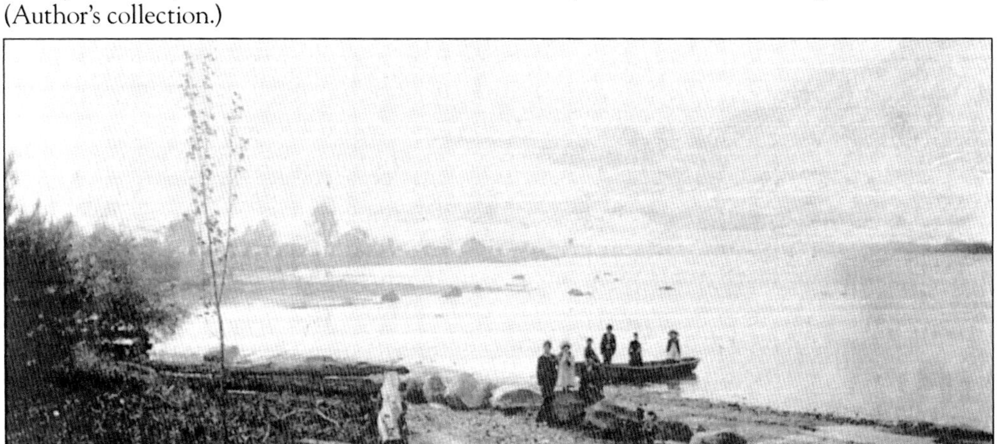

MILK RIVER BAY. The original name for Gaukler Point was Point à Guignolet, after a black cherry the French farmers used for making liquor. The British named it Milk River Point. The small bay where the Milk River flows into Lake St. Clair here became Milk River Bay. This area became a popular picnic site for boaters, as can be seen in this view from 1893. (Author's collection.)

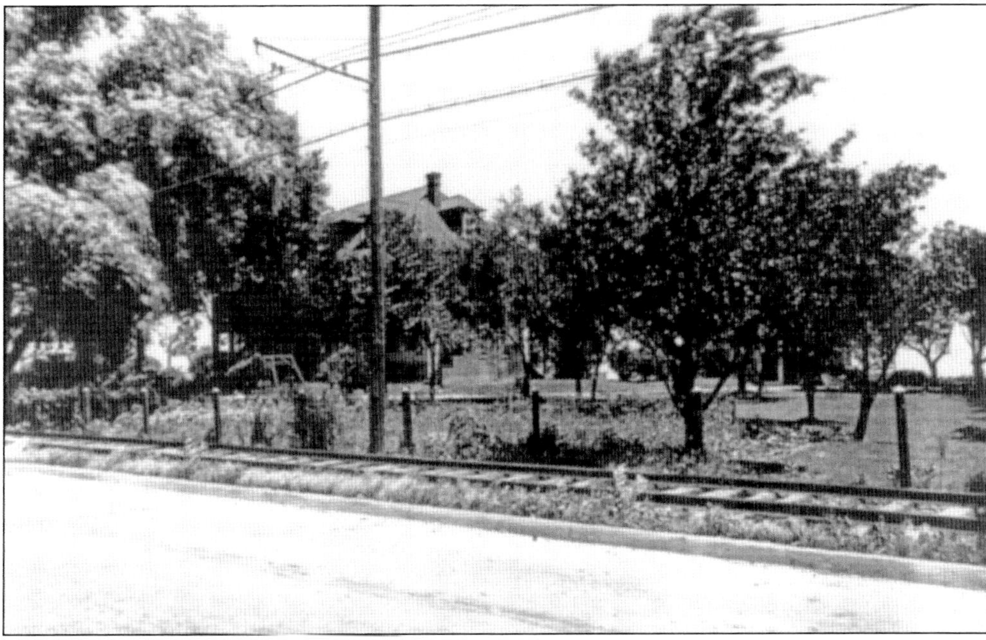

Gaukler Point Interurban Stop. This view dated 1917 shows the interurban track and stop at Gaukler Point. This is now part of the Edsel and Eleanor Ford property. Edsel Ford moved the road and the track when he purchased the land for his estate. The closeness of Lake Shore Road to the track is very clear in this image. (Courtesy of the St. Clair Shores Historical Commission.)

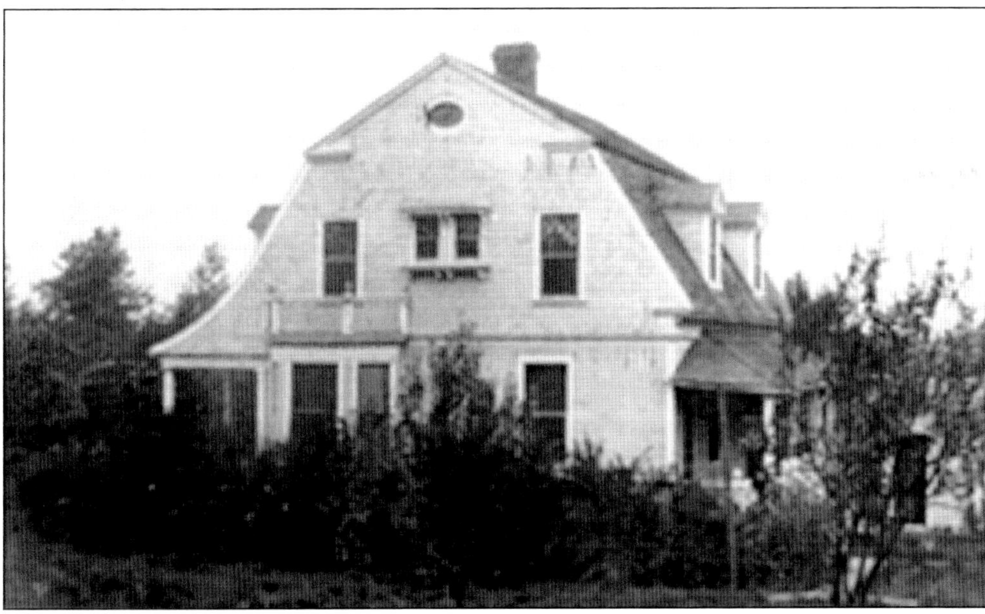

Doremus House, Gaukler Point. This cottage, seen in 1911, stood on Gaukler Point when Henry Ford purchased the property in 1914. Ford intended to live there while building an estate on the land, but then decided on a home in Dearborn instead. Ford allowed his neighbor and their daughter, Helen Doremus, to live here. When Edsel Ford built his home at Gaukler Point, this house was moved a short distance to Doremus Avenue in St. Clair Shores. (Courtesy of The Henry Ford.)

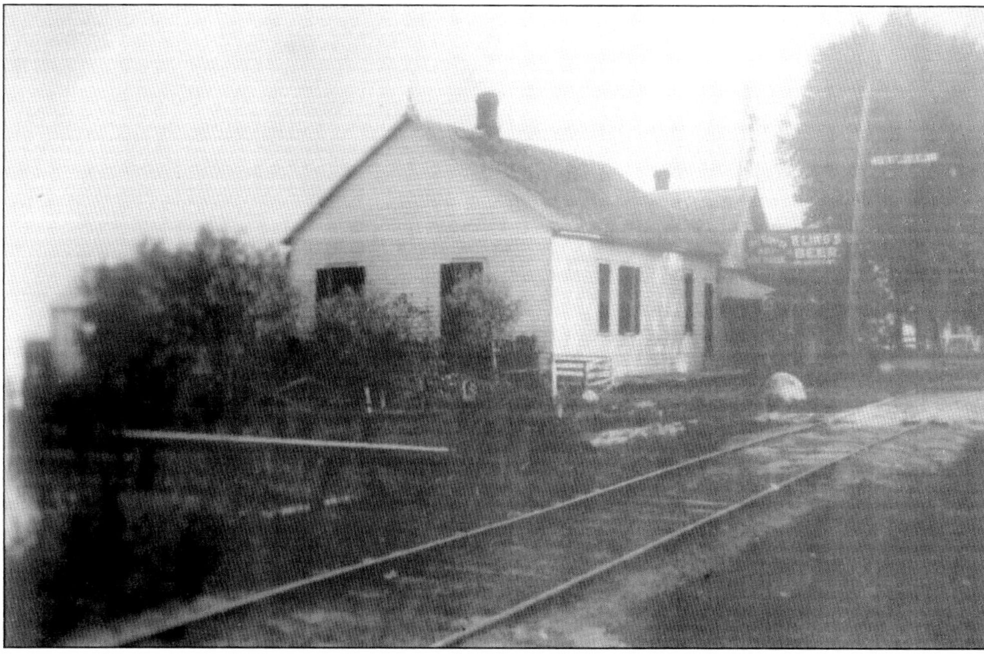

VERNIER ROADHOUSE. John Vernier opened this roadhouse on Lake Shore at Vernier Road in 1888. The eatery catered to travelers along the lake and adventurous Detroiters enjoying a day in the country. The menu included Vernier's famous chicken, fish, and frog leg dinners. Many of the visitors arrived via the interurban. Note the tracks passing in front of the roadhouse. Today, the Grosse Pointe Yacht Club gatehouse is located near the site of the roadhouse. (Courtesy of the Grosse Pointe Historical Society.)

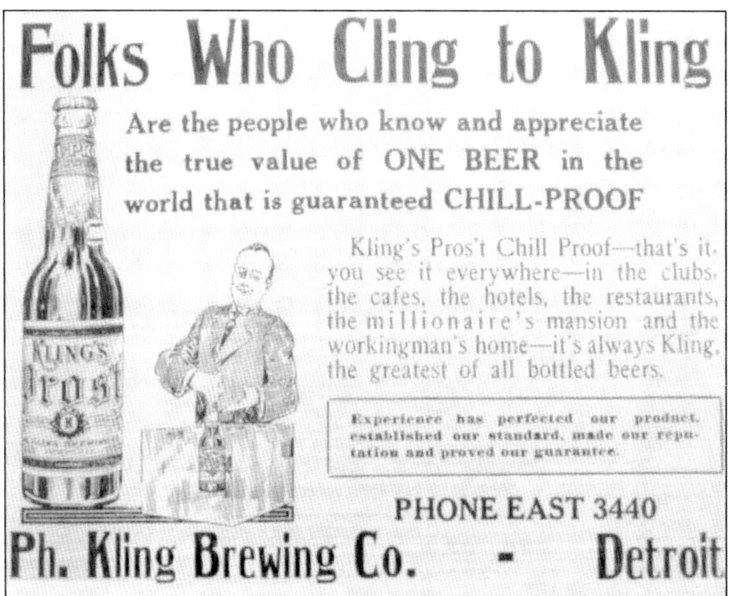

KLING BEER. Vernier's Roadhouse was noted for its chicken, fish, and frog leg dinners. With a meal, a diner could order a cold glass of beer, as the sign over the door in the view above clearly shows. The Kling Brewery was one of Detroit's largest breweries from the 1880s to the 1910s and was located off Jefferson Avenue near the present-day Belle Isle Bridge. (Courtesy of the St. Clair Shores Historical Commission.)

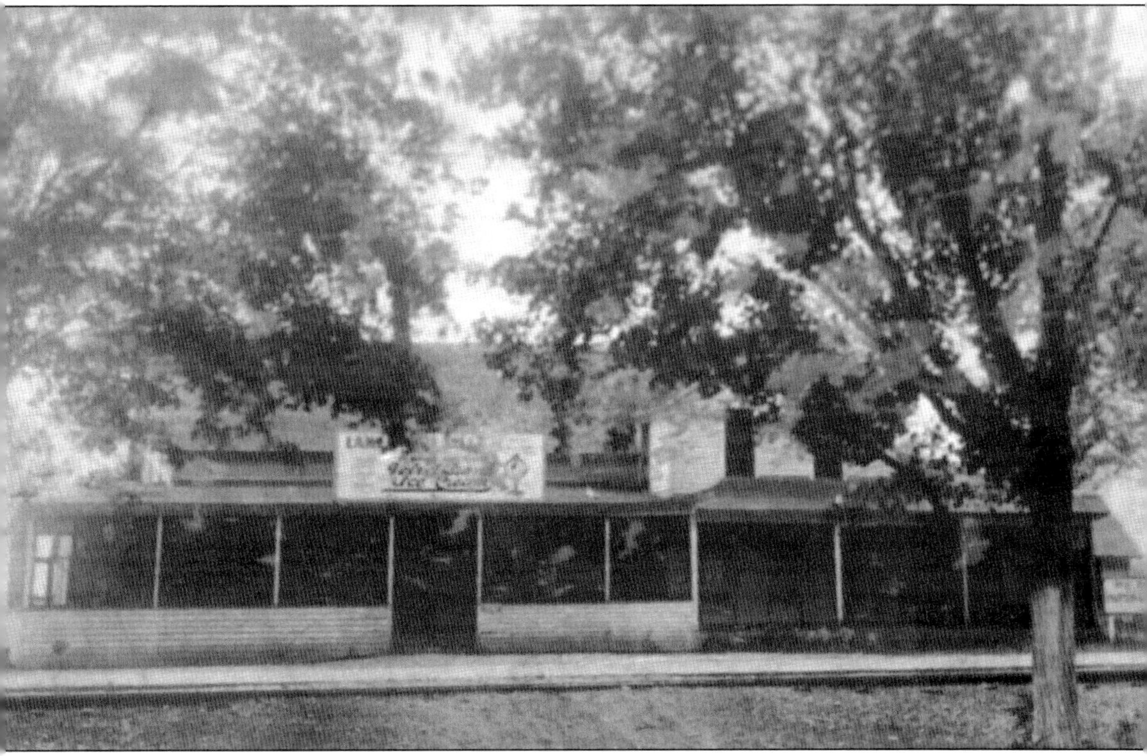

VERNIER ROADHOUSE AND HOTEL. In 1895, John Vernier sold his business to his cousin Edmund Vernier. Edmund moved the business to this larger building on the west side of Lake Shore Road just south of Vernier Road and added a hotel, seen here around 1900. Edmund was known for his hospitality, and the inn was one of the area's most popular. This roadhouse was also a popular gambling spot. In 1915, Edmund Vernier built another place on Vernier Road west of Lake Shore Road. Later, he served as Grosse Pointe Township clerk, treasurer, and, for many years, township supervisor. (Courtesy of the Grosse Pointe Historical Society.)

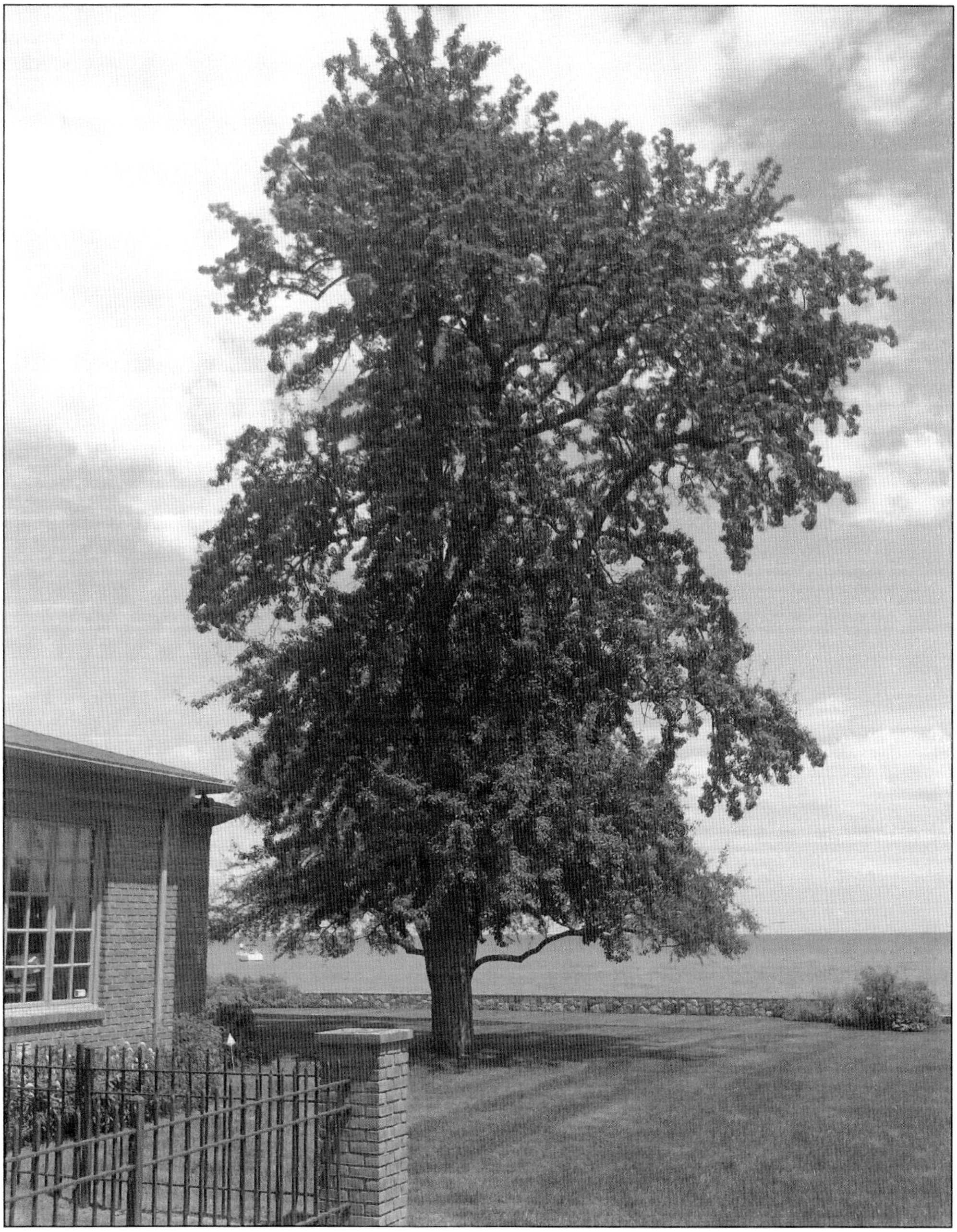

French Pear Tree. The French ribbon farms almost always contained an orchard of fruit trees, including pear trees. Legend has it that French settlers brought seeds or cuttings of pear trees to plant along the shore of Lake St. Clair and the Detroit River. These trees were known for their remarkable size and the quantity of their fruit. It was common for a French pear tree to reach a height of over 100 feet, with a circumference of eight to nine feet, producing 30 to 50 bushels of fruit per tree. Once common on the farms of the Village of Grosse Pointe Shores, only a few of these trees have survived. The magnificent tree pictured here is on the site of the former George Osius home. It is thought that George Osius planted this tree sometime between 1910 and 1920. (Courtesy of Kay Felt.)

Two

Mr. Osius's Village

By 1911, the village had changed and grown as new and more substantial homes were built all along Lake Shore Road, drawn by the stunning lake view. By this time, there was a movement within the community to incorporate in order to better manage local affairs. Following approval by residents formally establishing the Village of Grosse Pointes Shores, a new charter was ratified and the first council elected with George Osius as president. The first items approved by the new village council were the formations of a department of public safety and a department of public works. In the beginning, the council usually met at the home of George Osius, but it soon became apparent that a permanent location was needed. Thus, in the fall of 1914, voters approved a $22,000 bond issue to build a municipal building. Construction began immediately, and in December 1915, residents were invited to the dedication of the new village hall. This was followed by the building of a school and a municipal park and harbor. Almost immediately, the new village hall became a center for community activities including dances, motion pictures, and, in 1922, a public library. The growth of automobile use brought an end to the interurban railway, and in 1927, this service was discontinued. The interurban tracks were removed, and in 1930, the Wayne County Road Commission rebuilt and expanded Lake Shore Road. The 1920s also witnessed the development of the first subdivision in the village. The Great Depression brought difficult times to all of the Grosse Pointes, and of course, every resident young and old felt the effects of World War II. The war was followed by a period of prosperity and growth for the Village of Grosse Pointe Shores. To better oversee this growth, a planning commission was created in 1949, and in 1952, a master plan, the first in any of the Pointes, was approved by voters. This plan enabled the village to carefully control growth, which included new water and sewer lines, and of course, exceptional new homes and many subdivisions.

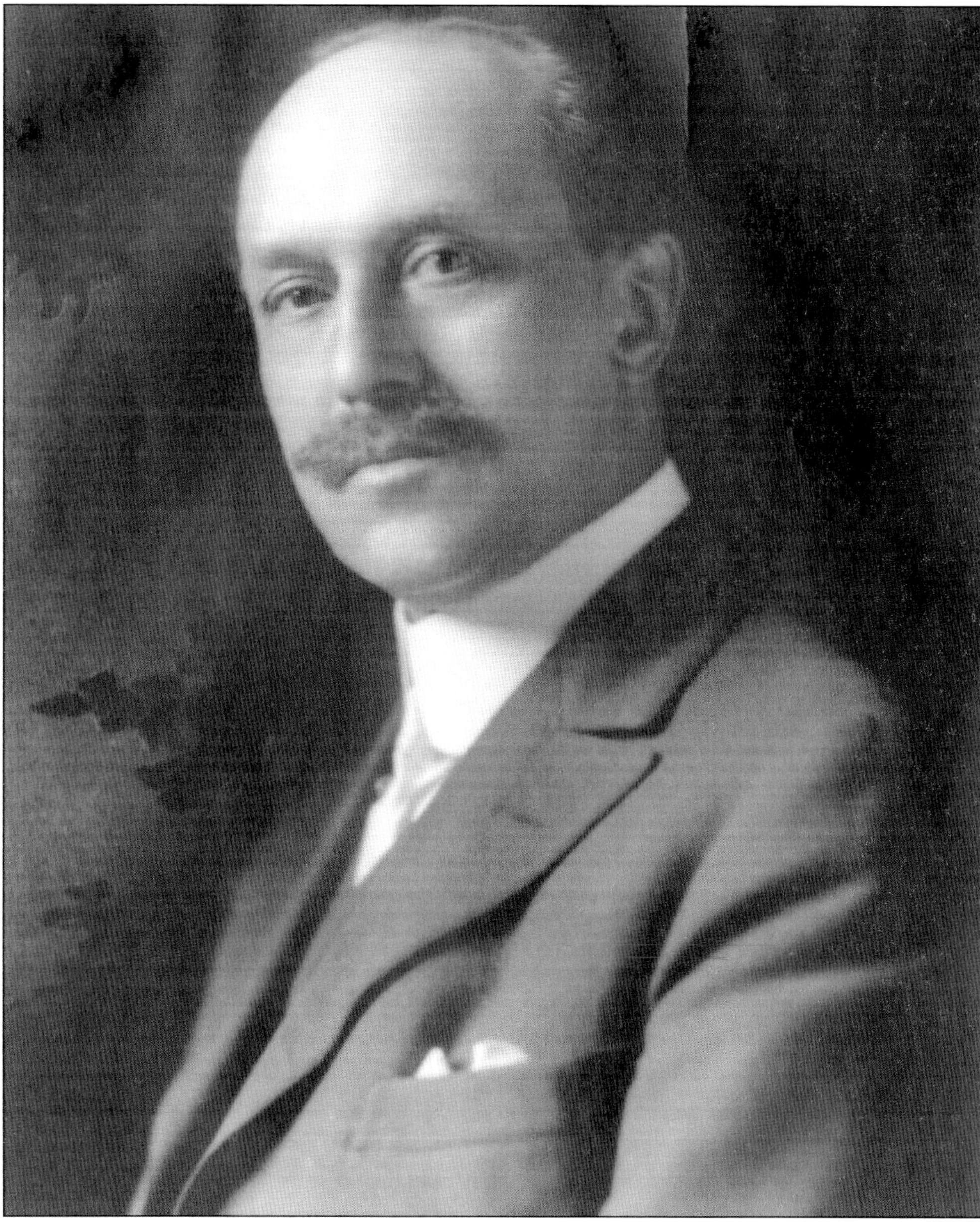

George Osius. George Osius was born in Bernkastel, Germany, in 1859 and came to the United States in 1878. He settled in Ann Arbor, where he soon opened a bookstore. In 1887, he sold the store and moved to Detroit, where he established the Michigan Ammonia Works. Before long, he became active in a variety of civic affairs. Osius served on the Detroit Public Library Commission and on the board of the Detroit Symphony Orchestra and as director of the Detroit Community Fund. He was also a leader in Detroit's large German-American community. In 1893, he married Elise Rickel. The Osius family moved to Grosse Pointe in 1901, and in 1911, built a gorgeous new home at 900 Lake Shore Road. As president of the charter commission, he was instrumental in establishing the Village of Grosse Pointe Shores in 1911, where he served as mayor from 1911 to 1928. He continued to serve on the village council and remained a leader in this community until his death in 1941. (Courtesy of the Burton Historical Collection, Detroit Public Library.)

Osius Family. George Osius was the first of his family to move to the United States but was soon followed by his brothers and sister. This c. 1914 photograph, taken on the lawn of his home in the Village of Grosse Pointe Shores, shows, from left to right, (sitting) sister Johanna Osius Molitor and their mother, Albertine Hyeden Osius; (standing) brother Theodore F.A. Osius, brother-in-law Edward Molitor, George Osius, and brother Rudolph Osius. The Molitors lived across Lake Shore Road from George and Elise. (Courtesy of the Osius family.)

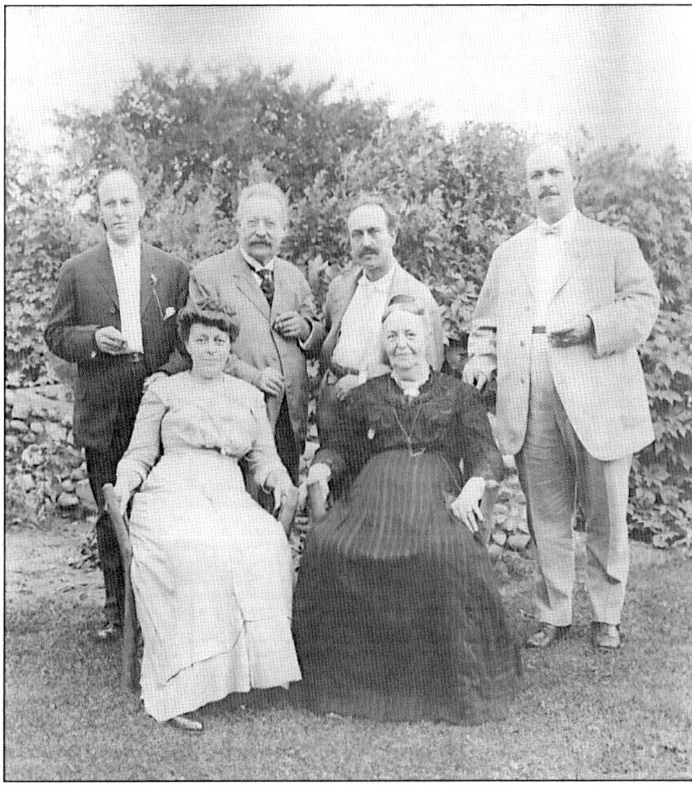

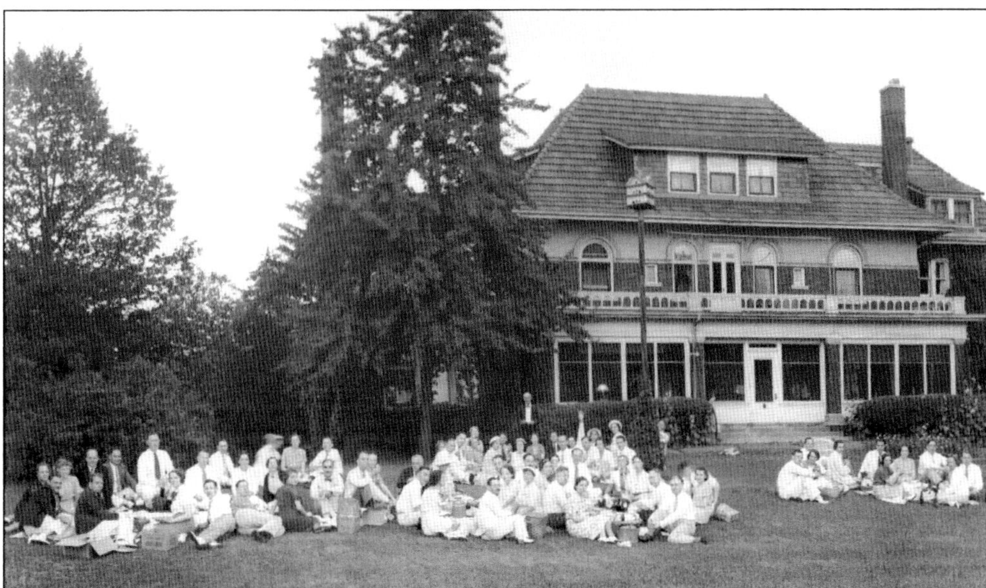

Osius Home. George and Elise Osius's new home became a social and civic center of the community. The house had many interesting features including a basement garage with a turntable for ease of moving automobiles, a very modern kitchen, and a study with a beautiful desk that had a myriad of intricate cubbyholes for papers. The property had almost 400 feet of lake frontage and extended back to what is now Mack Avenue. (Courtesy of the Osius family and Kay Felt.)

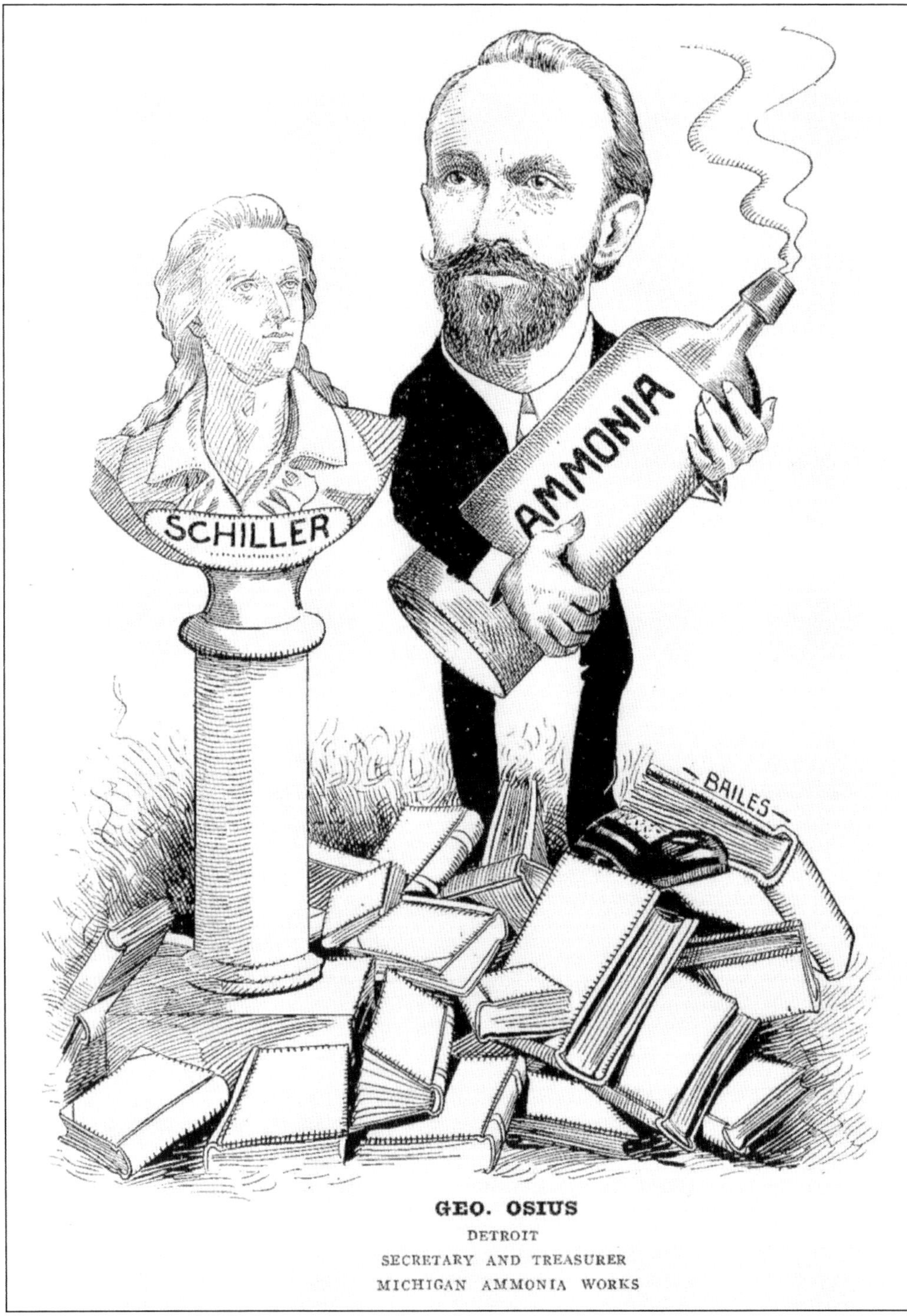

"As We See 'Em." In 1905, the Newspaper Cartoonists' Association of Michigan published a book of sketches of prominent men of Michigan. Titled *Our Friends As We See 'Em*, the collection included this caricature of George Osius, depicted holding a bottle of ammonia beside a bust of Schiller, surrounded by his beloved books. (Courtesy of the St. Clair Shores Historical Commission.)

SCHILLER MONUMENT. As an active member of Detroit's large German-American community, George Osius headed the Schiller Denkmal Executive Committee, which sponsored this statue of the German poet, philosopher, historian, and playwright Friedrich Schiller. Dedicated in 1905, the monument was placed in Detroit's Belle Isle Park where it can be seen today. (Courtesy of the Detroit Historical Society.)

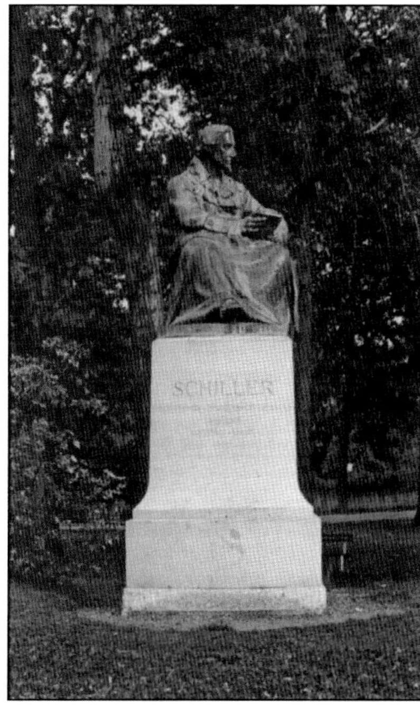

MICHIGAN AMMONIA WORKS. George Osius helped establish the Michigan Ammonia Works and quickly became general manager and then director of the company. The plant (circled on this 1916 real estate map) was located on the Detroit River near the foot of Meldrum Avenue adjacent to the Detroit Gas Works. The company soon had a plant in Toronto, Canada, and transacted business globally. Osius became a national leader in the industry, serving as chairman of the Ammonia Board for the War Department during World War I. In 1929, Osius retired, selling his company to the DuPont corporation. (Courtesy of the Detroit Historical Society.)

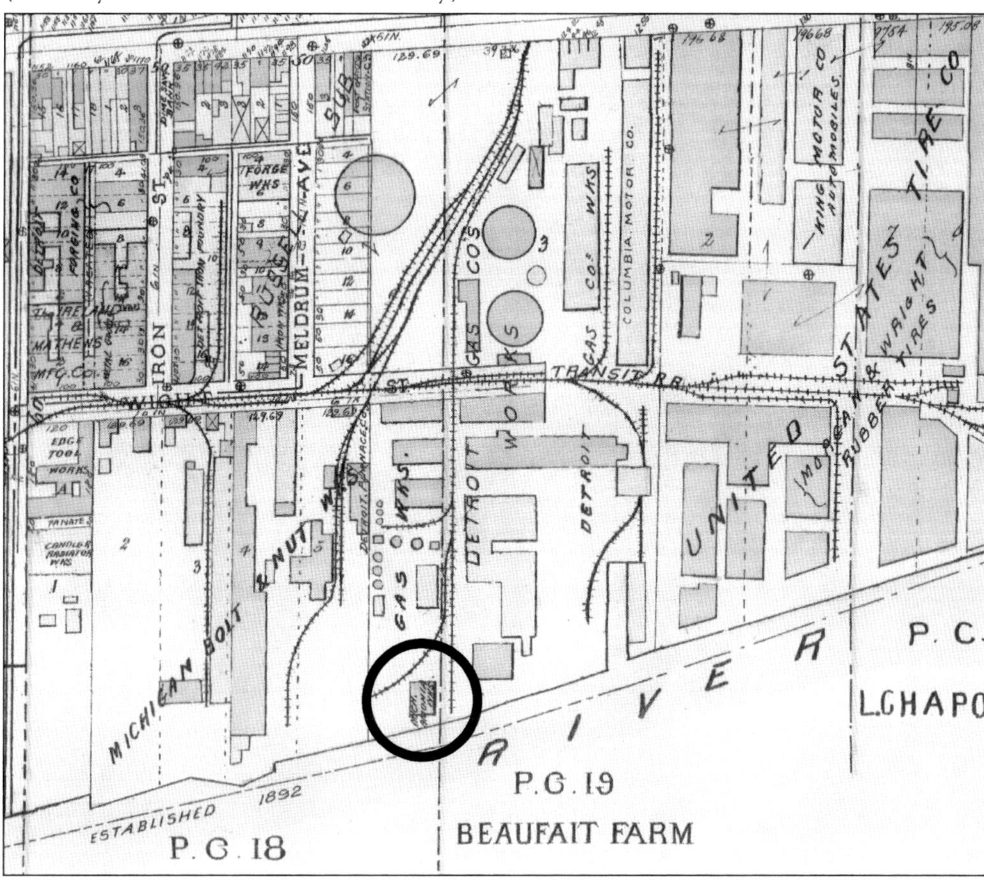

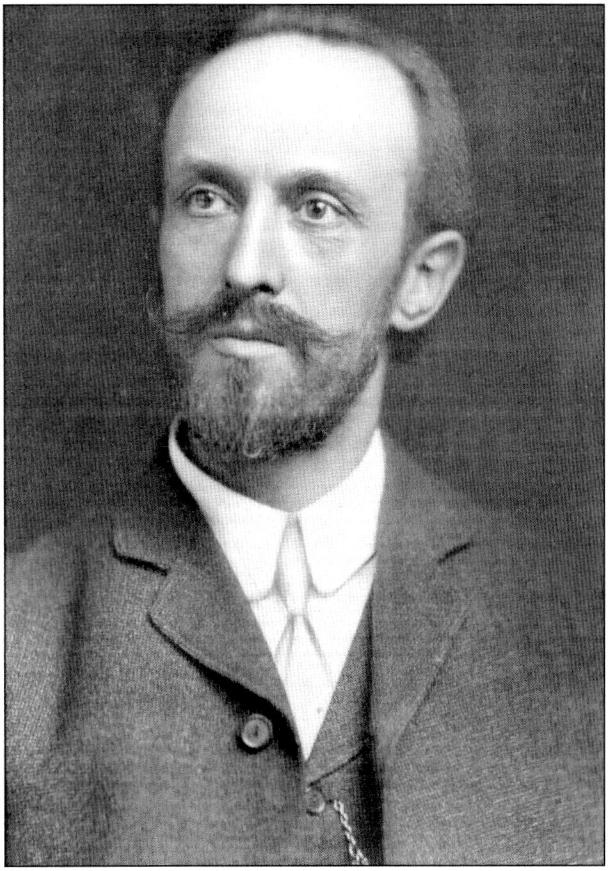

President, Detroit Library Commission. One of George Osius's proudest accomplishments was his service as a member of the Detroit Public Library Commission for 13 years (1900–1912), where he twice served as president. Osius was instrumental in bettering the salaries and working conditions of librarians and was a strong advocate of branch libraries. (Courtesy of the Burton Historical Collection, Detroit Public Library.)

Osius Branch Library. Upon leaving the Detroit Public Library Commission, Osius was honored by the naming of a new branch library built on Gratiot Avenue near Burns Avenue in the heart of Detroit's east-side German-American community. It was built at a cost of $40,000 with a gift from Andrew Carnegie. (Courtesy of the Burton Historical Collection, Detroit Public Library.)

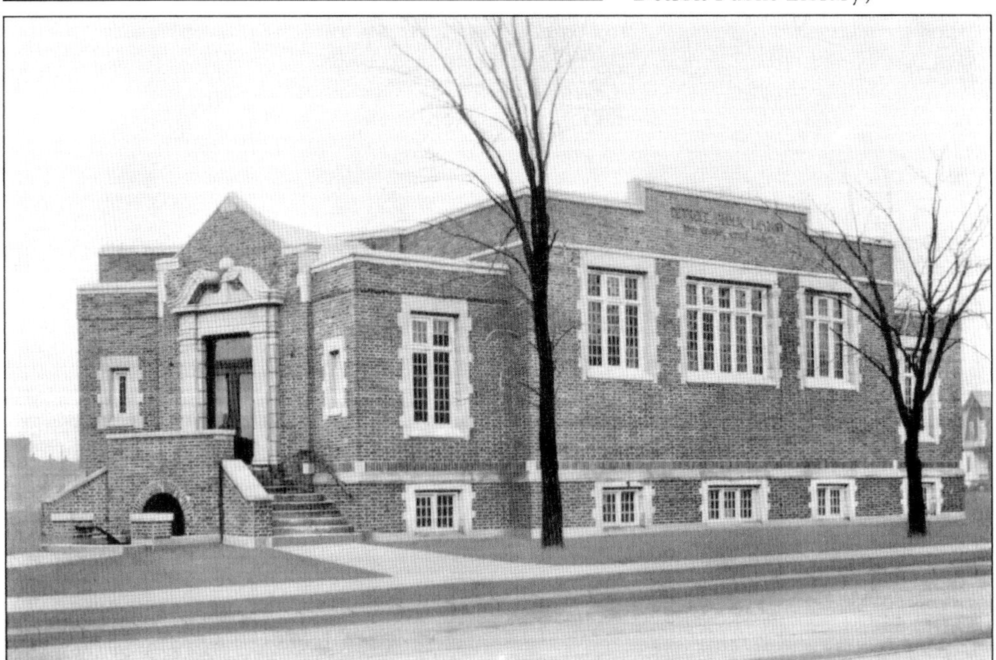

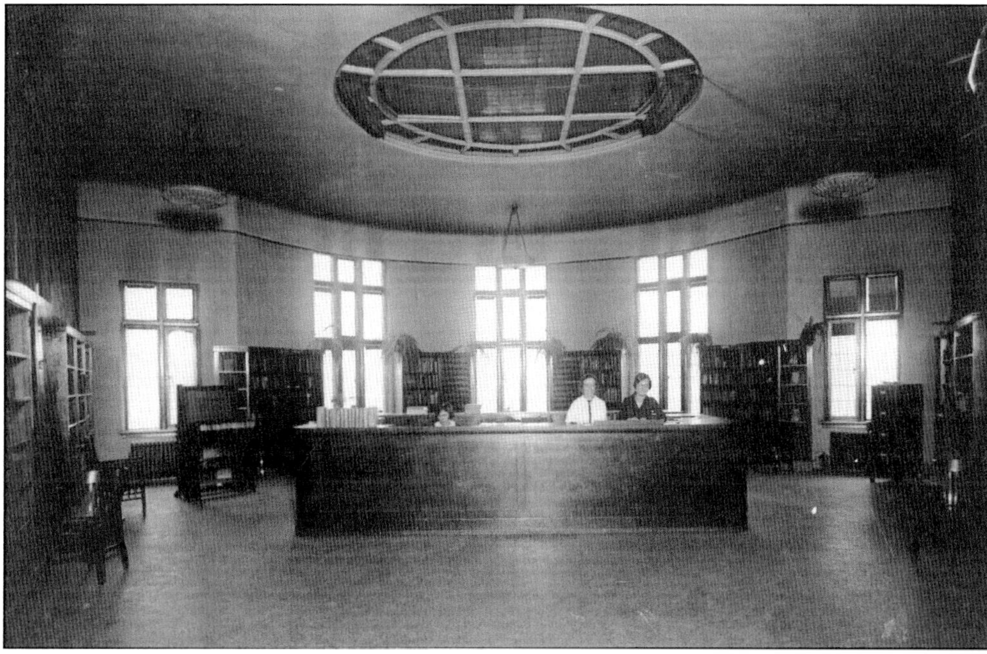

OSIUS BRANCH INTERIOR. This is the circulation desk in the main reading room shortly after the branch opened. From the very beginning, according to the annual report of the branch librarian, the library was extremely busy not only as a library but also as a community center. Book circulation was high, and neighborhood boys also used the 200-seat auditorium in the basement as a gym for their basketball league. (Courtesy of the Burton Historical Collection, Detroit Public Library.)

OSIUS BRANCH FLOOR PLAN. The Osius Branch continued to actively serve the community until 1939, when it was torn down due to the widening of Gratiot Avenue. It was replaced by the much larger Mark Twain Branch, which for many years served as a regional library. A bronze tablet was placed in this new library recognizing Osius's service to the community. (Courtesy of the Burton Historical Collection, Detroit Public Library.)

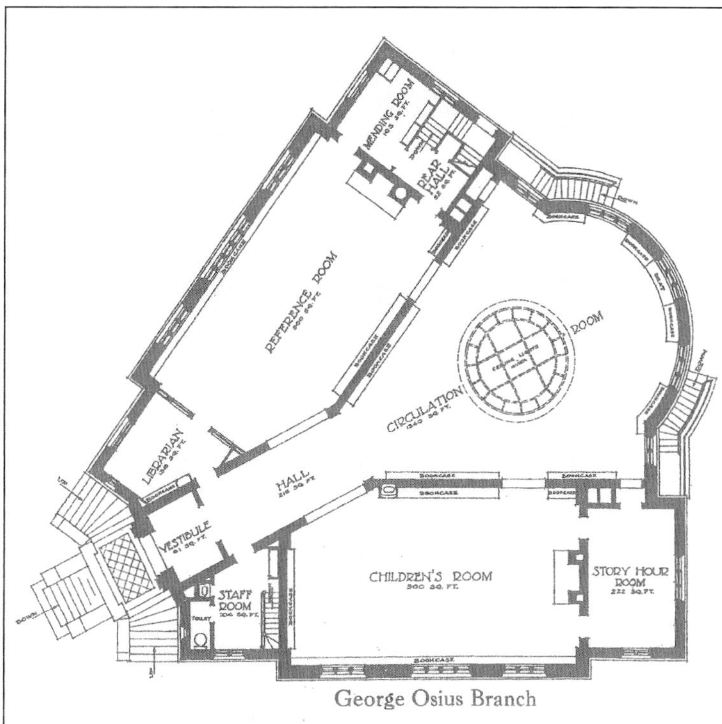

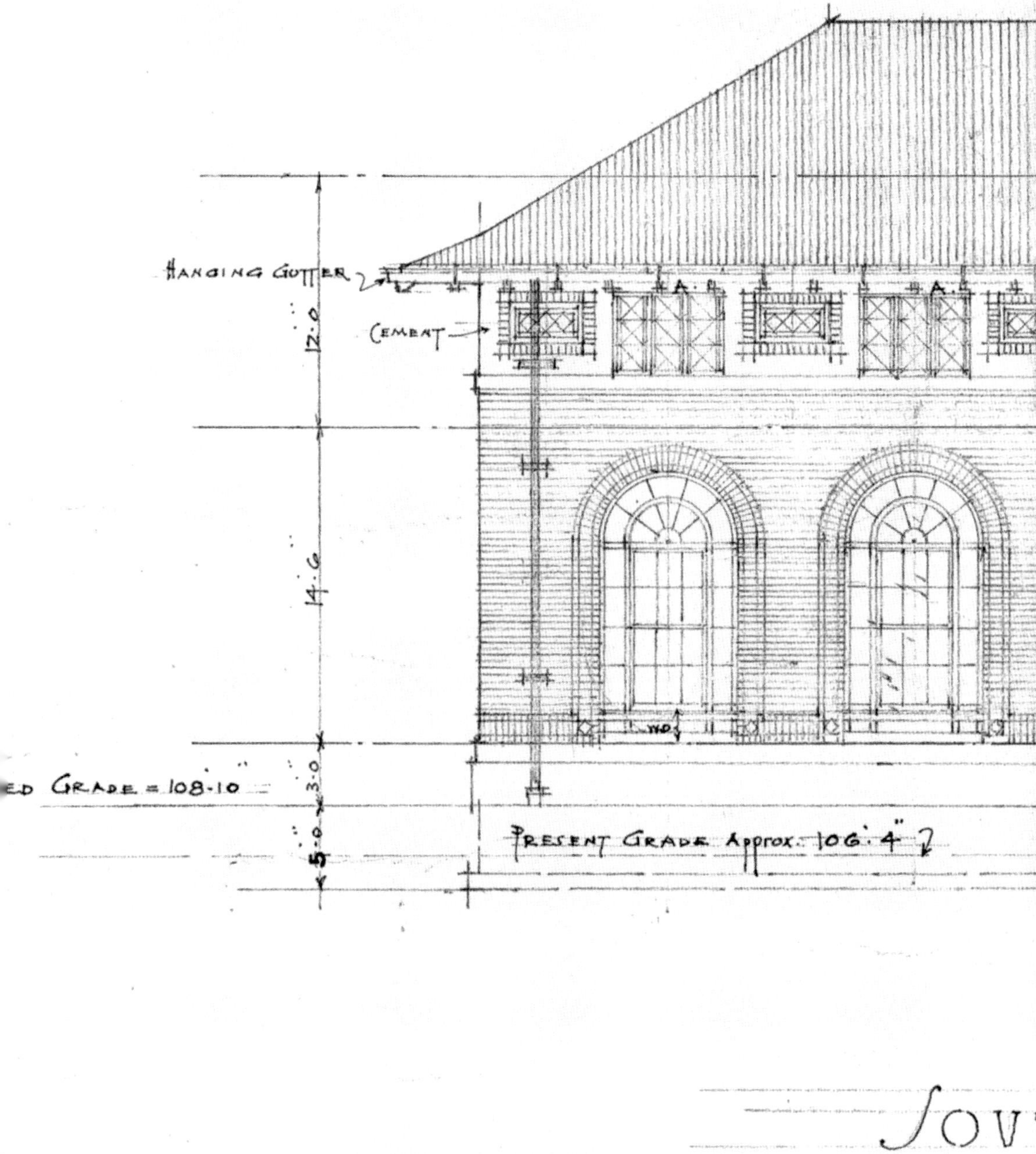

VILLAGE HALL. Following approval of the village charter on July 17, 1911, the council held its first meeting in the home of Pres. George Osius on July 24. Village business was conducted in private homes until October 1912, when the village leased a home on the southwest corner of Lake Shore and Vernier Roads. Purchase of the property where the village hall is presently located was approved in November 1913, and President Osius recommended the building of a new facility

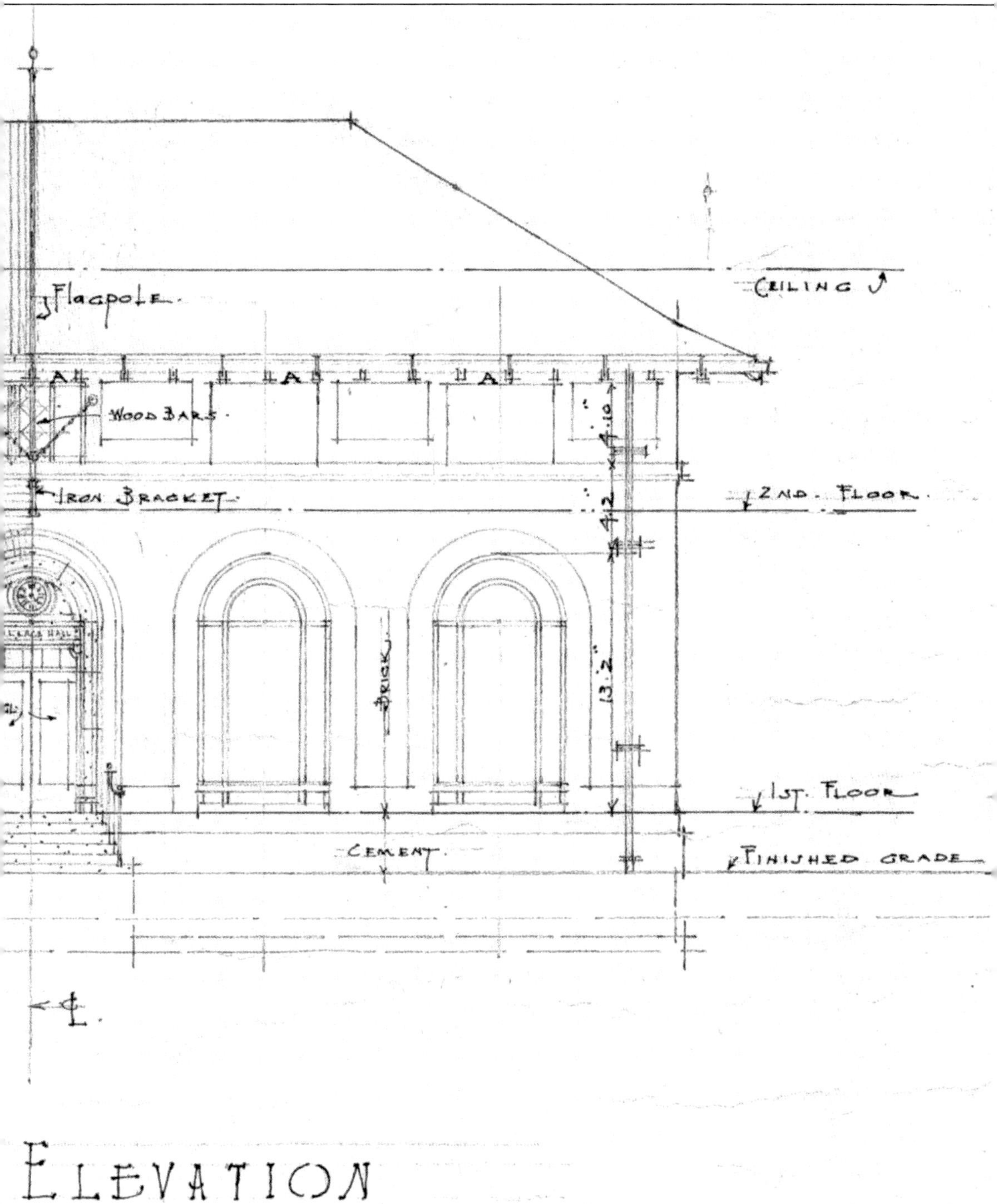

in April 1914. Detroit's most prominent architect, Albert Kahn, was retained to provide plans for the building. His design for the south elevation is seen here. An election was called, and the proposition to construct a new village hall at a cost of $22,000 was passed in November 1914. The village council met for the first time in its new home on November 1, 1915. (Courtesy of Albert Kahn Associates.)

THE DEDICATION OF THE
NEW VILLAGE HALL

WILL TAKE PLACE

FRIDAY, DECEMBER 10TH, 1915

AT 8 O'CLOCK P. M.

THE BOARD OF TRUSTEES

REQUEST THE PLEASURE OF YOUR PRESENCE

RECEPTION 8 P. M. DEDICATION 8:30 P. M.

DANCING 10 P. M.

VILLAGE HALL INVITATION. In addition to the council chambers and village offices, the new building provided a police and fire operating desk, a fire equipment room, and dormitory rooms at the rear of the second floor for firefighters. The large room over council chambers was used for community affairs such as dances and meetings. In 1916, a motion picture machine was purchased, and for a number of years villagers enjoyed movies here. (Courtesy of Albert Kahn Associates.)

VILLAGE HALL, 1927. This view of the village hall dates from 1927. Note the interurban tracks in the foreground and that Lake Shore Road is only a two-lane street. The first major change to the building came in 1929, when the second-floor spaces were converted into apartments for public safety officers. Thus, the village was able to increase staff and have personnel available for emergencies. (Courtesy of the Village of Grosse Pointe Shores.)

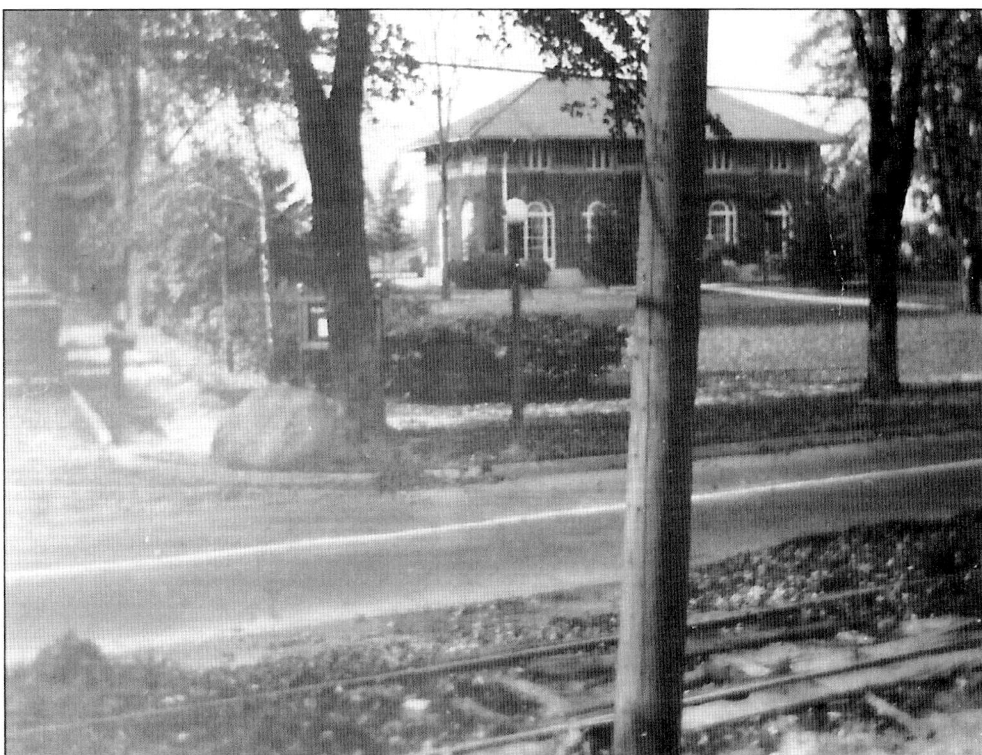

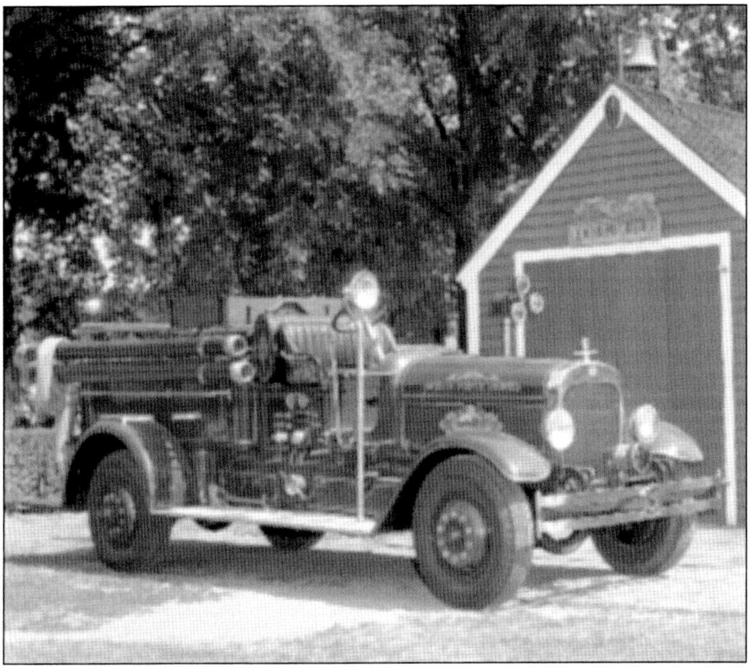

New Fire Truck. In 1924, the village purchased this Seagrave Pumper fire engine, replacing the old 1916 Model T La France fire truck. A 130-horsepower engine allowed the truck to pump 750 gallons of water per minute. After a major overhaul in 1938, this pumper continued in service until 1962. Following its decommissioning, it was donated to The Henry Ford, where it is on view today. (Courtesy of The Henry Ford.)

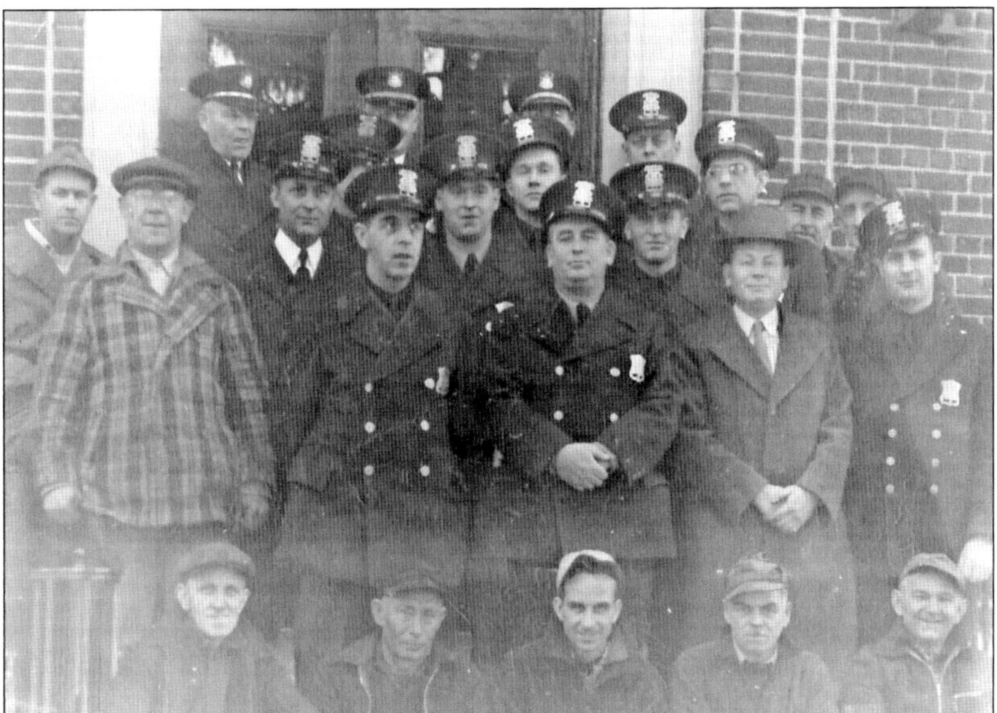

Village Employees. It was common at this time for village employees to send a special holiday greeting to all village residents. This photograph of the staff taken on the steps of the village hall was included with the 1947 card. (Courtesy of the Village of Grosse Pointe Shores.)

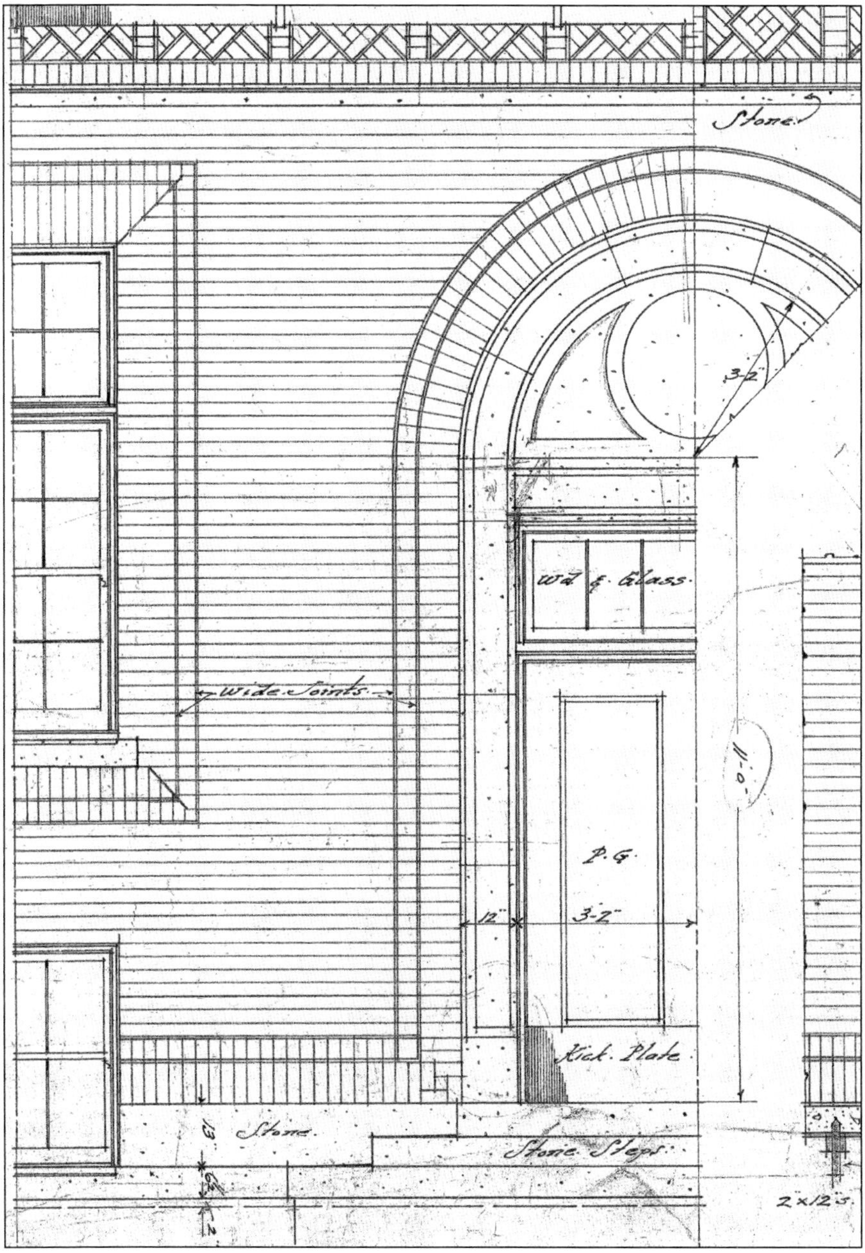

A New School. In 1915, the village turned to Albert Kahn once again—this time to build a school. His drawing of the school's front door is seen here. Construction began immediately following the design plan's approval. The building included seven classrooms on two floors. There were five rooms on the first floor, including the kindergarten and a room originally designated as a "dental clinic." One of the rooms even included a Pewabic tile fireplace decorated with figures of rabbits, ducks, roosters, and antelopes. The lower level (Kahn called it the basement) included the furnace room, janitor's room, and storage. It also included the girls' washroom and toilet and the boys' washroom and toilet. There were also two classrooms in the basement. On Kahn's original drawings, these were labeled "Manual Training" and "Domestic Science." (Courtesy of the Albert Kahn Collection, Bentley Historical Collection.)

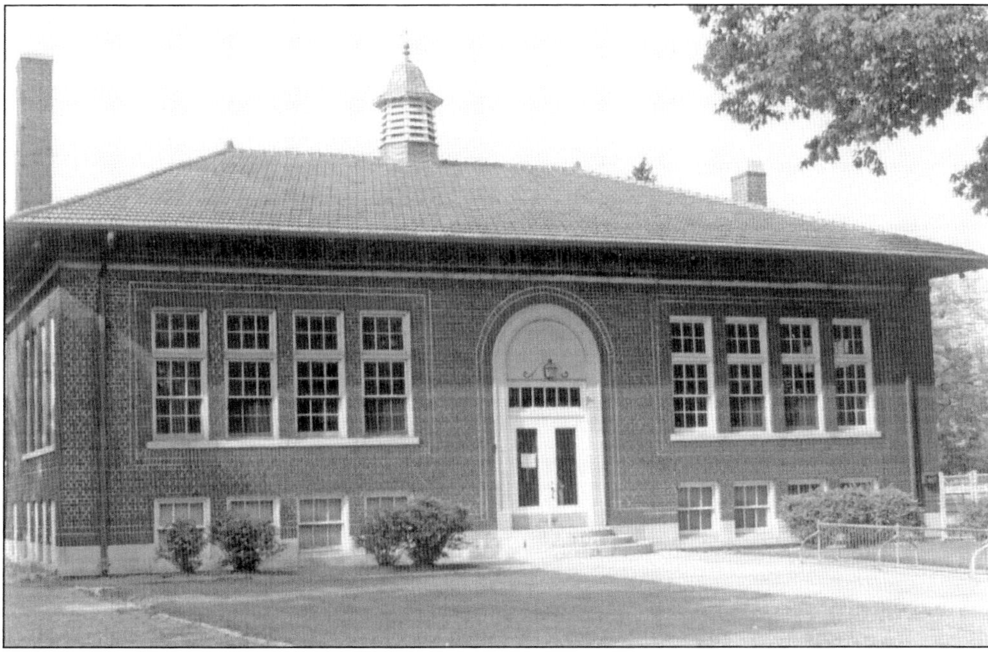

VERNIER SCHOOL. The school was built on property fronting on Vernier Road adjacent to the village hall and welcomed its first students in the fall of 1916. The Vernier School was part of the Rural Agricultural School District until 1922, when all Grosse Pointe schools were consolidated. (Courtesy of the Grosse Pointe Historical Society.)

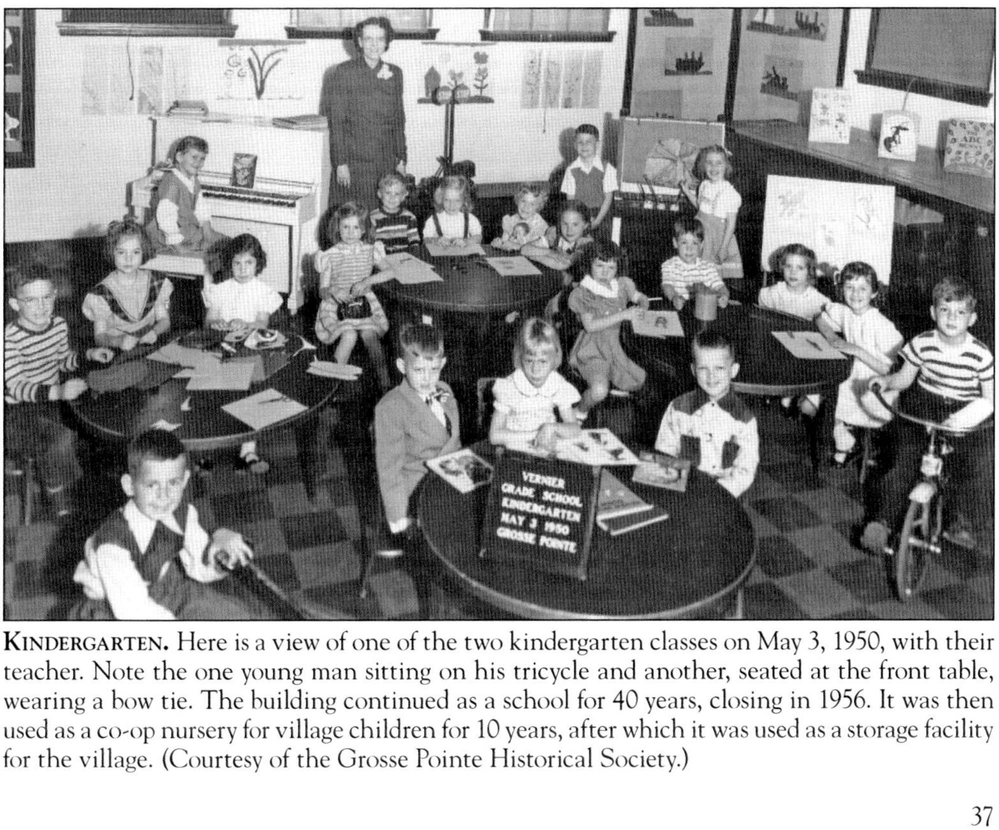

KINDERGARTEN. Here is a view of one of the two kindergarten classes on May 3, 1950, with their teacher. Note the one young man sitting on his tricycle and another, seated at the front table, wearing a bow tie. The building continued as a school for 40 years, closing in 1956. It was then used as a co-op nursery for village children for 10 years, after which it was used as a storage facility for the village. (Courtesy of the Grosse Pointe Historical Society.)

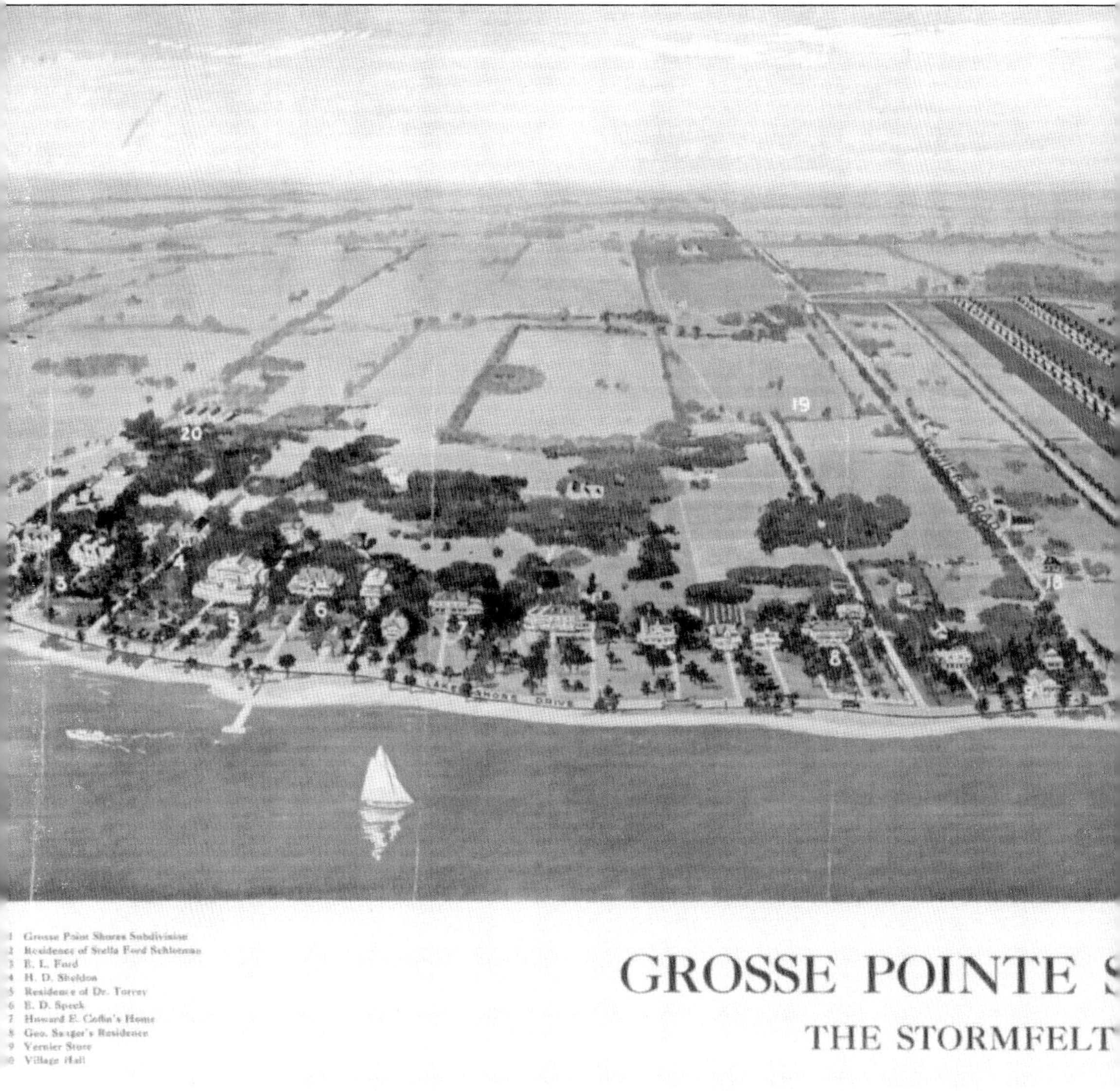

Bird's–Eye View. By the 1920s, the first subdivisions for the village were being planned. The Stormfeltz-Loveley Company published this panoramic view as an advertising piece to interest buyers in property along what appears to be present-day Hampton and Roslyn Roads. Today, this image is of particular historical interest as it identifies the location of many of the Lake Shore Road estates. The date can be guessed by noting what is (and what is not) identified. Gaukler Point is listed with Edsel Ford's name, but their house is not shown, so it must be pre-1929. The

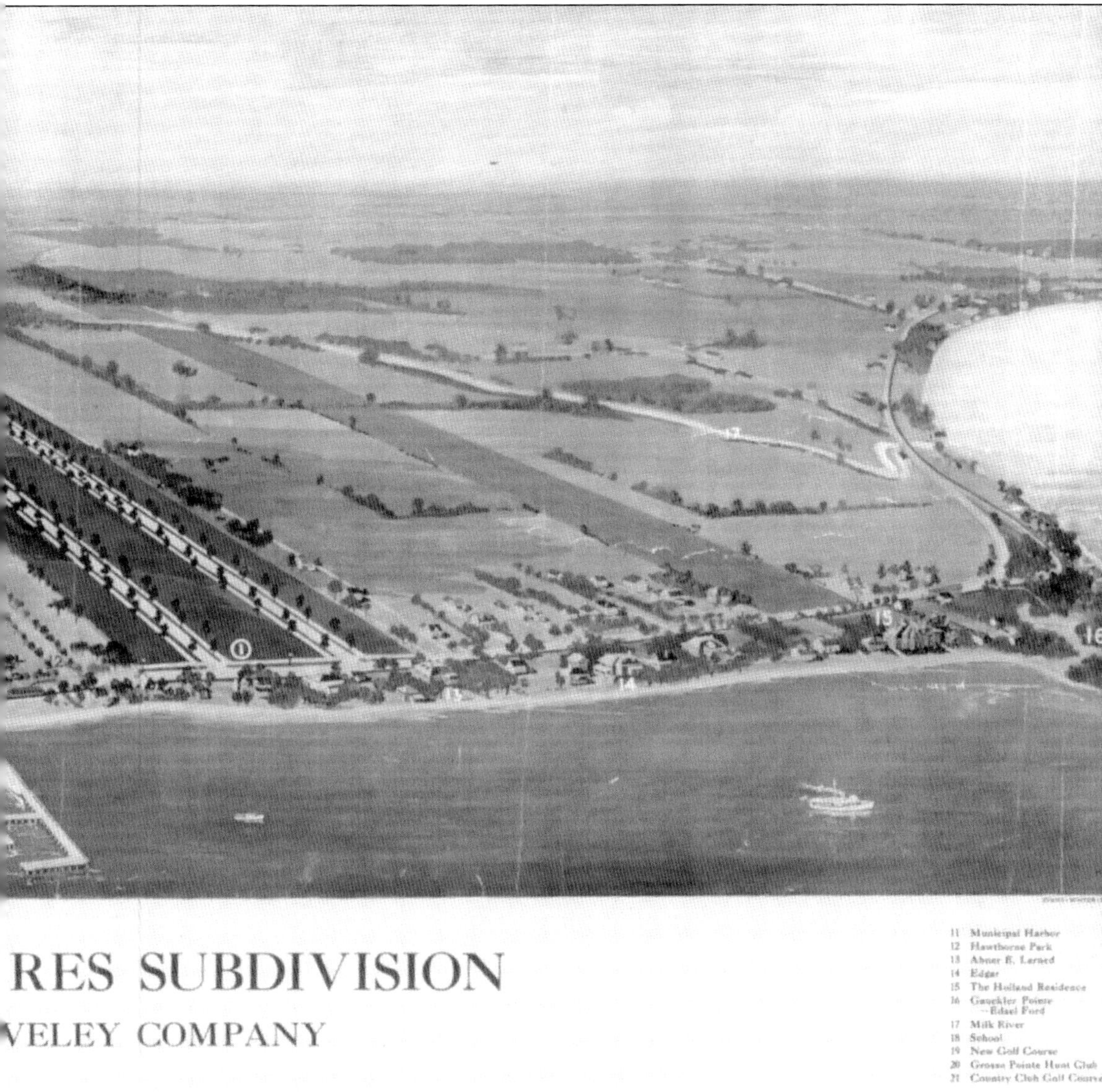

newly expanded municipal pier and harbor dates from 1927, but there is no indication of the Grosse Pointe Yacht Club clubhouse, which opened in 1929. The village hall dates from 1915 and the school from 1916. The "New Golf Course," Lochmoor, opened in 1917. The interurban tracks are shown with cars operating. The interurban ceased operation along Lake Shore Road in 1927. Thus, by using these indicators, the print dates from the mid-1920s. It is a most interesting view of the Village of Grosse Pointe Shores. (Courtesy of the Grosse Pointe Historical Society.)

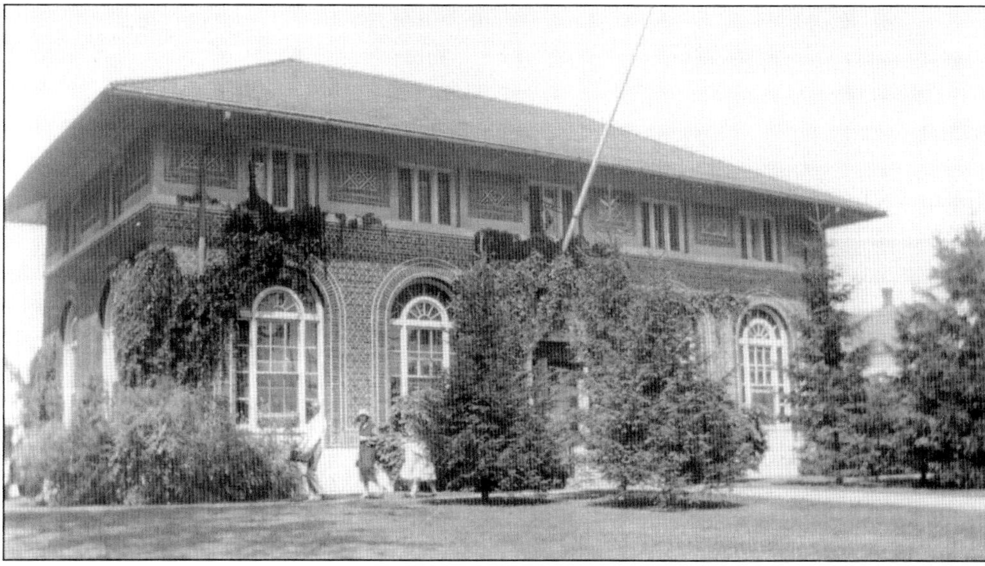

A Branch Library. In 1922, the first public library in the Grosse Pointes was opened in a room in the Grosse Pointe Shores Village Hall. The library was operated as a branch of the Wayne County Library System, following its mission statement that "the Grosse Pointe villages are entitled to books and the administrative services of a trained librarian." (Courtesy of the Grosse Pointe Public Library.)

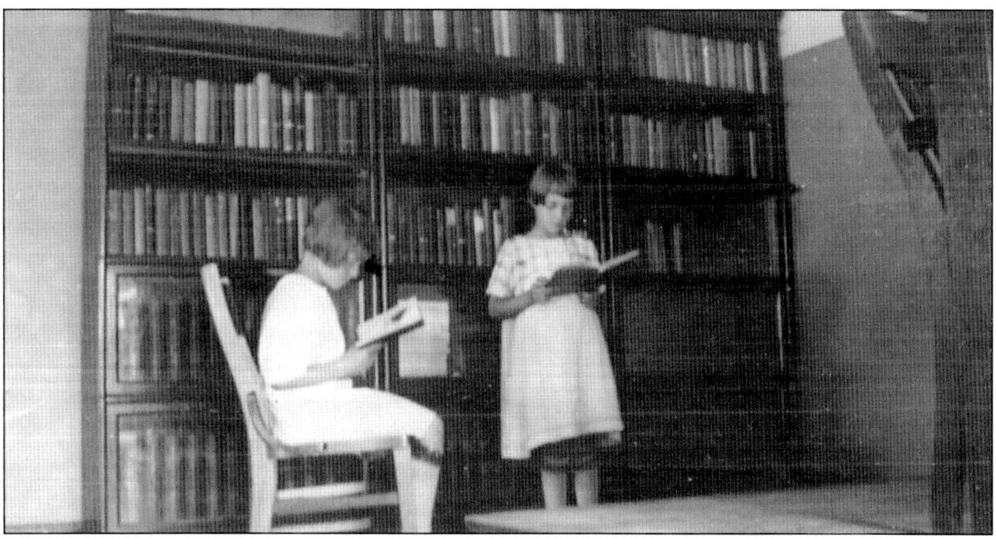

Selecting a Book to Read. Here, two young residents choose books from the shelves of the newly opened public library at the Grosse Pointe Shores Village Hall. In 1928, the Wayne County Library opened a branch library building at Waterloo and St. Clair Avenues in the City of Grosse Pointe. (Courtesy of the Grosse Pointe Public Library.)

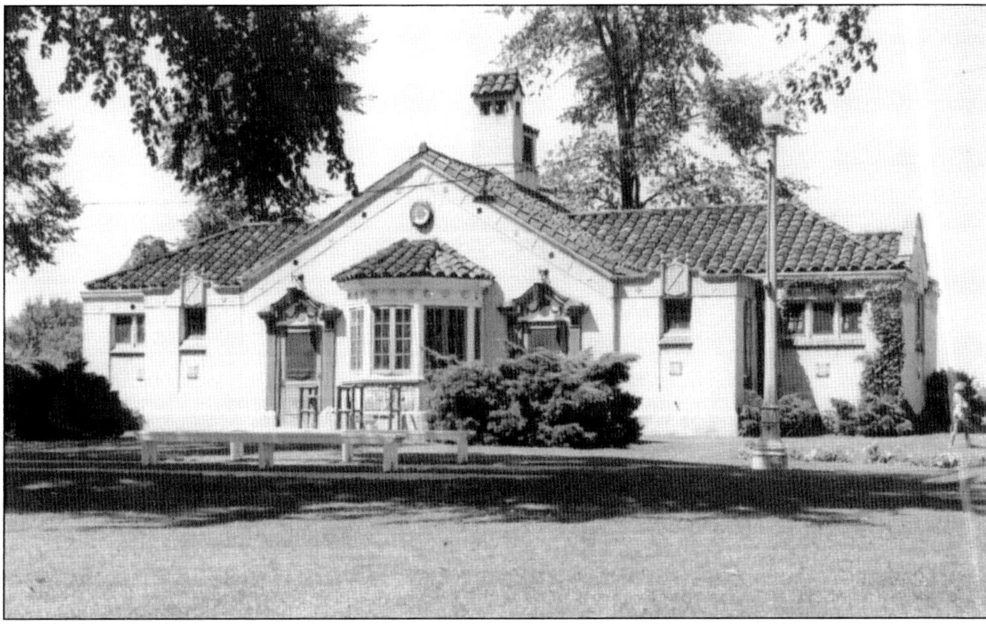

GEORGE OSIUS MUNICIPAL PARK AND NEW BATHOUSE. In 1915, the village began construction of a waterfront park at the foot of Vernier Road. This was the first municipal park to be built in the Pointes. A 1,300-foot wooden pier was built with a rectangular enclosure at its end to form a boat harbor, giving residents a place to keep sailboats and small power craft. A beach was created at the shoreline for swimming, and a small building with lockers was constructed. In 1926, the village acquired additional land, and in 1927, a bond issue was approved enabling the village to fill in the shoreline creating a six-acre park, build a new bathhouse, and install a more permanent pier and seawall. In 1932, the park was officially named George Osius Municipal Park, and a handsome plaque and monument were dedicated honoring Osius for his years of public service. (Both, courtesy of the Grosse Pointe Historical Society.)

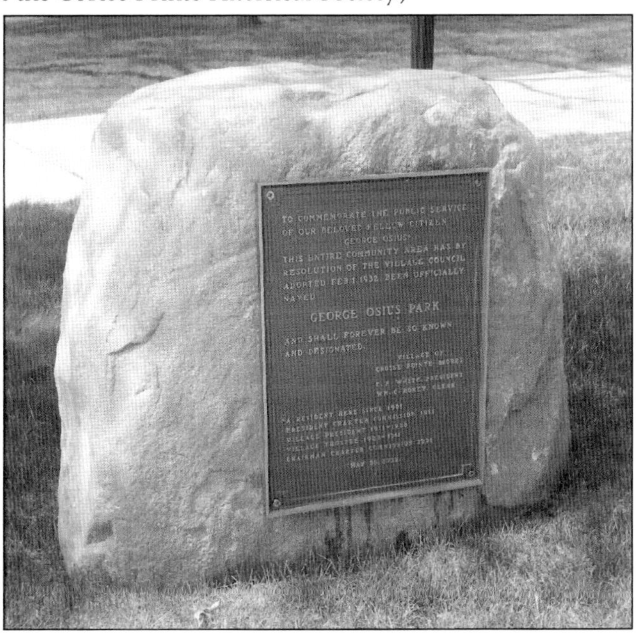

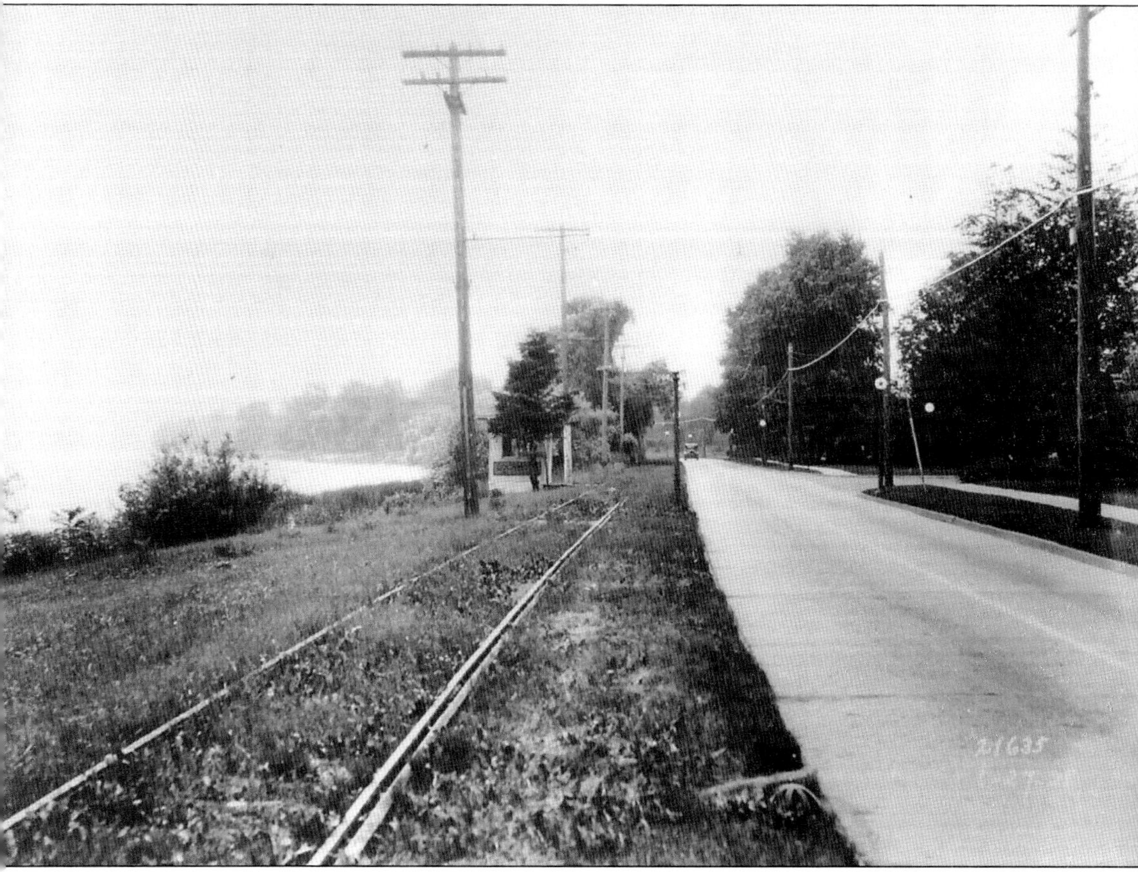

The End of the Interurban. With the end of the interurban system, plans were begun to widen Lake Shore Road. The abandoned tracks are seen here in 1928. They were soon taken up, and in 1930 and 1931, the Wayne County Road Commission began construction of the road using fill taken from the excavations of the new skyscrapers being built in Detroit. The wooden shelter seen here was at Lochmoor Boulevard. On Lochmoor off of Lake Shore Road was the home of Brace Beemer; from 1941 to 1954, Beemer was the voice of the Lone Ranger on radio station WXYZ in Detroit. Beemer also portrayed Sgt. William Preston of the Yukon on *Challenge of the Yukon* for a brief time after *The Lone Ranger* series ended. Following his death in 1965, Beemer's house was torn down and the property divided into three lots. (Courtesy of Kenneth Schramm.)

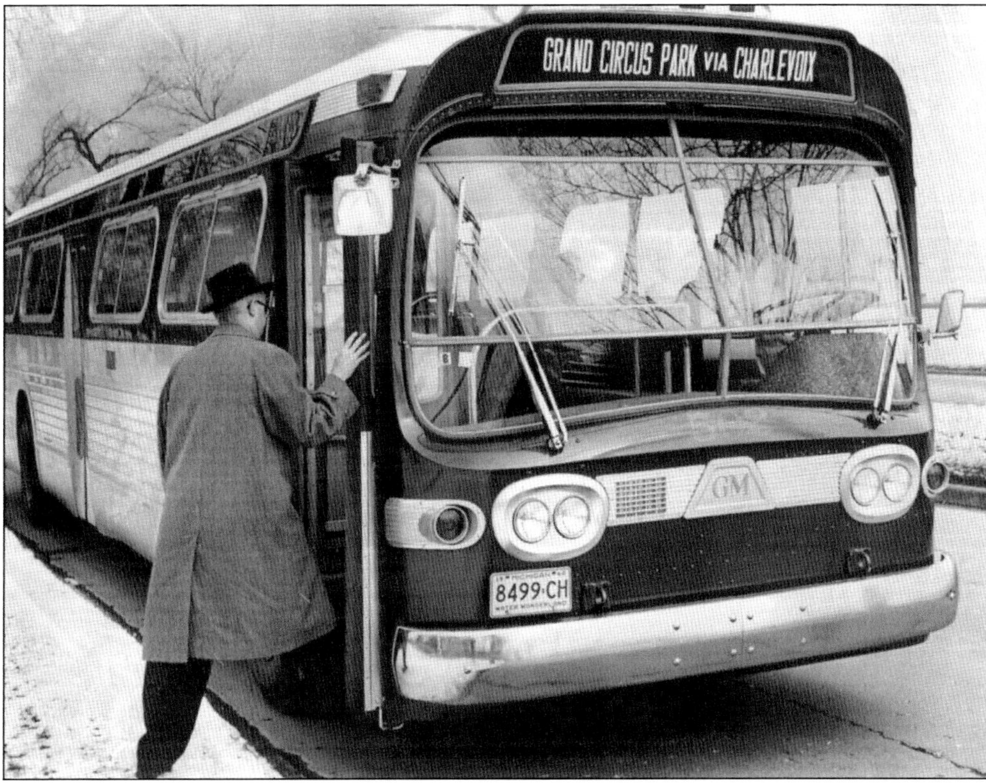

New Bus Service. The motorbus system replaced the old interurban rail system. Here, a bus of the Lake Shore Line is seen loading passengers for the trip out to Grosse Pointe in the 1960s. Bus service to the Pointes was taken over by SEMTA (Southeast Michigan Transit Authority) in 1973. (Courtesy of Kenneth Schramm.)

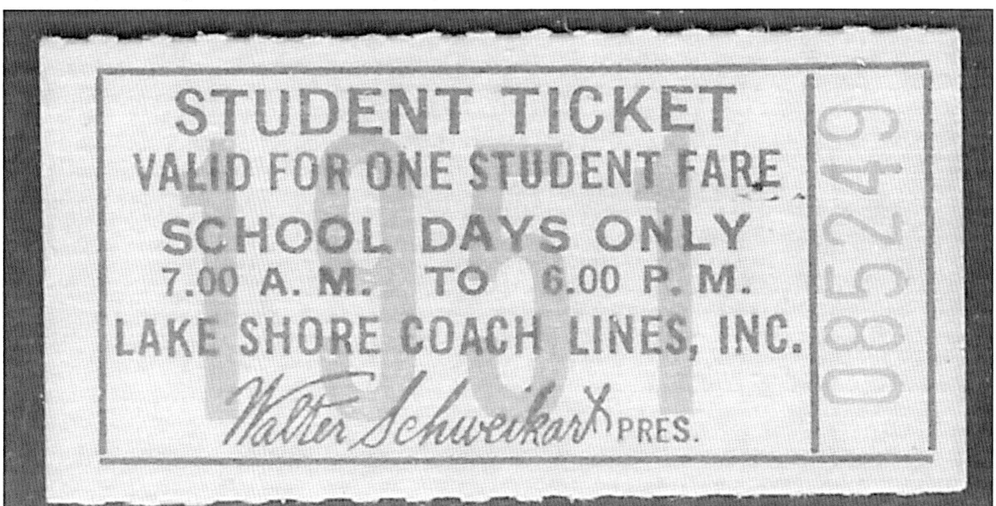

Student Ticket. Public bus service was used by students as transportation to and from school in the 1950s. Schoolchildren were able to purchase tickets at a substantial savings. However, a ticket could be used only at certain times, like "school days only," as this Lake Shore Coach Line ticket from 1951 clearly states. (Courtesy of Kenneth Schramm.)

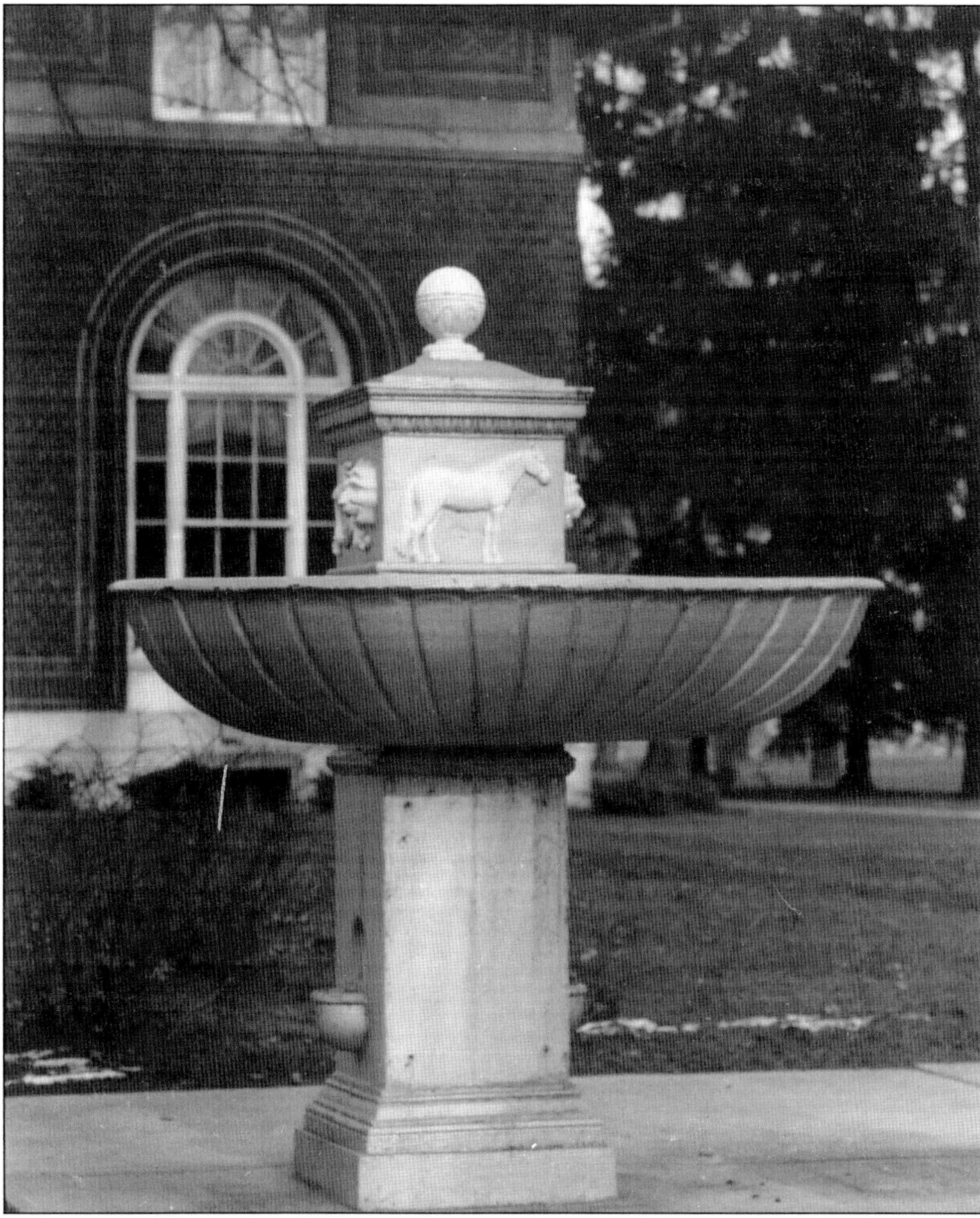

The Fountain. The Animal Welfare Committee of the 20th Century Club appeared before the village council on July 21, 1913, to request the installation of a permanent drinking fountain for horses and dogs. The corner of Vernier and Lake Shore Roads was suggested as a location for the fountain, which was donated by the Good Cheer Club of the Girls Friendly Society. The site was approved, and the fountain was installed on April 15, 1914. The fountain featured a large basin for horses, a small basin below for dogs, and a bubbler on the side for pedestrians. Unfortunately, the widening of Vernier Road left the fountain, as seen here, dangerously close to the roadway; in 1980, it was struck almost head-on by an automobile. Supporting rods broke, and the cast iron fountain exploded into its component parts. The parts were gathered and the fountain was completely reassembled and moved across the road to the George Osius Municipal Park. (Courtesy of the Grosse Pointe Historical Society.)

Three

The Mansions of Lake Shore Road

Beginning in the first years of the 20th century, more than a dozen mansions were built along Lake Shore Road in the Village of Grosse Pointe Shores as year-round estates for some of Detroit's wealthiest and most successful families. These homes represented a variety of architectural styles including English Tudor, French Renaissance, Italianate, Georgian, Regency, and of course, the more informal yet still grand Colonial. These great homes were designed by such nationally known architects as Detroiter Albert Kahn, Albert H. Spahr of Pittsburgh, and Ralph Adams Cram of Boston and New York. The architects took advantage of the magnificent lake views, and the houses were intentionally linked with formal terraces, gardens, and lawns. These grand estates included Deeplands, built in 1911 for Henry D. and Caroline Shelden; Claireview, built in 1913 for Dr. Harry N. and Nell Torrey; and possibly the grandest of them all, Stonehurst, built for Joseph and Stella Schlotman in 1917. This construction movement continued into the 1920s and even into the difficult years of the 1930s with homes for Oscar and Marjorie Webber in 1927, Alvan and Estelle Macauley in 1930, and Standish and Lotta Backus in 1934. All of these magnificent homes were built to last, but in reality, most survived for only a relatively short time. After the passing of the patriarchs and matriarchs, family members subdivided many of the estates, and the properties were rebuilt with luxury homes, unique in design and style, incorporating modern building techniques and modern amenities. The Village of Grosse Pointe Shores took the lead in a successful effort to prudently control this new real estate development as the village evolved into the beautiful community that it is today.

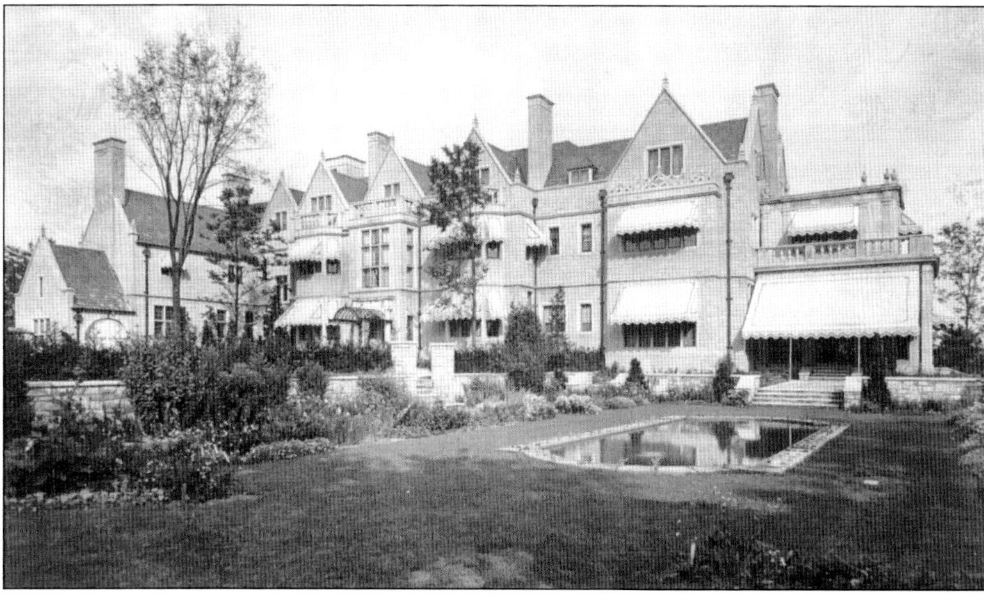

Schlotman House. In 1914, upon returning from a three-month honeymoon abroad, Joseph Schlotman and his bride, Stella Ford, began construction of their house at 500 Lake Shore Road, which they named Stonehurst. This would be one of the grandest of the great mansions that once lined Lake Shore Road in the Village of Grosse Pointe Shores. The Schlotmans hired Albert Spahr of Pittsburgh to design their 40-room Early English Renaissance manor that would occupy a 30-acre site. (Courtesy of Manning Brothers Historic Photograph Collection.)

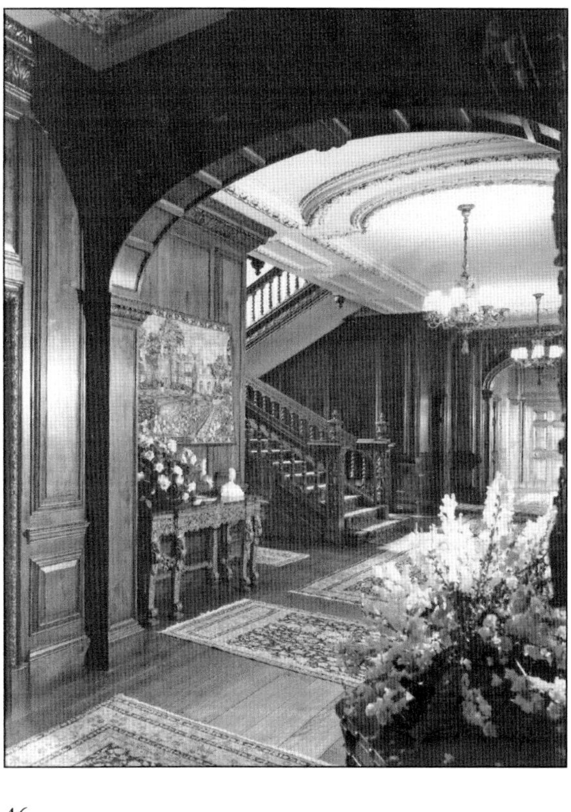

Schlotman House Main Hall. The Schlotman mansion was built about 500 feet from the lakeshore and was flanked by the estates of Stella's three siblings, Hetty (Mrs. Elmer R. Speck); Nell (Mrs. Harry N. Torrey); and their brother, Emory L. Ford (no relation to Henry Ford). One entered Stonehurst at the great hall with its carved-oak paneling, ornate ceilings, and grand staircase. Directly ahead of this main hall was the marble and stone atrium. (Courtesy of the Grosse Pointe Historical Society.)

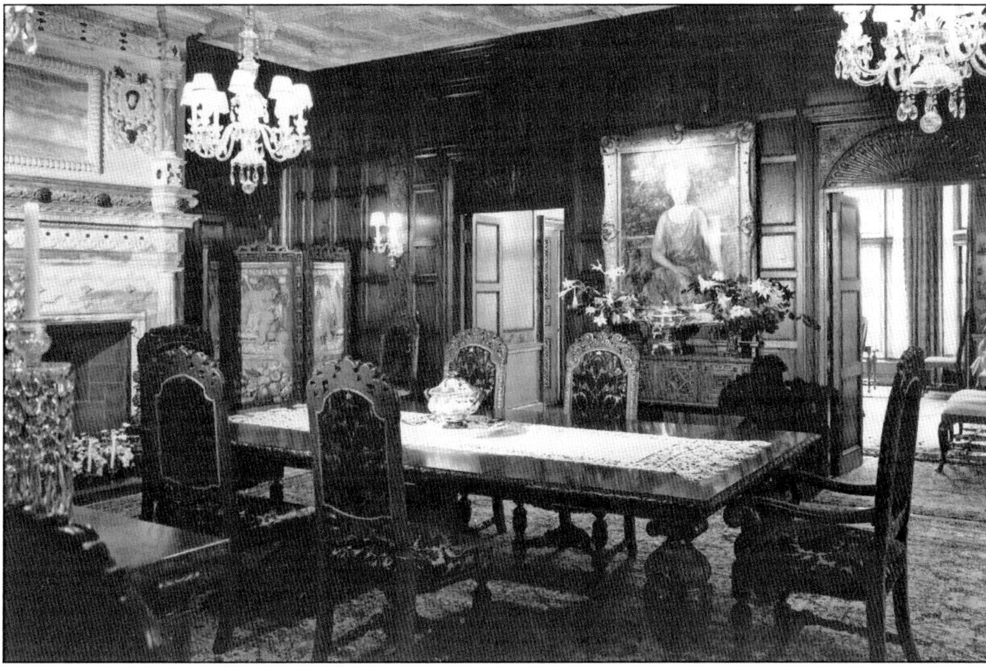

SCHLOTMAN HOUSE DINING ROOM. Located off the atrium was this elegant dining room. At the opposite end of the atrium were the paneled library, the magnificent music room brought from England, and a sun porch. A spacious ballroom occupied the lower level. On the garden side of the house were the formal gardens, terraces, and porch. Farther back on the property were the greenhouse, the seven-car garage, and the head gardener's and chauffeur's houses. (Courtesy of the Grosse Pointe Historical Society.)

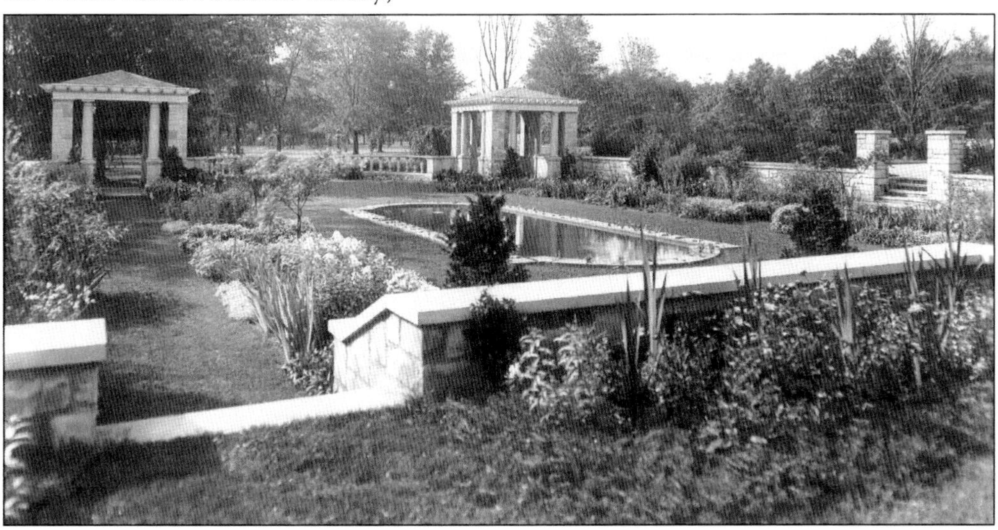

SCHLOTMAN HOUSE GARDEN. After her husband's death in 1951, Stella Schlotman continued to live at Stonehurst, and it remained the scene of parties, debuts, and charity events. Stella Schlotman died in January 1974 at the age of 95. Stonehurst had survived 57 years. The house was demolished in 1974, and the property, by then reduced to about 10 acres, was subdivided into more than 20 lots for new homes. All that remains today is the low stone wall fronting on Lake Shore Road. (Courtesy of the Grosse Pointe Historical Society.)

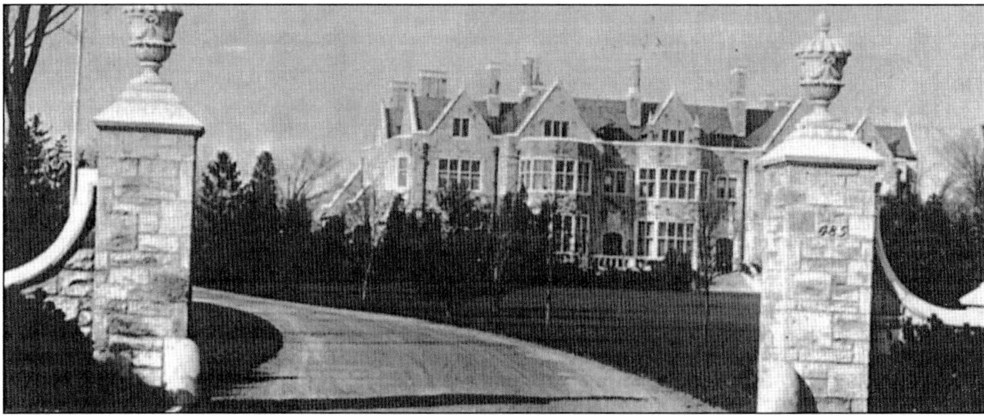

E.L. Ford House. The Emory L. Ford House, built in 1916 at 485 Lake Shore Road, was also designed by Albert H. Spahr. Emory Ford and his sisters were grandchildren of Capt. John B. Ford of Pittsburgh, founder of the Pittsburgh Plate Glass Company and the Michigan Alkali Company at Wyandotte. For many years, Emory Ford was president of the latter company. The stone entrance pillars remained after the demolition of this home in the 1950s and can still be seen on Lake Shore Road. (Courtesy of Manning Brothers Historic Photograph Collection.)

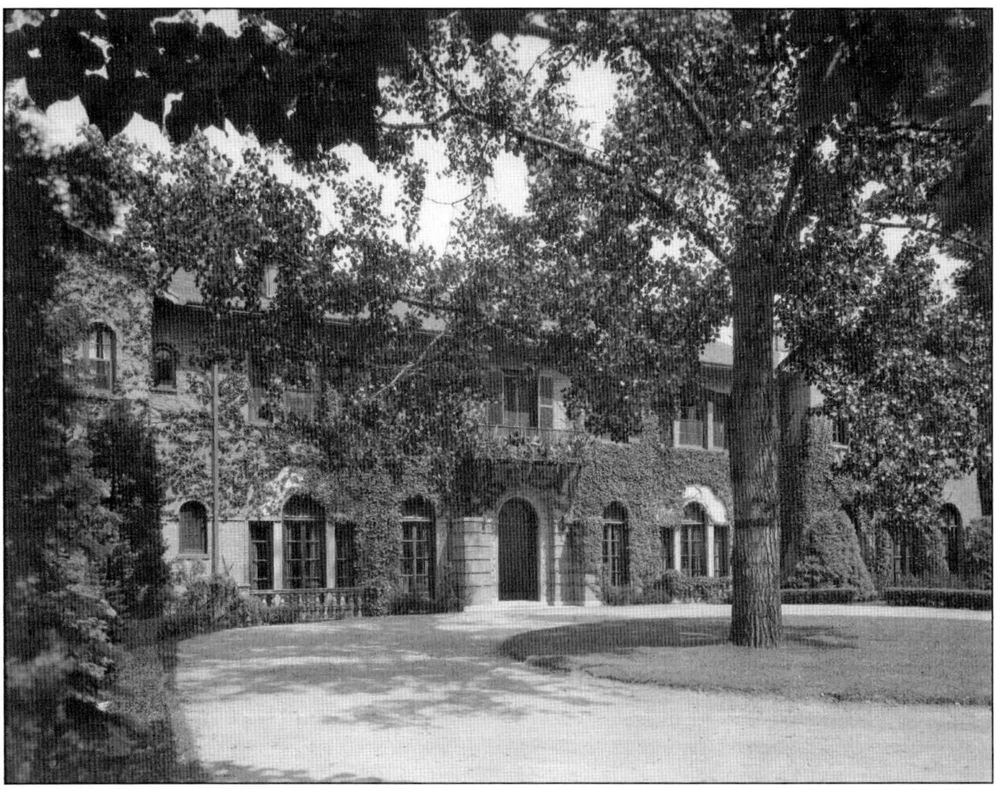

Shelden House Entrance. In 1911, this house was built for Mr. and Mrs. Henry D. Shelden at 525 Lake Shore Road. The architect was Arthur Huen of Chicago. The exterior walls of the house were faced with grayish-yellow bricks, and the roof tiles were green. French doors opened onto an inviting terrace flanked by projecting bays. The entrance, approached by a driveway, was at the rear of the house. (Courtesy of the Grosse Pointe Historical Society.)

SHELDEN HOUSE WALKWAY. The house could be seen from Lake Shore Road at the end of this long wooded walkway. The property consisted of some 80 acres, having approximately 1,100 feet of frontage on Lake St. Clair with a portion extending inland about 3,000 feet. (Courtesy of the Grosse Pointe Historical Society.)

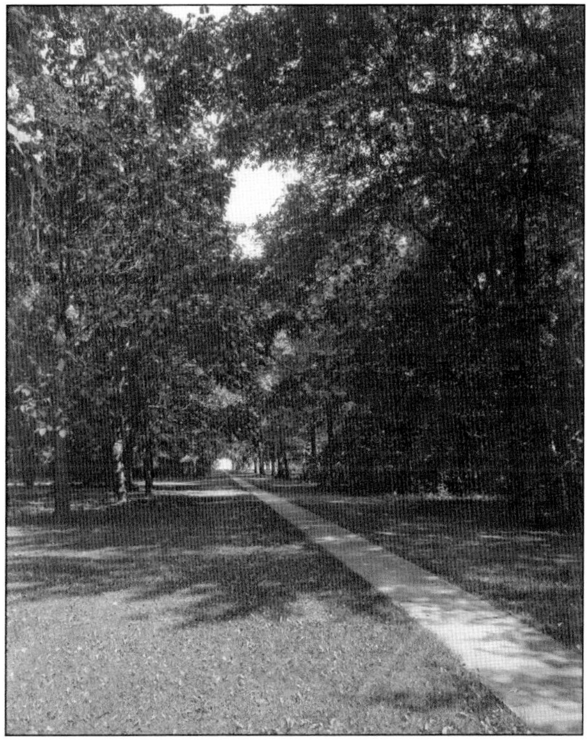

SHELDEN HOUSE LIBRARY. Mrs. Shelden was the daughter of Civil War general Russell A. Alger, former governor and senator from Michigan. Many of the furnishings for the Shelden House came from the Alger family home in Detroit. The library, seen here, was filled with family portraits and heirlooms. The heads in the library all came from family hunting trips. (Courtesy of the Grosse Pointe Historical Society.)

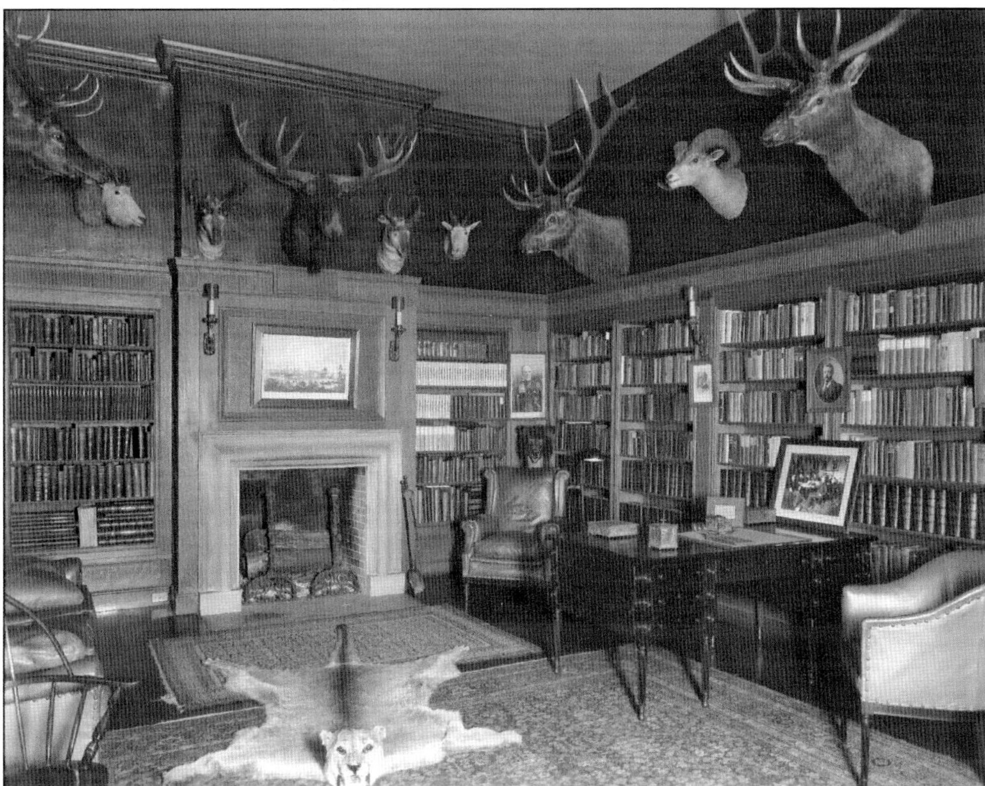

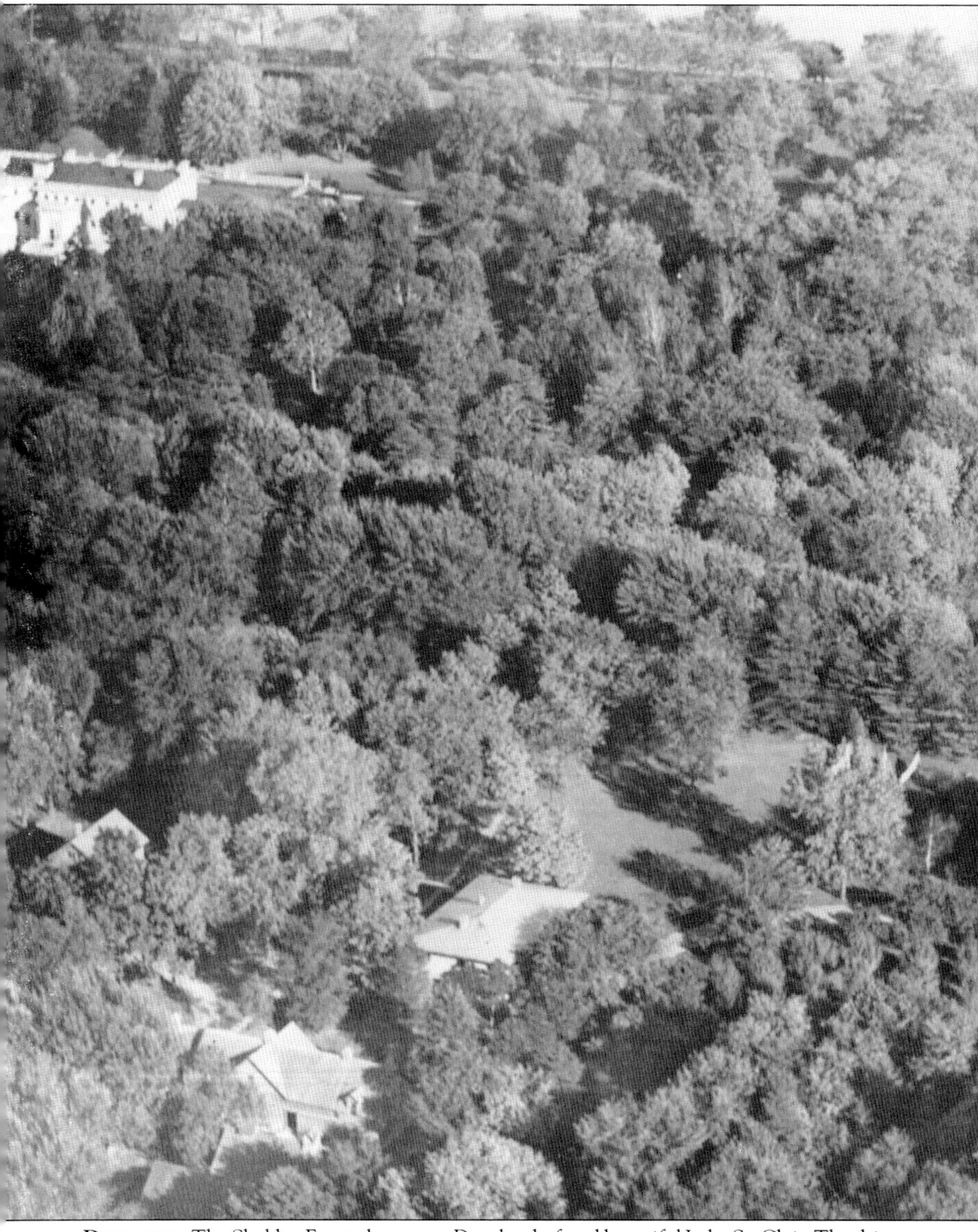

DEEPLANDS. The Shelden Estate, known as Deeplands, faced beautiful Lake St. Clair. The driveway came through the trees to the right in this aerial view. The three smaller buildings included a four-car garage, the gardener's house, and the stable. A vista was cut through the trees to afford a view of the lake. The house to the left belonged to Dr. and Mrs. Harry N. Torrey. The estate

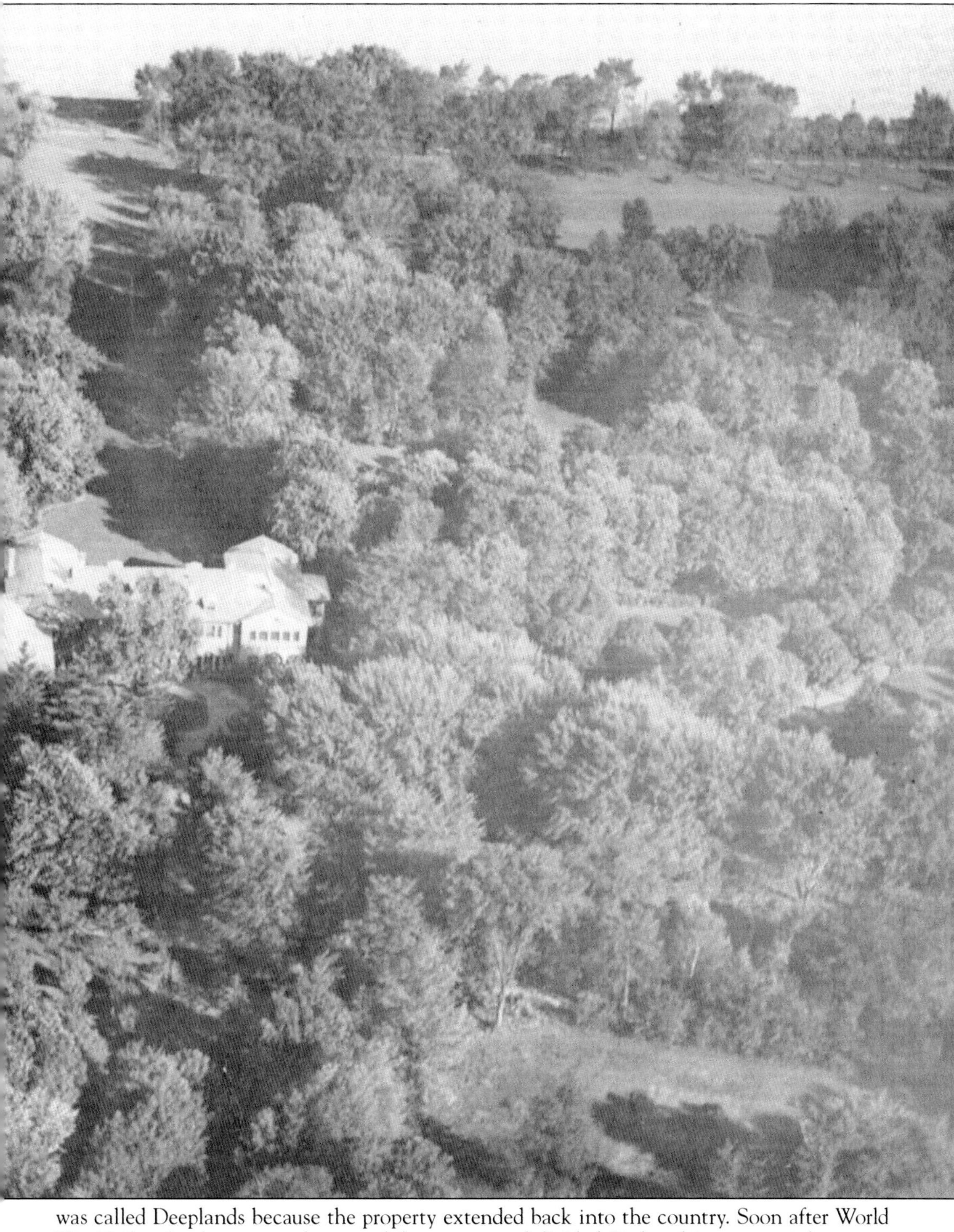

was called Deeplands because the property extended back into the country. Soon after World War II, Deeplands was torn down, and the property subdivided. Today, this property is known as Deeplands subdivision. (Courtesy of the Grosse Pointe Historical Society.)

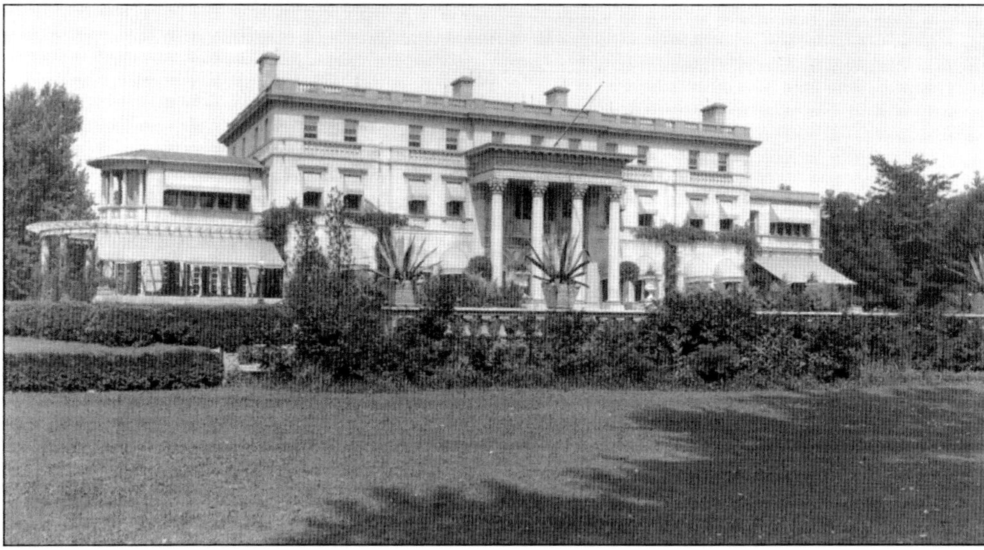

Torrey House and Dining Room. Detroit architect John A. Scott, who had just completed the Wayne County Building in downtown Detroit, designed this Italian Renaissance–style home. Built between 1911 and 1913 on the site of the former Claireview Jersey Stock Farm, the house burned in 1959 and was torn down in 1960. This home was built for Dr. Harry N. Torrey and his wife, Eleanor "Nell" Ford Torrey, sister of Stella Ford Schlotman. As can be seen in the view of the dining room below, the Torreys created an elegant setting for entertaining. According to an account in the *Detroit News*, royalty and statesmen danced across the home's marble floors. Dr. Torrey, a noted surgeon, yachtsman, and big game hunter, hosted a medical convention for 1,200 at the mansion in 1916. (Both, courtesy of the Grosse Pointe Historical Society.)

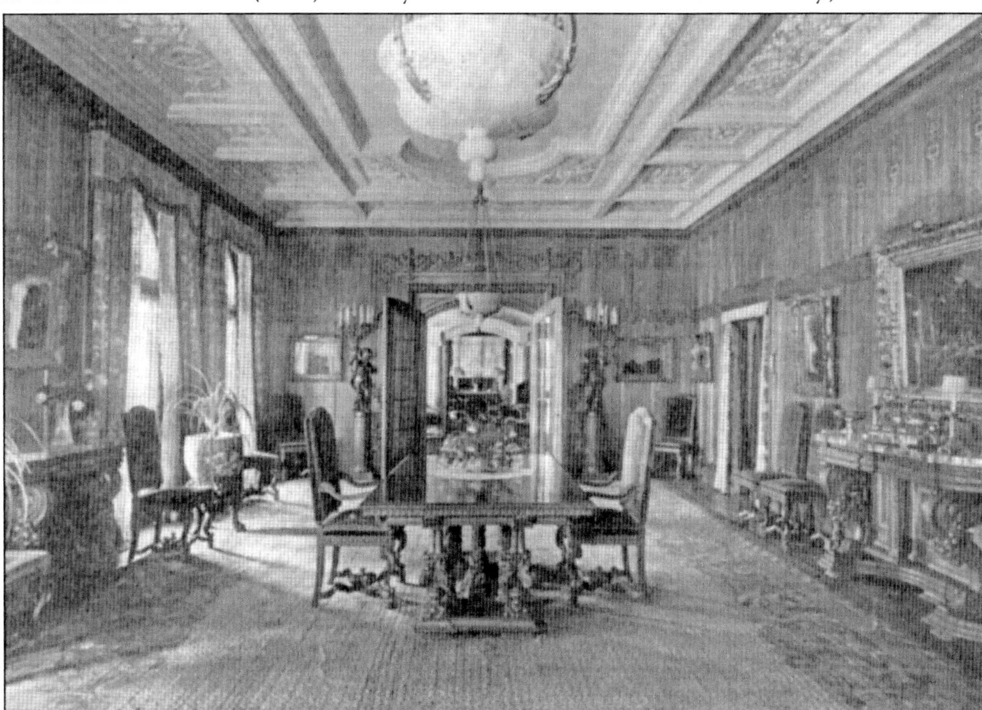

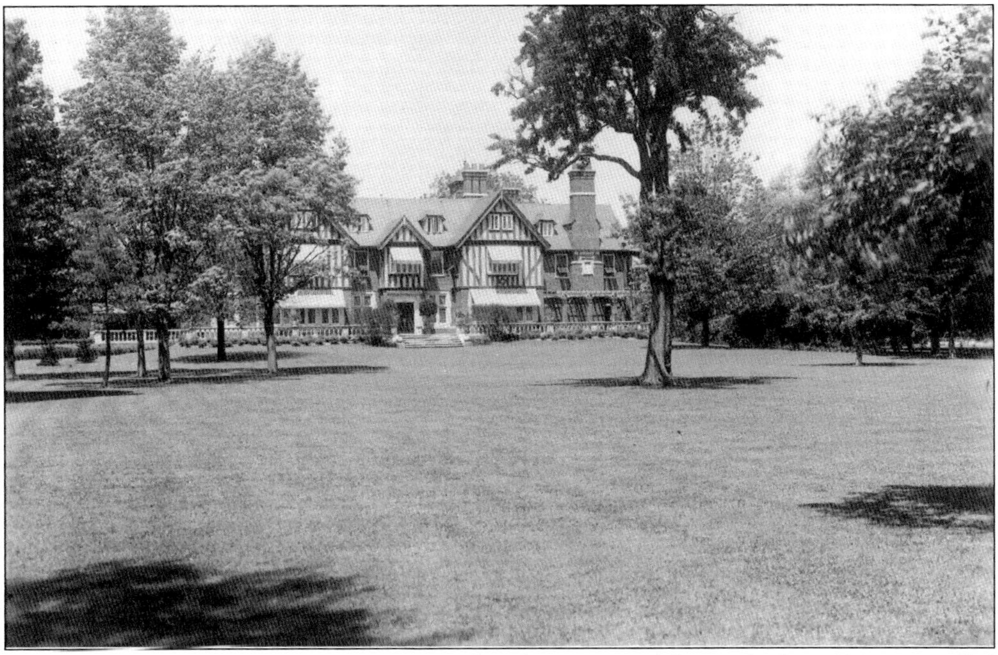

Speck House and Speck House Garden. The Elmer R. Speck house, built in 1914, was called Fairholme. Architect Albert H. Spahr of Pittsburgh designed the half-timbered Tudor-style mansion at 585 Lake Shore Road. Hetty Ford Speck was the sister of Stella Ford Schlotman, Nell Ford Torrey, and Emory L. Ford. These four siblings were the grandchildren of Capt. John B. Ford, originally of Pittsburgh. The origin of the family no doubt accounts for their choice of an architect from Pittsburgh for the Speck, Schlotman, and E.L. Ford houses. (Both, courtesy of the Manning Brothers.)

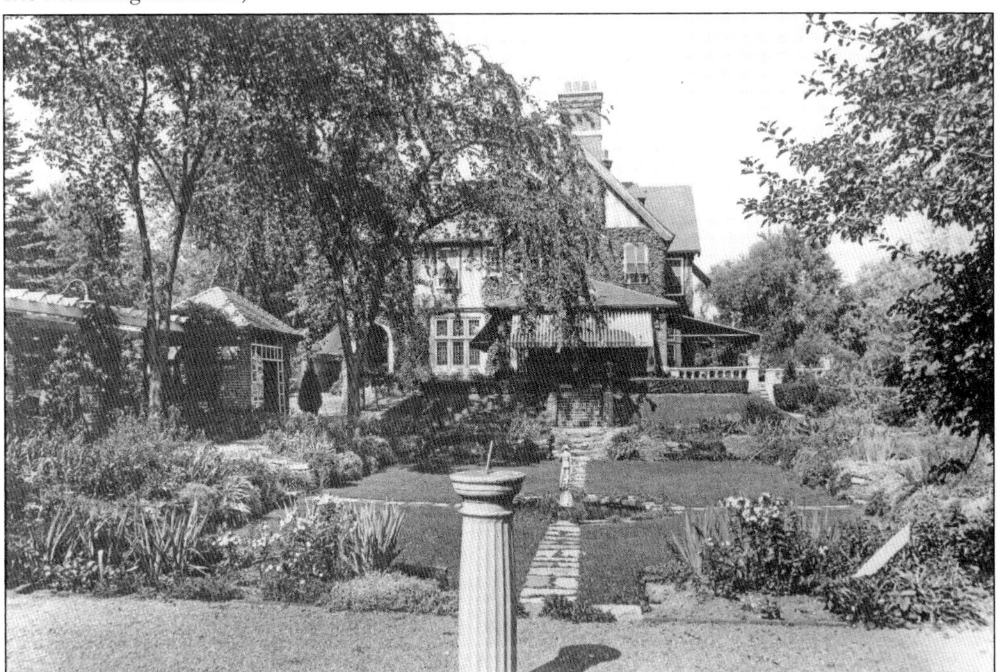

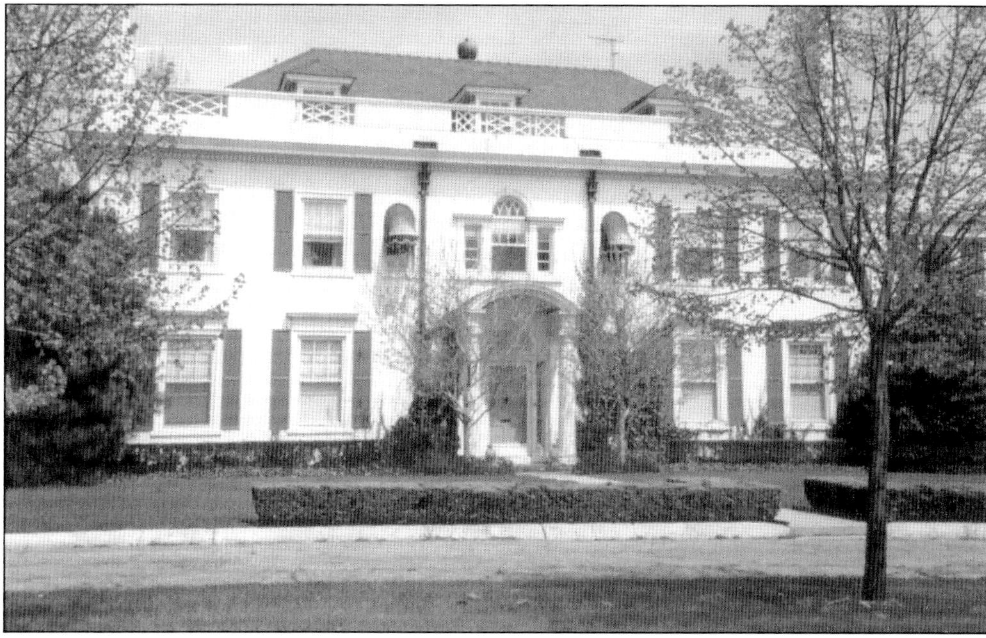

Ballantyne House. Built in 1914 at 2 Claireview Road at Lake Shore Road, this Colonial Revival house, with Classical details, was the home of Ford Ballantyne, secretary-treasurer of the Michigan Alkali Company of Wyandotte. The adjoining residence, Fairholme, was owned by Ballentyne's mother, Hetty Speck. (Courtesy of the Grosse Pointe Historical Society.)

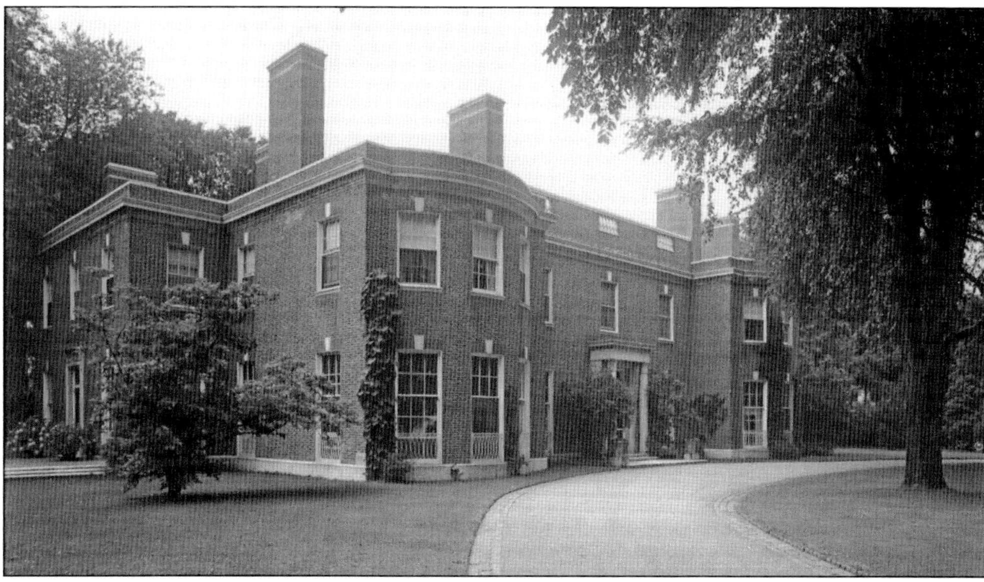

Clark House. Located at 635 Lake Shore Road, this home was built in 1934 for Emory W. Clark, then president of First National Bank of Detroit. Architect Hugh T. Keyes, an associate of Albert Kahn, designed it. Regency in flavor with curved bay windows and delicate iron grillwork railings, this home was beautifully landscaped. Later it was the home of Benson Ford, vice president of the Ford Motor Company and son of Edsel and Eleanor Ford. Benson served on the Village of Grosse Pointe Shores Council during the 1950s. (Courtesy of the Manning Brothers Historic Photograph Collection.)

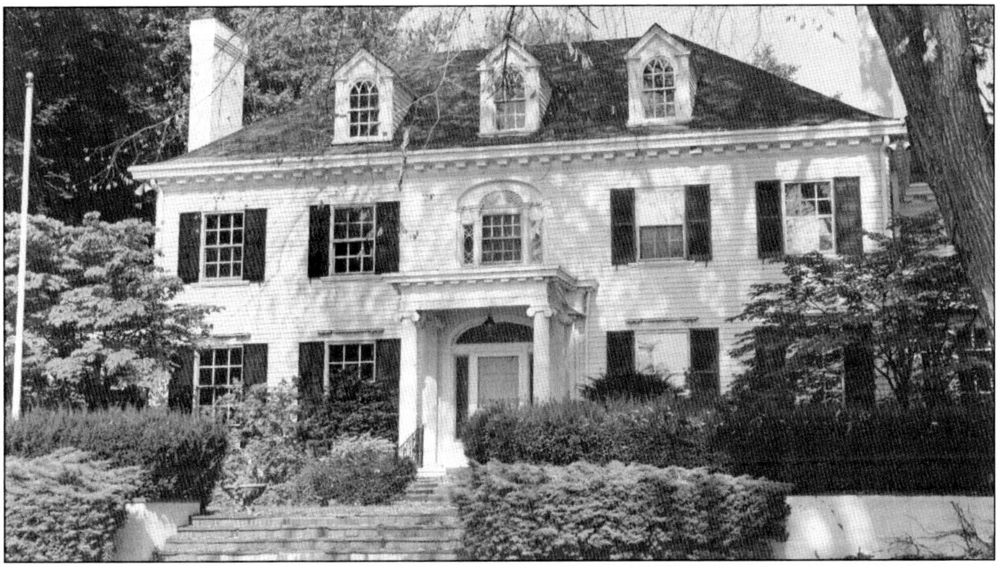

JEWETT HOUSE. Walter MacFarland designed this home at 625 Lake Shore Road in 1909 for Harry M. Jewett, president of the Paige-Detroit Motor Company. It was a Georgian-style clapboard home originally used as a summer cottage. In addition to the house, the estate included a boathouse, reflecting pools, a gazebo, and an orchard. Robert and Victoria Liggett presently own this home; they completed an extensive restoration of the house, naming it Ellenhall. Today, this 7,500-square-foot home sits on more than two acres with a panoramic view of Lake St. Clair. (Courtesy of the Grosse Pointe Historical Society.)

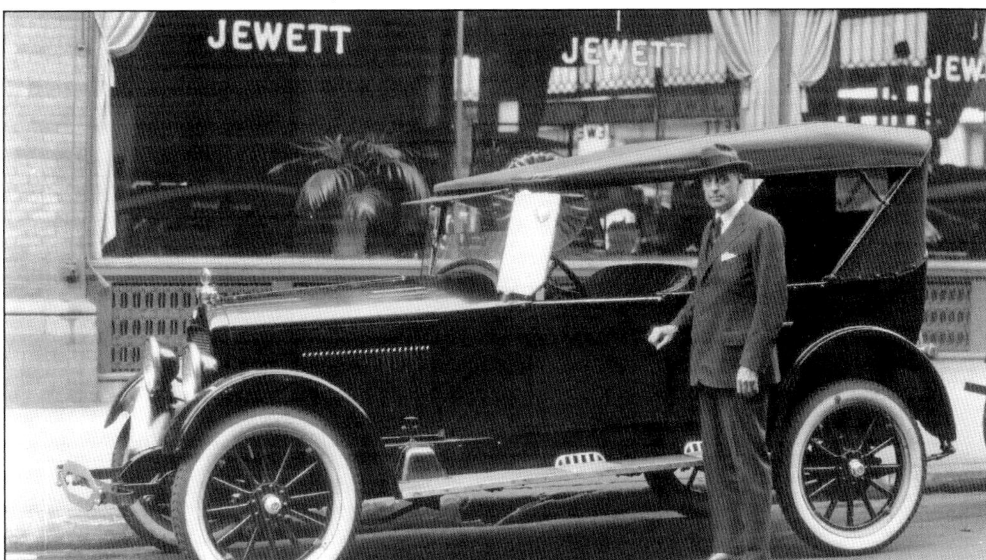

HARRY M. JEWETT. A civil engineer, Jewett was hired as president of the newly formed Paige-Detroit Motor Car Company in 1909. From 1923 to 1926, the company also built the Jewett car, seen here in front of a Detroit dealership. Harry Jewett was long active in civic affairs for the Village of Grosse Pointe Shores, serving on the first village council in 1911 with George Osius. Jewett was also an early member of the Grosse Pointe Yacht Club, serving as commodore from 1919 to 1925. (Courtesy of the National Automotive History Collection, Detroit Public Library.)

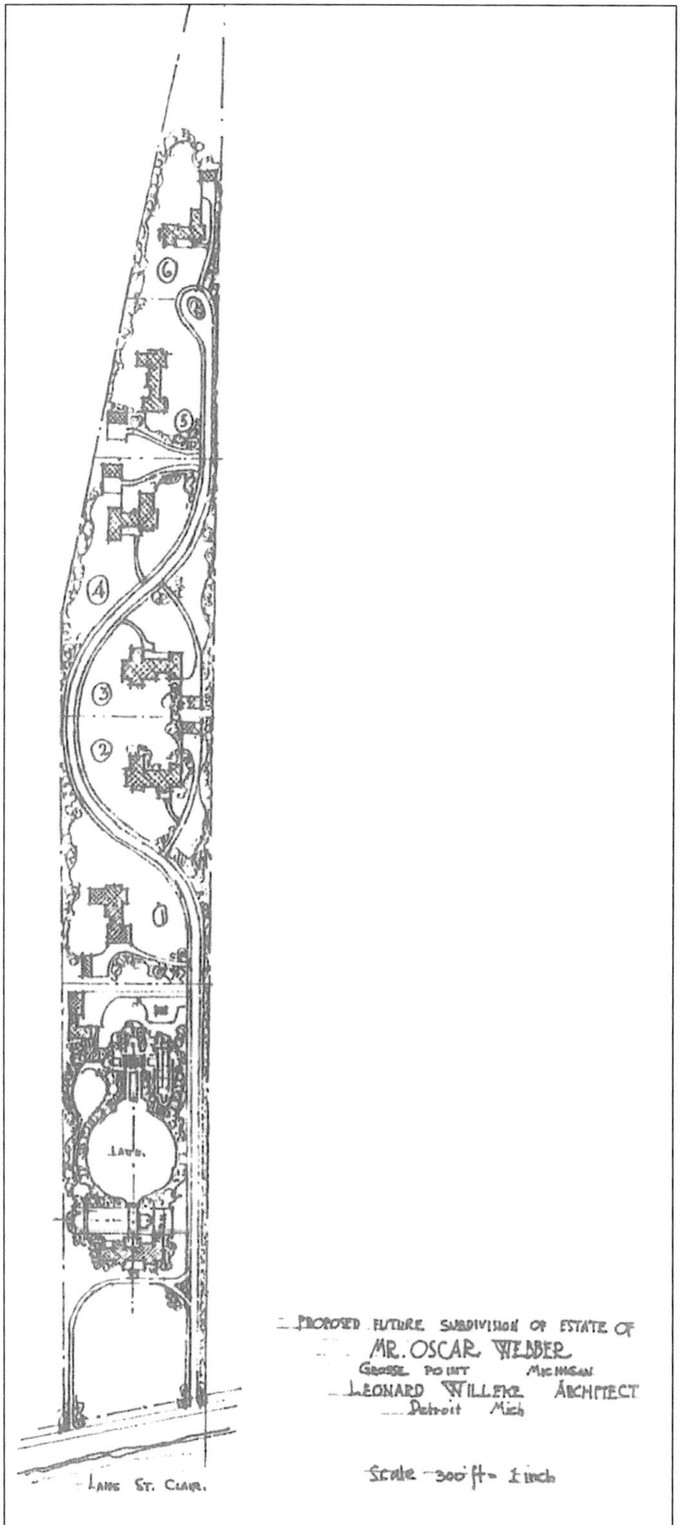

WEBBER HOUSE PLAN. Noted architect Leonard B. Willeke built this mansion for Oscar and Marjorie Webber at 619 Lake Shore Road. This map is Willeke's 1924 scheme for the future subdivision of the Webber estate. The plan allowed for the construction of six houses at the rear of the property while maintaining the integrity and gracious front lawn of the Webbers' mansion. (Courtesy of Thomas W. Brunk.)

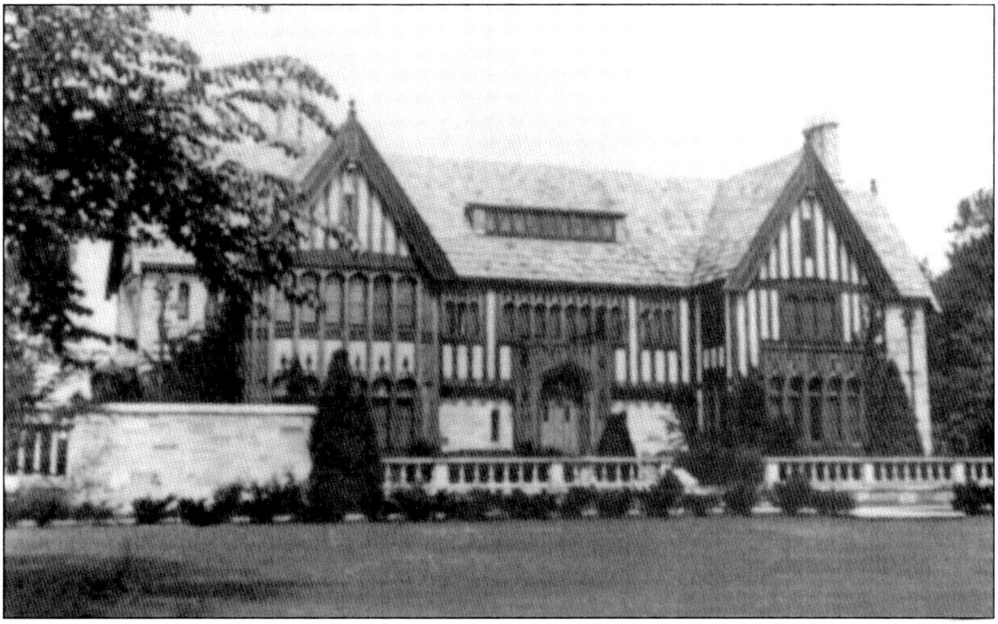

WEBBER ESTATE. This is a view of the front of the mansion after the addition of the large terrace balustrades and garden wall around 1935. One of the most important aspects of this beautiful home are the features of the exterior woodwork—birds, vines, flowers and grapes—that are repeated throughout the interior, notably on the doors, the main staircase, fireplaces, and cornices. This is one of the few of the great Lake Shore Road mansions still standing. (Courtesy of Thomas W. Brunk.)

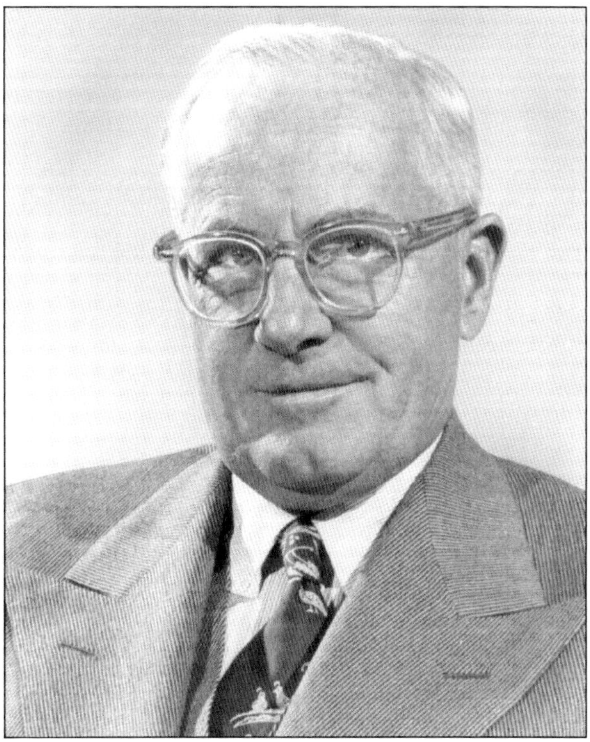

OSCAR WEBBER. Oscar Webber was one of four brothers, all nephews of Joseph L. Hudson, to hold an executive position in the great Detroit J.L. Hudson department store. He started as a cash boy in 1903. He graduated from the University of Michigan in 1910 and became vice president and general manager of the store in 1912 and president in 1948. Webber was connected with the store's later expansion, including the building of Northland Center. (Courtesy of the Grosse Pointe Historical Society.)

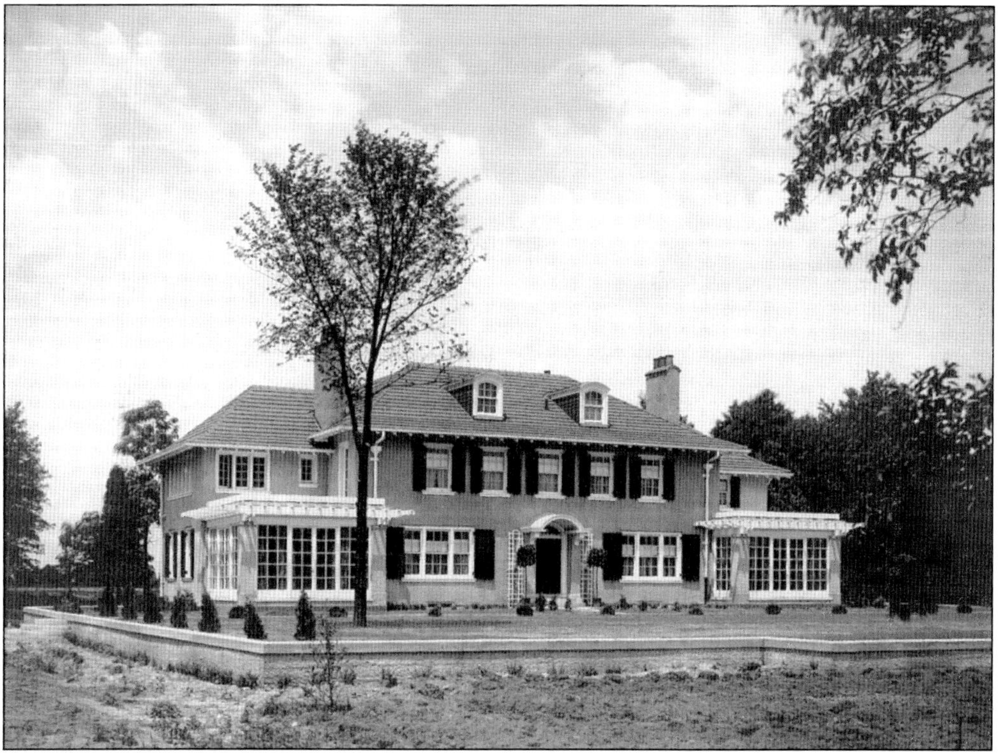

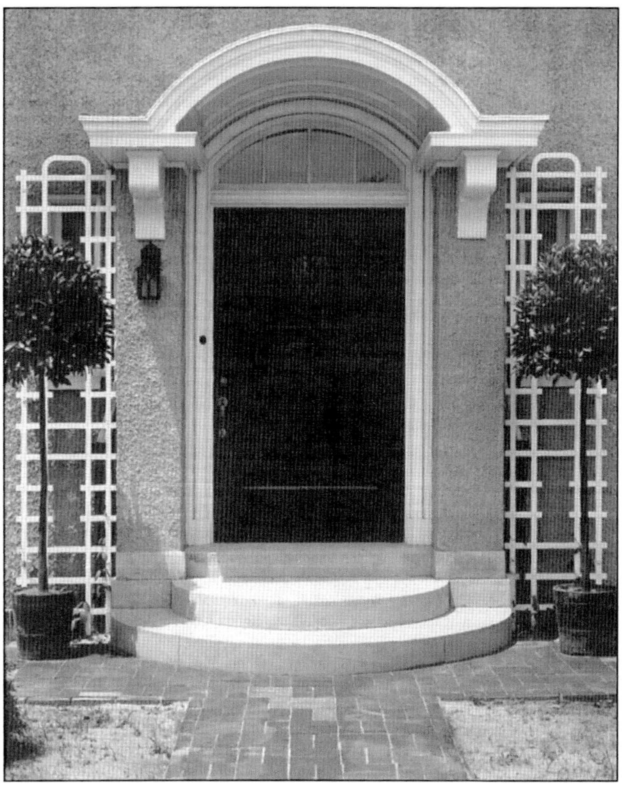

COFFIN HOUSE AND FRONT DOOR DETAIL. This attractive house at 633 Lake Shore Road was one of the five Albert Kahn houses in the Village of Grosse Pointe Shores. It was built in 1910 for Mr. and Mrs. Howard E. Coffin. He attended the University of Michigan, majoring in mechanical engineering. An automobile engineer and industrialist, Coffin was one of the founders of the Hudson Motor Car Company with Roy D. Chapin. He was also a charter member of the Society of Automotive Engineers, serving as president in 1910. During World War I, Coffin served as chairman of the Aircraft Board, which organized aircraft production and industrial mobilization. Coffin retired from Hudson in 1930 but served as a consultant until his death in 1937. (Both, courtesy of Albert Kahn Associates.)

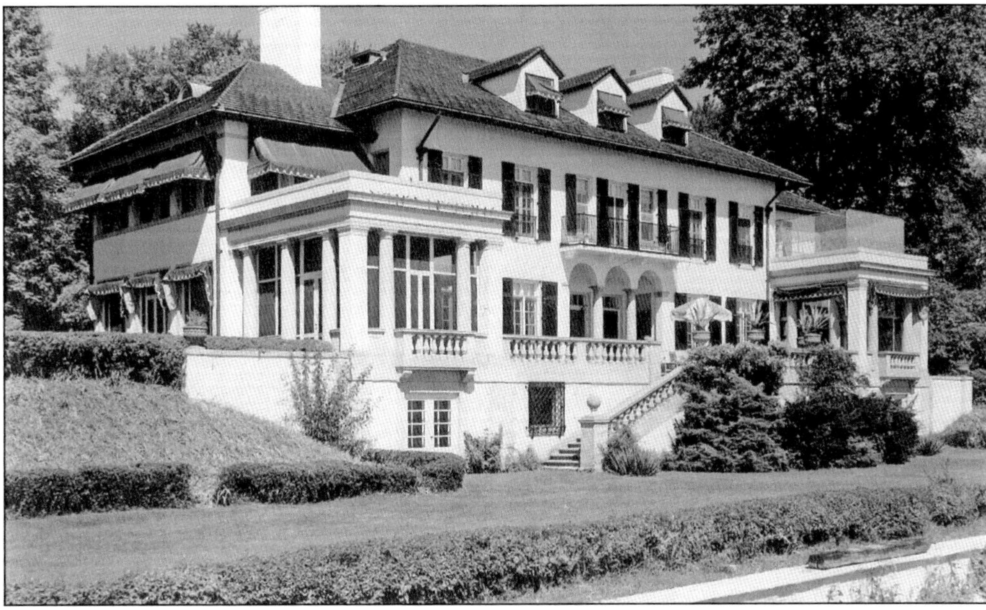

Edgar House and Terrace. This home was built in 1910 by Albert Kahn for C. Goodloe Edgar, president of Edgar Sugar House, dealers in sugar and molasses. The house has Italian Renaissance influences and is similar to the Moorings, the Russell Alger Jr. house. Albert Kahn was a great admirer of architect Charles A. Platt of New York, who designed a series of estates in Grosse Pointe including the Alger house, one of Platt's most important designs. Kahn actually recommended Platt to the Algers as the architect for their house. Kahn's design of the Edgar house is similar in many ways to the Alger house. However, it is simpler and smaller. The terrace of the Edgar House is higher above the level of the lake and thus "is more intimately related to the living quarters," according to W. Hawkins Ferry in *Buildings of Detroit*. (Both, courtesy of Albert Kahn Associates.)

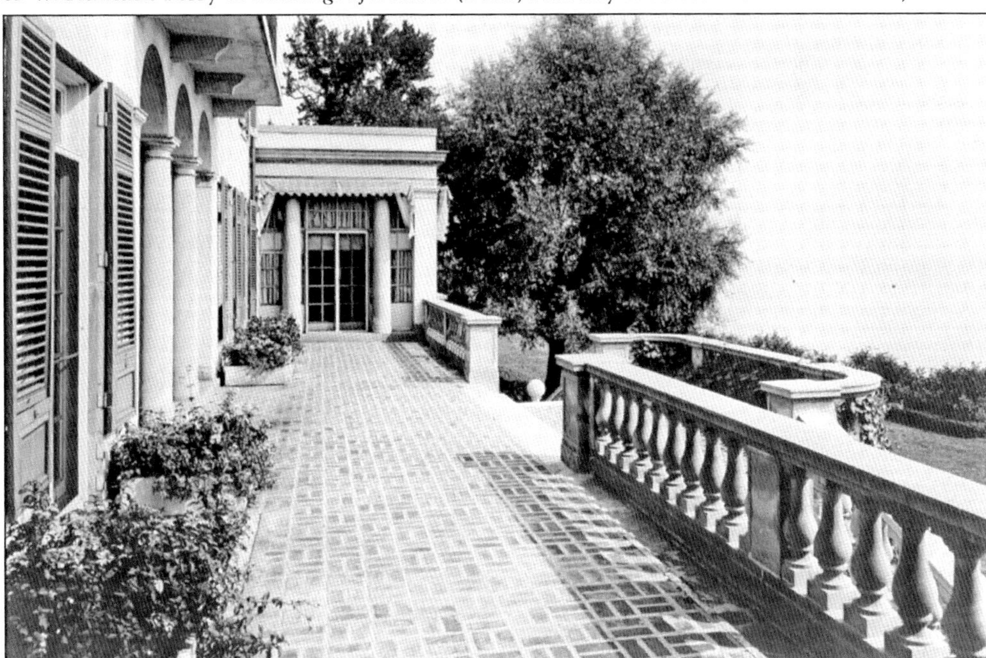

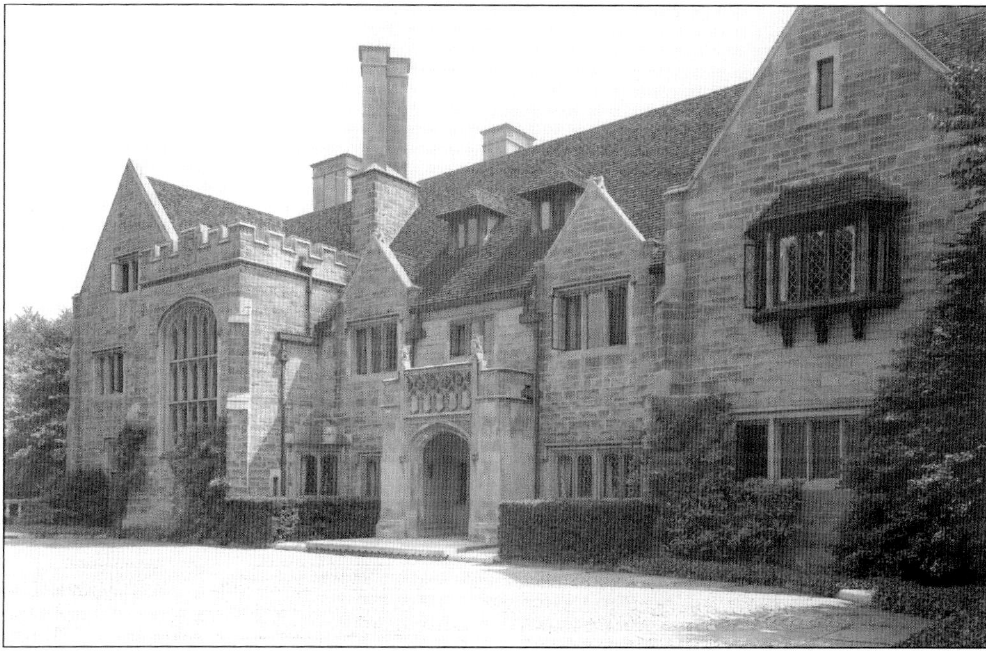

BACKUS HOUSE ENTRANCE. One of the last of the great estates to be built in the Village of Grosse Pointe Shores, and one of the grandest, was the home of Mr. and Mrs. Standish Backus, located on a 12-acre site at 725 Lake Shore Road. The Backus mansion was the result of Mr. Backus's boyhood dream of one day becoming an architect. Instead, he was a lawyer, engineer, industrialist, one of the organizers of the Cadillac Motor Car Company, and later, until a year before his death in 1943, president of Burroughs Corporation. (Courtesy of the Manning Brothers Historic Photograph Collection.)

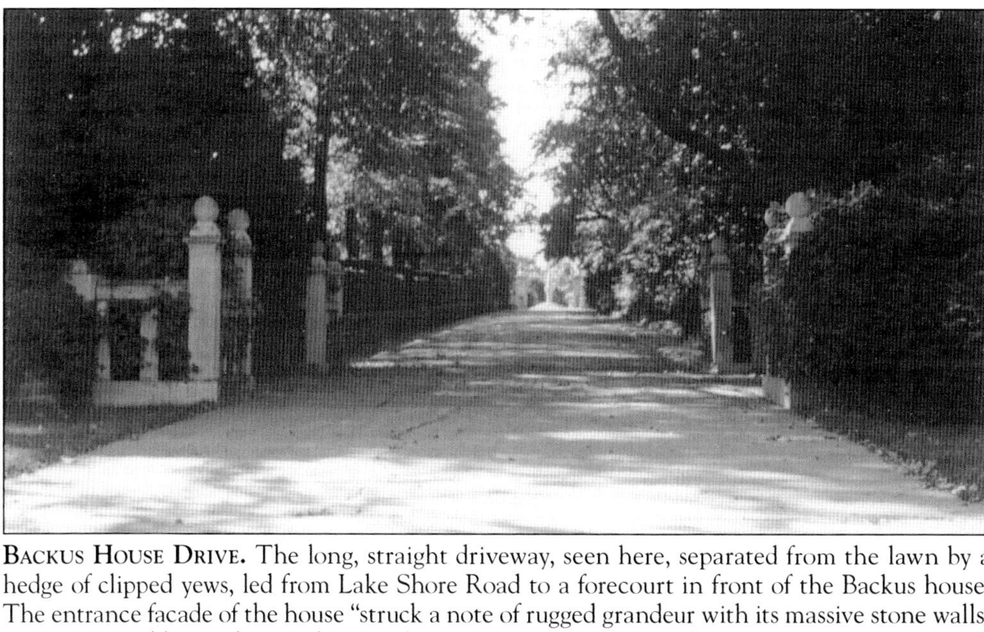

BACKUS HOUSE DRIVE. The long, straight driveway, seen here, separated from the lawn by a hedge of clipped yews, led from Lake Shore Road to a forecourt in front of the Backus house. The entrance facade of the house "struck a note of rugged grandeur with its massive stone walls, picturesque gables, and ornately carved entry," Ferry wrote in *Buildings of Detroit*. (Courtesy of the Grosse Pointe Historical Society.)

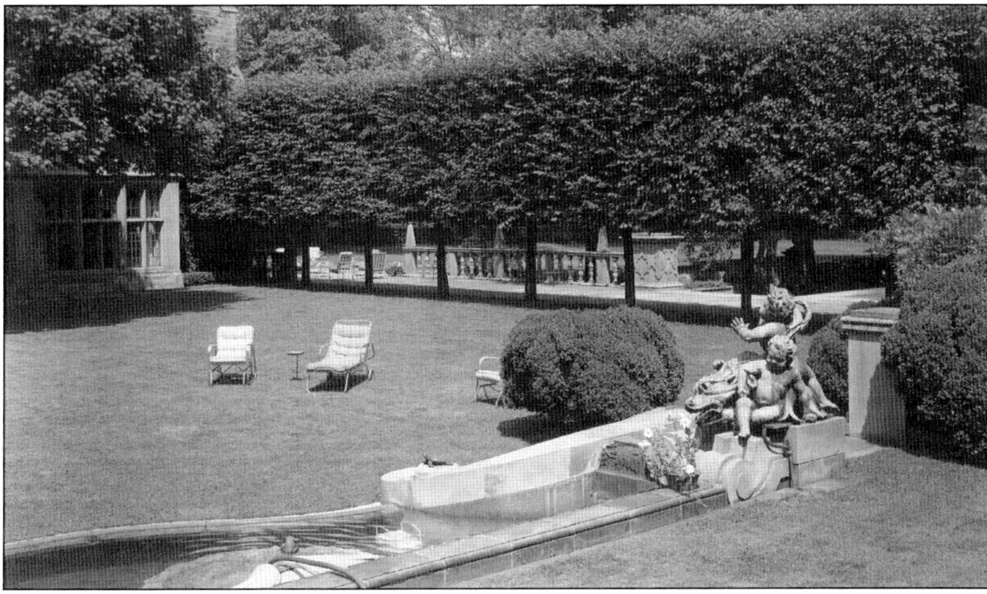

Backus House Garden. Landscape architect Fletcher Steel of Boston designed the gardens of the Backus house. He worked closely with architect Robert O. Derrick to create a beautiful setting for the house. Sweeping lawns were bordered by clumps of box bushes and rows of clipped European linden and beech trees. The gardens were recognized nationally for their beauty and style. (Courtesy of the Manning Brothers Historic Photograph Collection.)

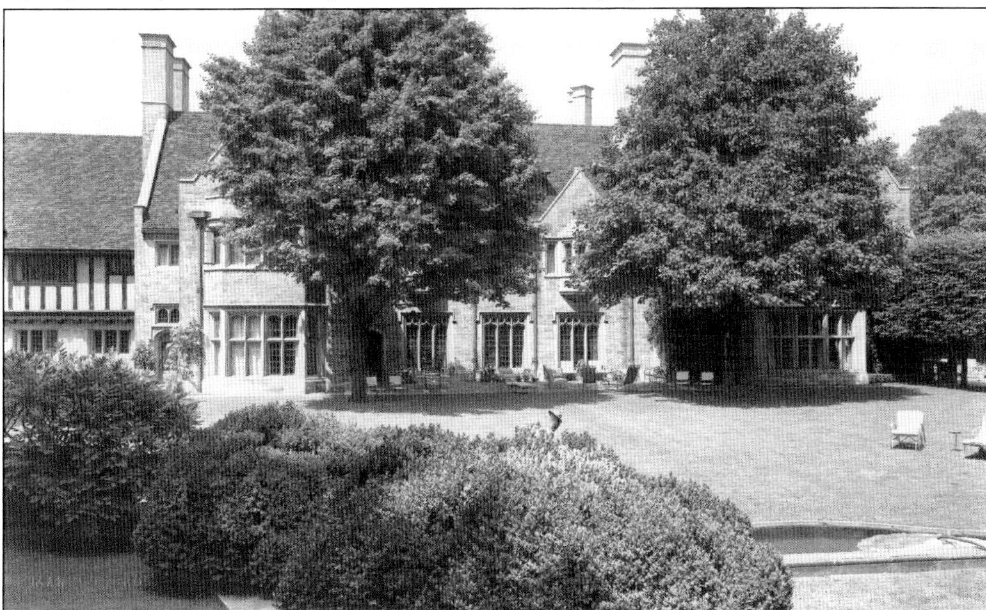

Backus House Rear. The first party that the family gave when they moved into their new home was in February 1933 to announce the engagement of their daughter. It was a grand party, but Mr. Backus kept a dark secret that night. He had been told Detroit's banks would not open the following Monday. The guests danced away the evening unaware of this disastrous news. Mrs. Backus continued to live here until her death in 1965. Shortly thereafter, the house was demolished, and the property subdivided. (Courtesy of the Manning Brothers.)

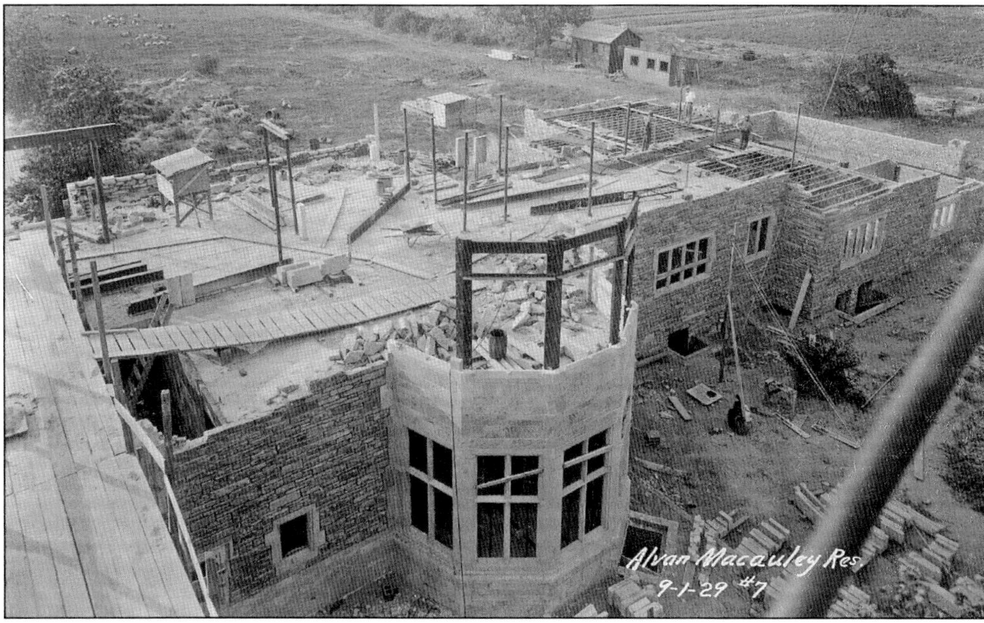

Macauley House Construction. Somewhat similar to the Edsel & Eleanor Ford House was the great mansion that Albert Kahn built in 1930 at 735 Lake Shore Road for Alvin Macauley, president of the Packard Motor Car Company. This view of the home under construction gives a sense of its size and the extent of the property of one of the grandest mansions of Lake Shore Road. (Courtesy of Albert Kahn Associates.)

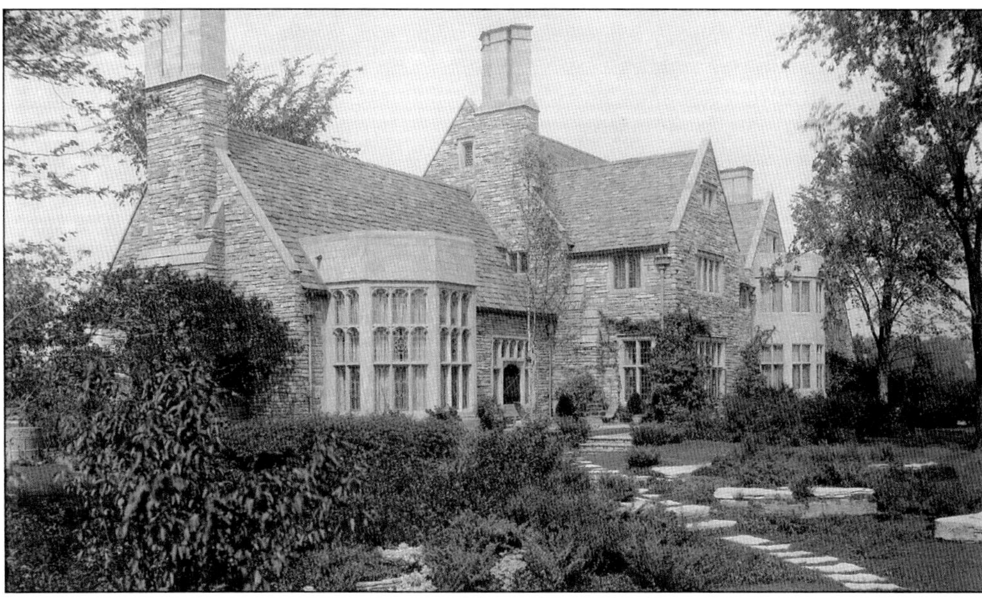

Macauley House Exterior. Like their neighbors the Fords, the Macauleys were also partial to the Cotswold style, and in preparation for the building of their house they spent weeks in England studying the local architecture. The proportions of the house were carefully planned, and a pleasing effect was secured by a variety of details and a contrast in textures. The excellent quality of the masonry was assured by the employment of several craftsmen with years of experience, supervised by a Cotswold foreman. (Courtesy of Albert Kahn Associates.)

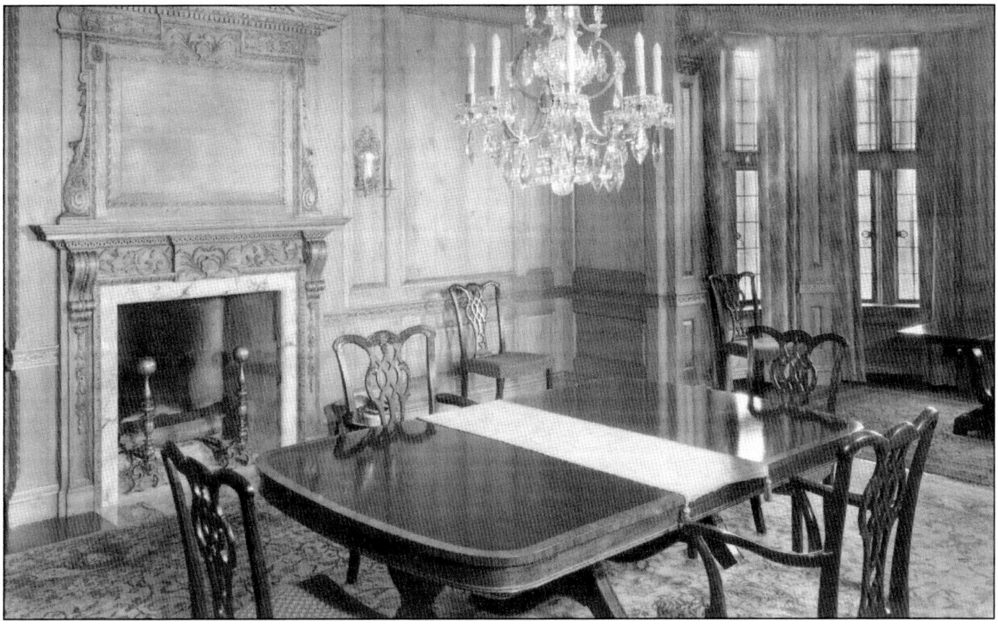

Macauley House Dining Room. The skilled woodcarving of the distinguished interior was executed under the direction of the Hayden Company of New York. In the living room, which occupied an entire wing, there was paneling that combined the medieval linefold motif with later Renaissance ornament. The dining room, seen here, was George I in style. (Courtesy of the Albert Kahn Collection, Bentley Historical Society.)

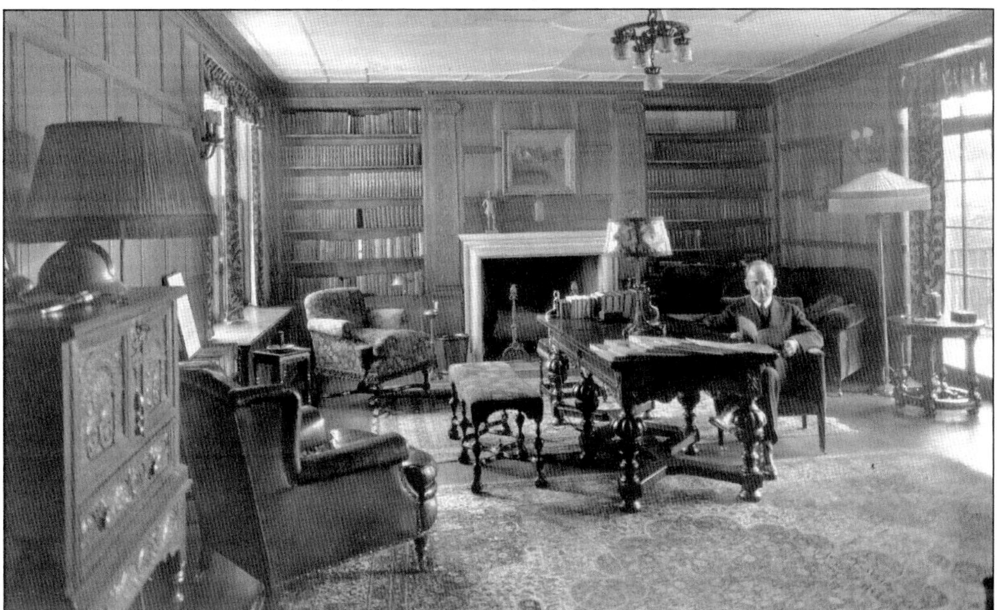

Macauley House Library. The exquisite detail, paneling, and workmanship of the ceiling are seen here in the library with Mr. Macauley seated at his desk. Alvin Macauley became president of Packard in 1916. He oversaw an era when Packard was the leader in the luxury car market. He stepped down as president in 1939 but continued on as chairman of the board until 1948. (Courtesy of the Albert Kahn Collection, Bentley Historical Society.)

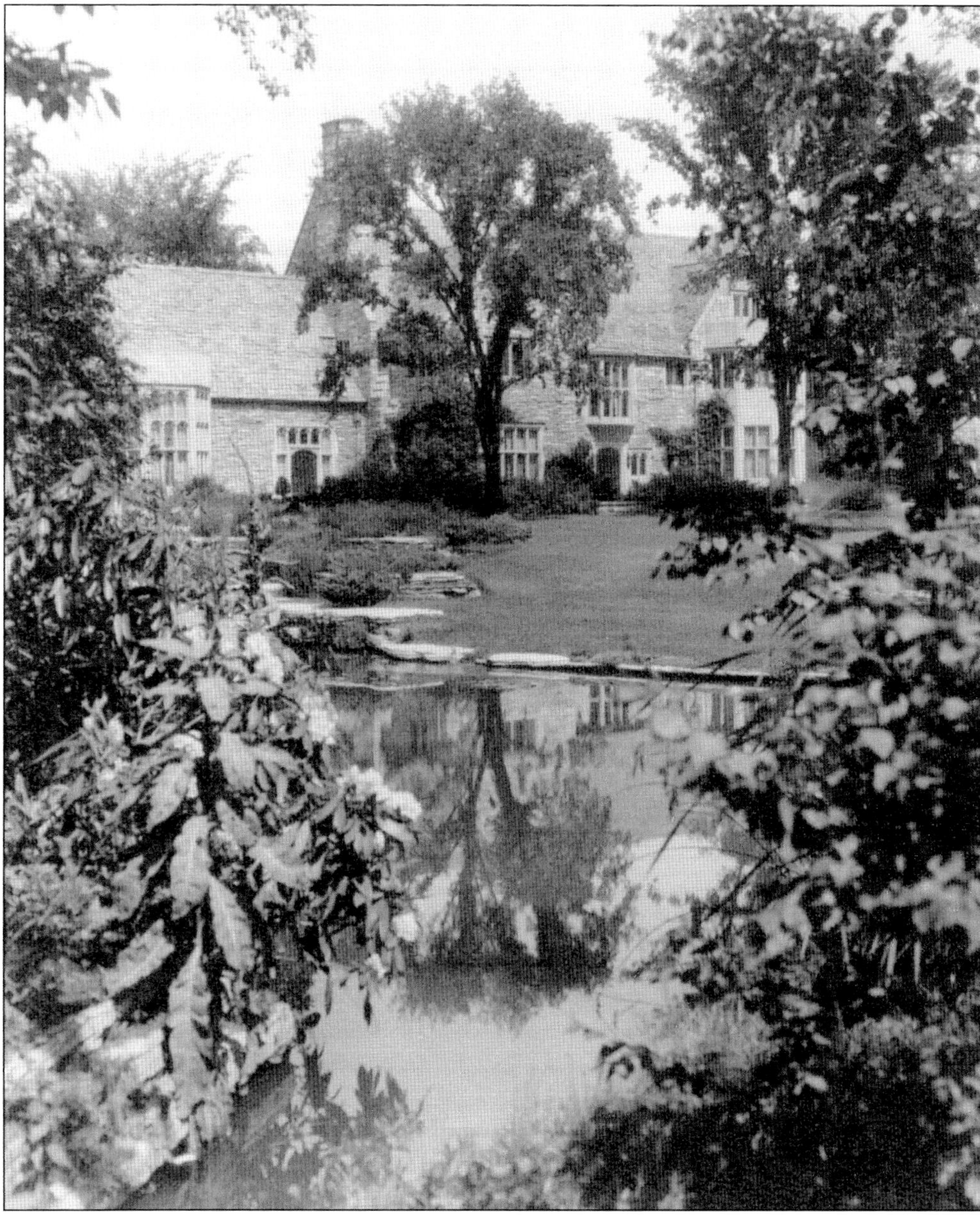

Macauley House Garden. Less secluded than the Ford House, the Macauley house stood proudly in the open, amid sweeping stretches of lawn, which provided a splendid setting and gave it the air of a great landed estate. As famed architectural historian W. Hawkins Ferry noted, "The landscape architect Edward A. Eichstaedt avoided any suggestion of artificial restraint or stylization in the landscaping of the Macauley house. Utilizing the natural characteristics of the terrain as a keynote, he emphasized broad unhampered areas bordered with native trees and shrubs." A terrace of generous dimensions provided a view across the lawn toward Lake St. Clair. The Macauley house was one of the finest examples of the grand mansions that once lined Lake Shore Road. In later years, this grand estate was the home of the Alfred R. Glancy Jr. family. The Glancys lived here until Mr. Glancy's untimely death in 1973. The home was demolished shortly thereafter. (Courtesy of the Albert Kahn Collection, Bentley Historical Society.)

Four

The Grosse Pointe Yacht Club

One of the unique features of the new Village of Grosse Pointe Shores was that many of the residents, living on the shore of Lake St. Clair, were avid sailors and owners of fine sailing yachts and powerboats. In the winter months, many of the younger men joined in the sport of iceboating. It was this interest in sailing, both in the warmer days of summer and the coldest days of winter, that led a group of 25 village residents to found in 1914 the world-class Grosse Pointe Yacht Club. R. George Marsh was elected the first commodore and led the club in that position for the next four years. Originally open only to residents of the village, club members first met in each other's homes. That soon changed. At a special club meeting in July 1926, the membership authorized the board to execute a lease for property at Vernier and Lake Shore Roads with the Village of Grosse Pointe Shores for the site of a clubhouse. Guy Lowell of Boston was then engaged as the architect. His plan called for an 18th-century Italian Renaissance building combining sun-washed stucco walls with terra-cotta tile, topped by a 187-foot bell tower. Tragically, Lowell died at sea before the new clubhouse was finished, but his senior associates saw the project to completion. Construction began in 1928, and the stunning new clubhouse opened amid great fanfare on July 4, 1929, virtually on the eve of the Great Depression. Fortunately, the club was able to survive the difficult economic times and the world war that followed. Over the years, club facilities have been updated and modernized several times. Today, in addition to the enlarged and improved harbor, the club facilities include a bowling alley, a fine Olympic-size swimming pool, several clay tennis courts, two lighted paddleball courts, and a sailing center with a fleet of club-owned sailboats. The club has prospered and grown since 1914 and is today one of the most prestigious yacht clubs in the nation.

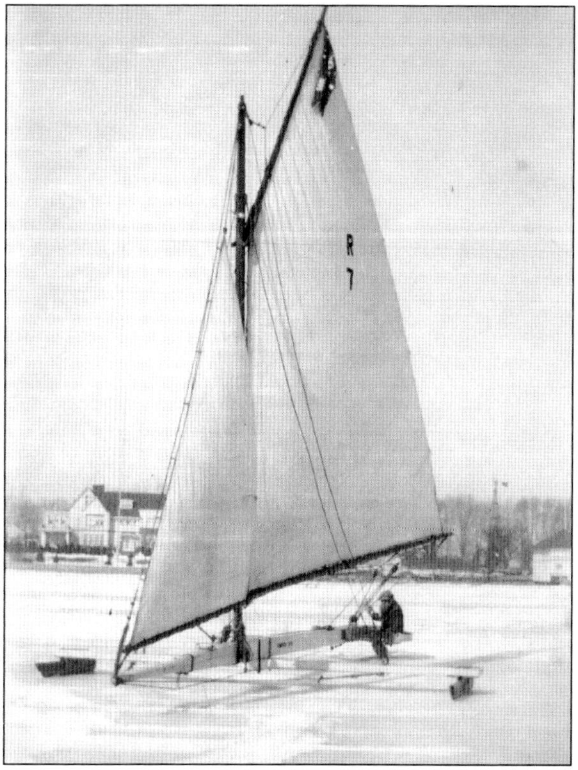

ICEBOATING. Iceboating was a principal interest of many of the founding members of the Grosse Pointe Yacht Club. Pictured here around 1920 is G. Russell French at the tiller of this boat *French Boy*, owned with his brother John H. French Jr. Their father, John H. French Sr., would later serve as commodore of the Grosse Pointe Yacht Club. Sailing on frozen Lake St. Clair, these boats could reach speeds of 50 to 60 mph. *French Boy* is now on permanent display at the Grosse Pointe Yacht Club. The house at 936 Lake Shore Road is visible in the background. (Courtesy of the Grosse Pointe Historical Society.)

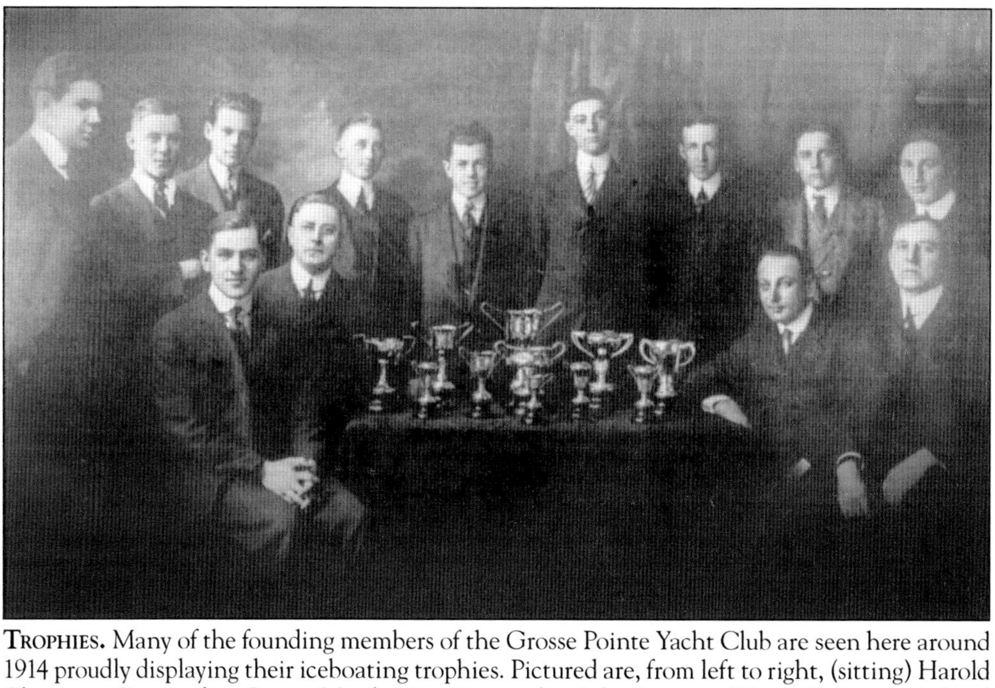

TROPHIES. Many of the founding members of the Grosse Pointe Yacht Club are seen here around 1914 proudly displaying their iceboating trophies. Pictured are, from left to right, (sitting) Harold Chapeton, Commodore George Marsh, Vice Commodore John Long, and Frank Center; (standing) Bill Long, George Hendrie, Carlyle Long, Ignatius Backman, William C. Roney, Bill Hendrie, Wilfred Bachman, Wally Hock, and John Aukland. (Courtesy of Thomas P. Kliber.)

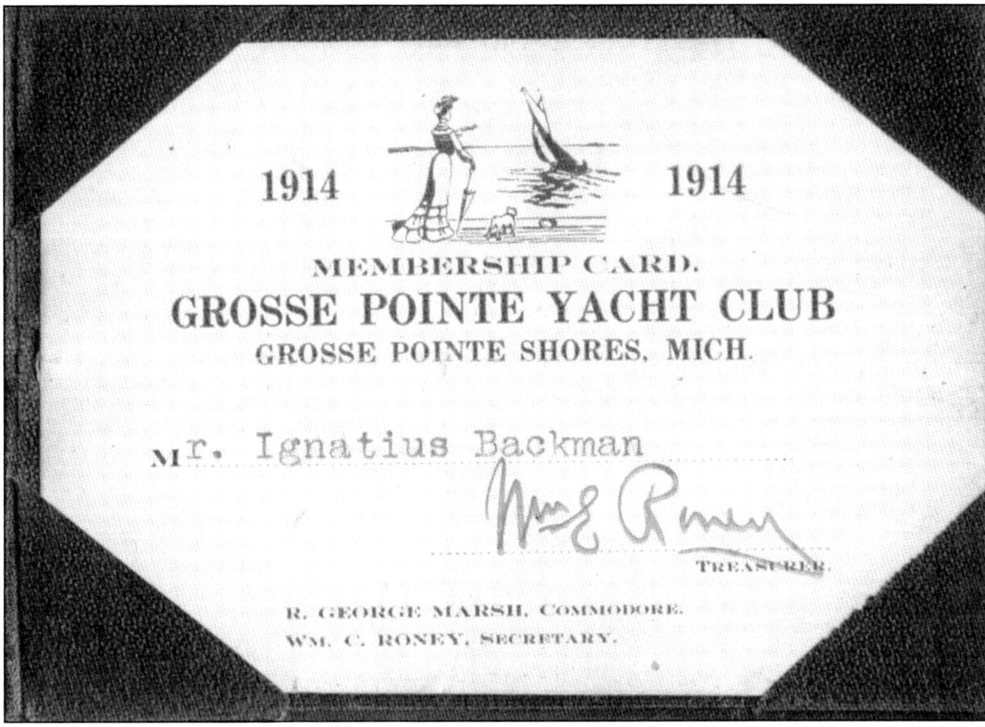

Club Card. One of the first Grosse Pointe Yacht Club membership cards was issued to Ignatius Backman, signed by treasurer William C. Roney. Backman was an avid iceboater. Lake St. Clair, partially in the area offshore near the Village of Grosse Pointe Shores, was prized by the boaters for its clear unpolluted waters, which froze clean and solid during the winter months. (Courtesy of Thomas P. Kliber.)

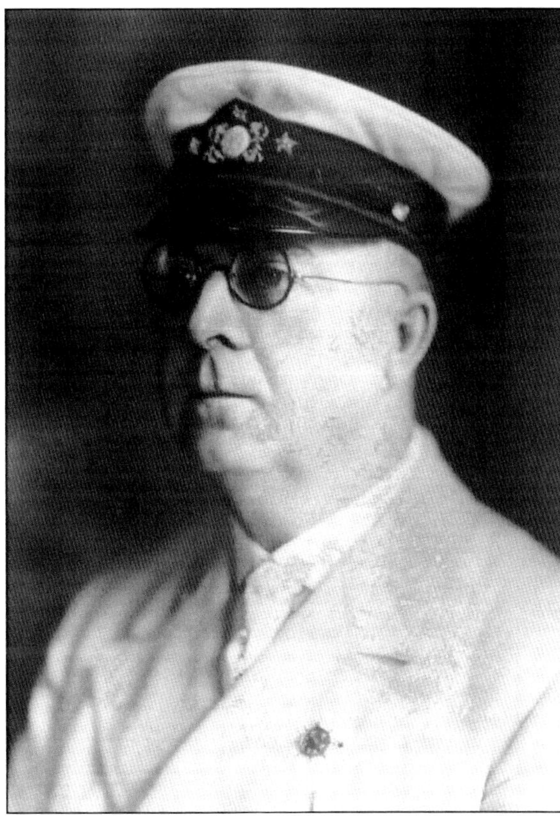

Commodore R. George Marsh. One of the founding members of the Grosse Pointe Yacht Club was R. George Marsh. The organizational meeting of the club was held at his home in 1914. Marsh was elected the club's first commodore, guiding the organization through its formative years. He served until 1918, followed by Harry H. Jewett, commodore from 1919 to 1925. Marsh served again as commodore from late 1925 until August 1926. (Courtesy of the Grosse Pointe Yacht Club.)

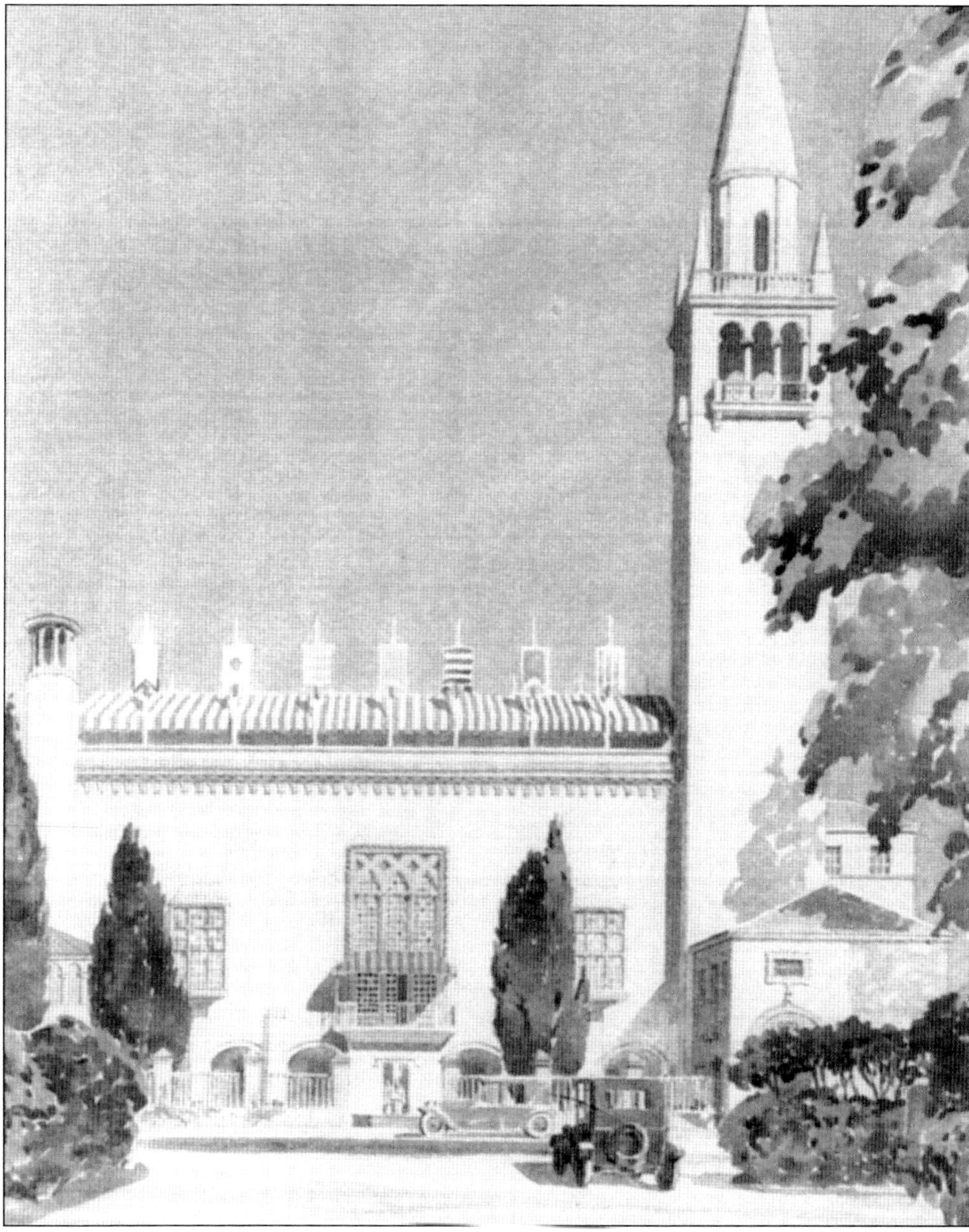

Architect's Rendering. It was only a matter of time before plans were begun for the construction of a clubhouse. In 1926, the yacht club purchased its first piece of lakefront property at the southwest corner of Lake Shore and Vernier Roads. In January 1927, a second piece of property, just to the south, was purchased. At this time, the club's board of directors engaged Guy Lowell, a world-renowned architect from Boston, to design their clubhouse. Lowell, himself a highly regarded yachtsman, began work immediately. Sadly, Lowell died suddenly while on a trip to the Portuguese Madeira Islands less than a month after preparing his first preliminary designs. Fortunately, Lowell's senior associates were able to take over the project, including this rendering, and see the building of the clubhouse through to its successful completion. (Courtesy of the Grosse Pointe Yacht Club.)

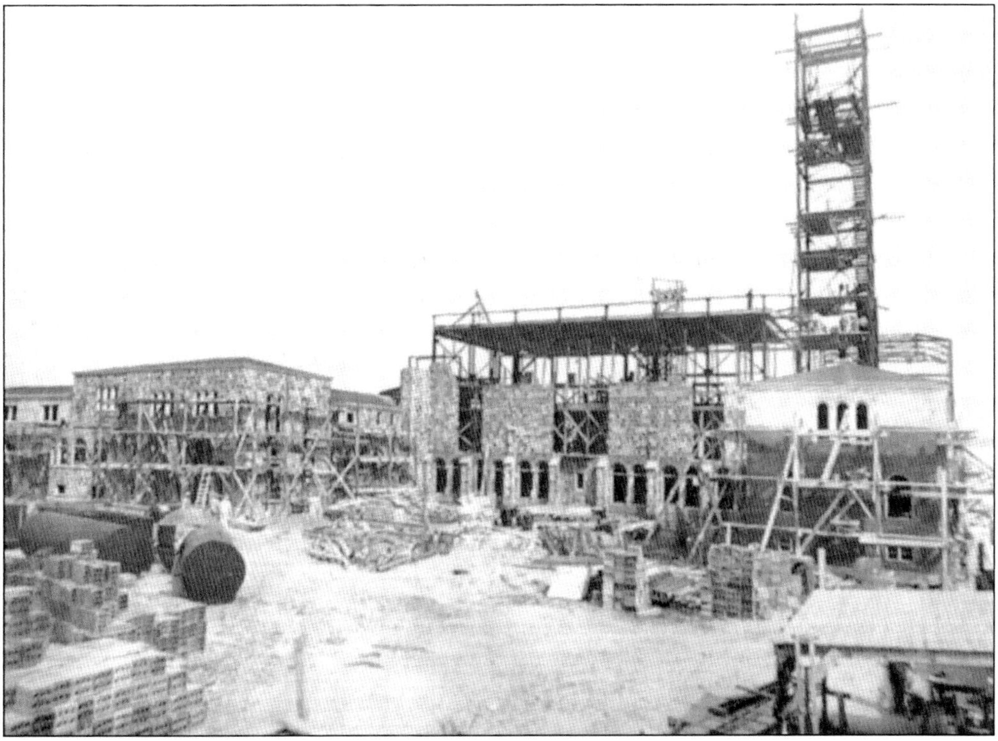

Under Construction. Construction of the clubhouse began in early 1928 after the board of directors let the $400,000 contract to Corrick Brothers Company. Visible here in its skeletal stage of construction is the notable 187-foot tower. Construction took only 16 months from the ground breaking in February until the grand opening and dedication on July 4, 1929. (Courtesy of the Grosse Pointe Yacht Club.)

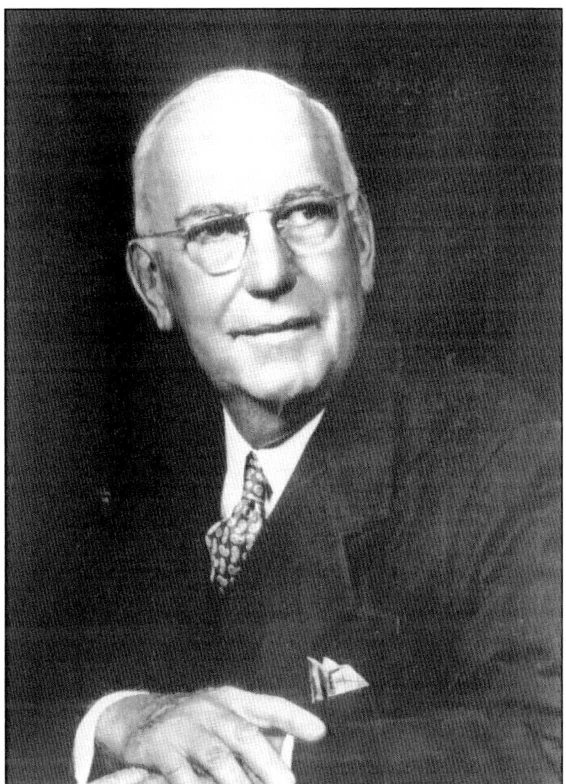

Commodore John H. French. An avid iceboater, John H. French served as commodore from 1926 to 1931, leading the club during the years of construction of the new clubhouse. French's 124-foot motor yacht *Siele* was one of the many large yachts in the yacht club harbor on July 4, 1929. (Courtesy of the Grosse Pointe Yacht Club.)

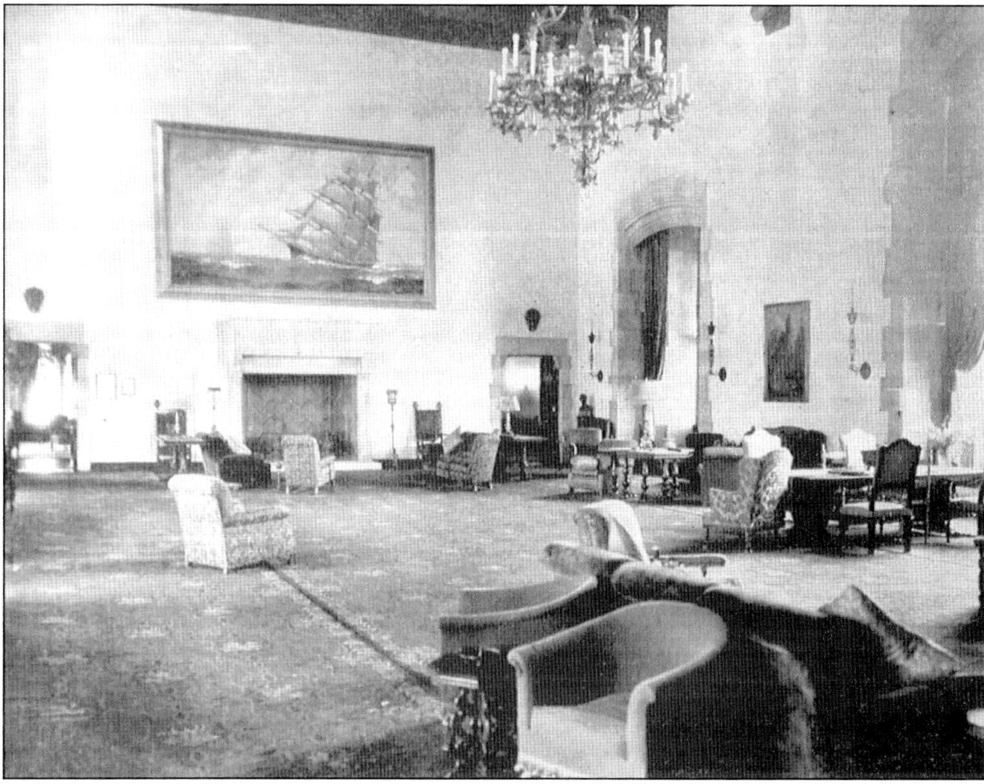

BALLROOM. Conversational groupings of overstuffed furniture and rich oriental rugs reflect the decor of the 1920s and early 1930s. The original chandelier, as seen in this early photograph of the ballroom, still hangs in the same spot today. This photograph was taken shortly after Commodore John H. French donated the fine 10-foot-by-29-foot marine painting *Sea Witch* by Frank Vining Smith of Boston. (Courtesy of the Grosse Pointe Yacht Club.)

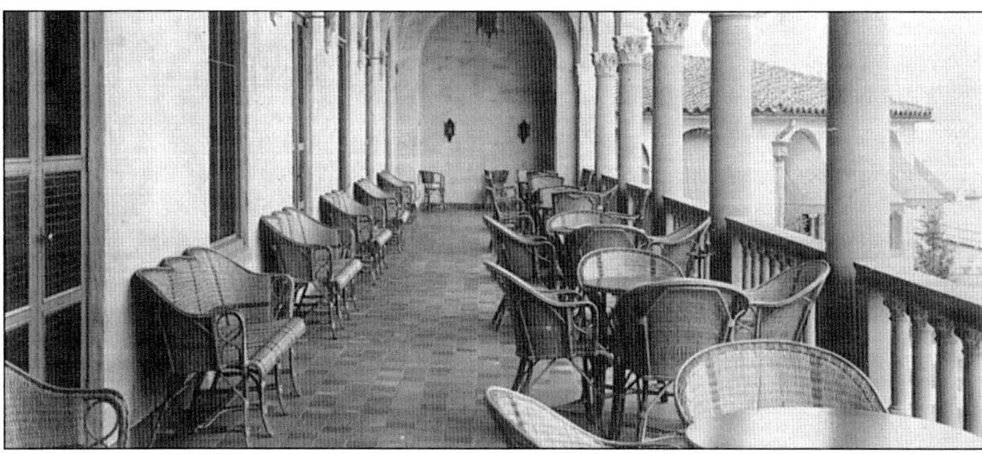

VERANDA. This original spacious Italian-style veranda of the 1929 Grosse Pointe Yacht Club offered fresh air and fresh breezes from Lake St. Clair. The veranda has since been enclosed, remodeled, and renamed the Binnacle—the club's lakeside dining area. (Courtesy of the Grosse Pointe Yacht Club.)

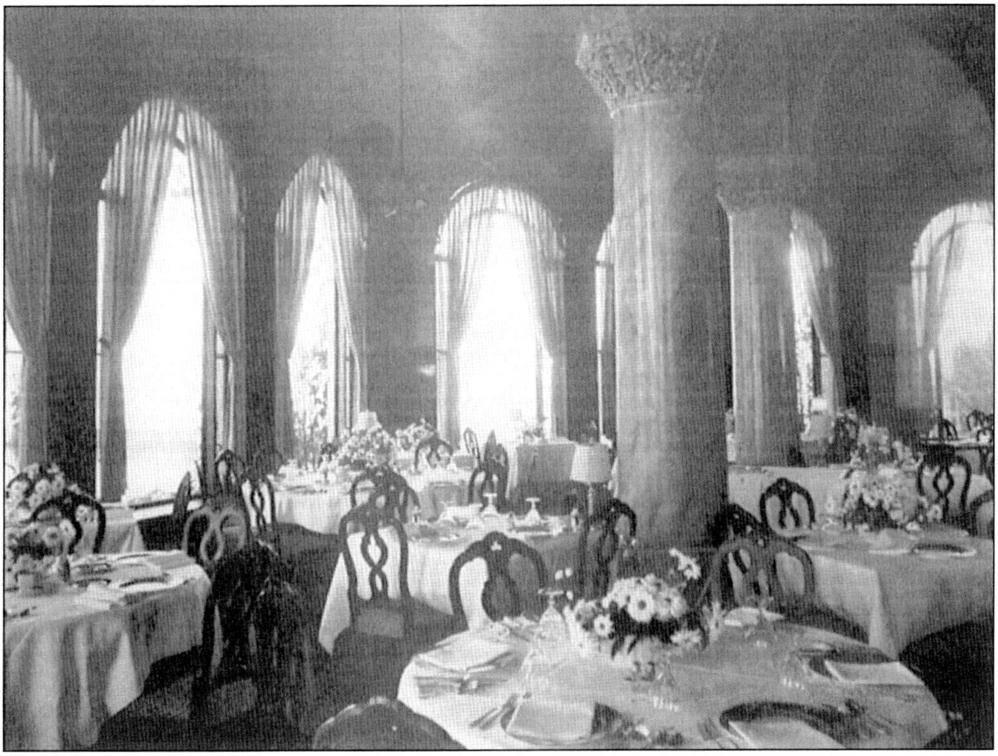

MAIN DINING ROOM. The main dining room was called one of the most cheerful rooms of the new clubhouse. The central area, surrounded by marble columns, was originally intended as a dance floor for the dining tables that surrounded it. The appointments of the dining room included china imported from Bavaria, glassware from the Netherlands, and lighting fixtures from Florence, Italy. (Courtesy of the Grosse Pointe Yacht Club.)

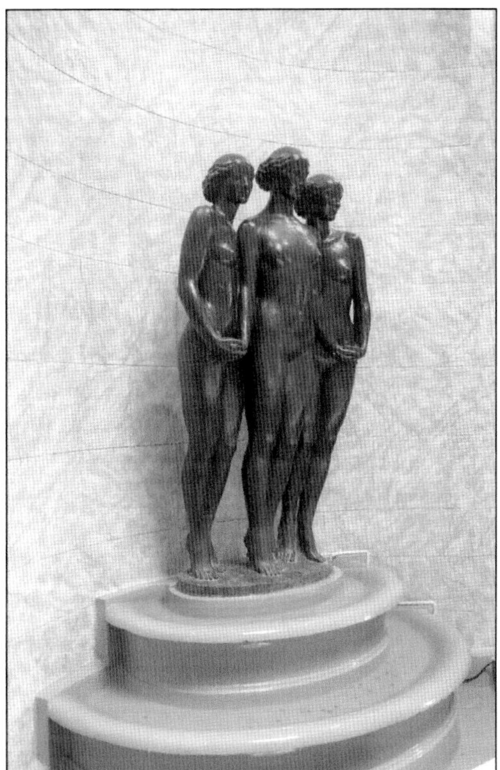

THE RHYTHM OF THE WAVES. This bronze sculpture, located in the rotunda, the center point of the clubhouse, was given as a gift by member Clarence L. Ayers in 1930. Created by sculptor Wheeler Williams, the piece is said to be based on the free-spirited dancer Isadora Duncan and two of her dance students. This work is flanked by two bronze figures, titled *East Wind* and *West Wind*. (Courtesy of Thomas P. Kliber.)

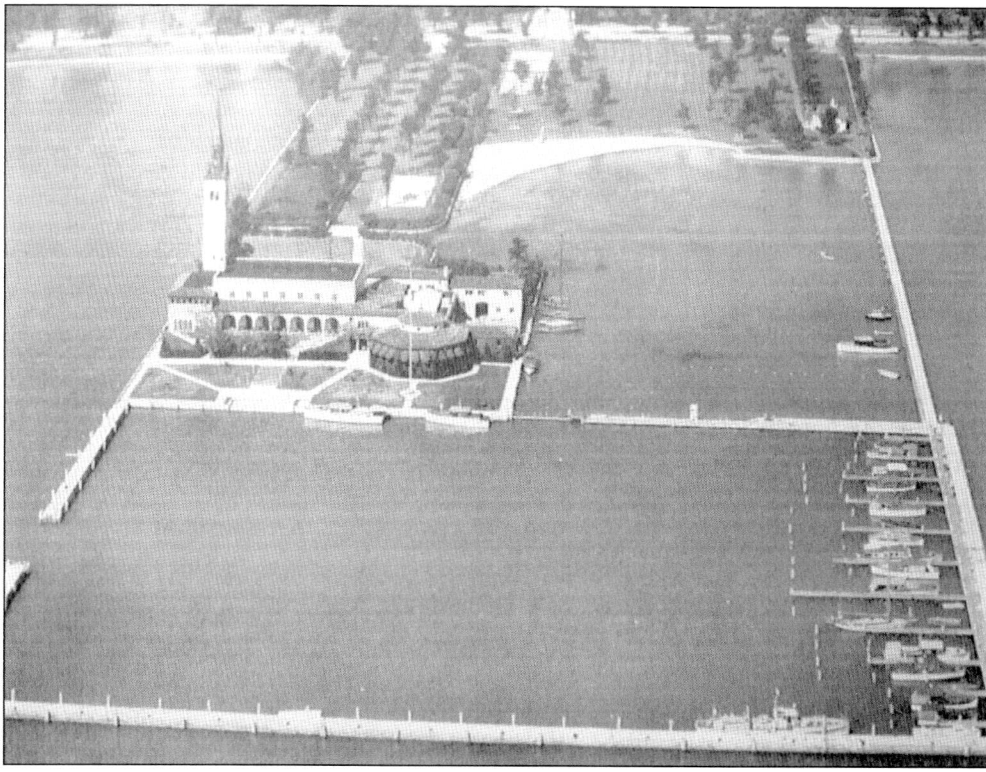

Aerial View. This aerial view from 1930 shows the original club harbor. The grand opening of the new clubhouse was followed in a few months by the Great Depression and the closing of all of Detroit's banks. Despite all efforts by the officers and board, the financial burden of the bonds for the new clubhouse was too great. By late 1935, the Grosse Pointe Yacht Club, more than $1 million in debt, went into receivership. (Courtesy of the Grosse Pointe Yacht Club.)

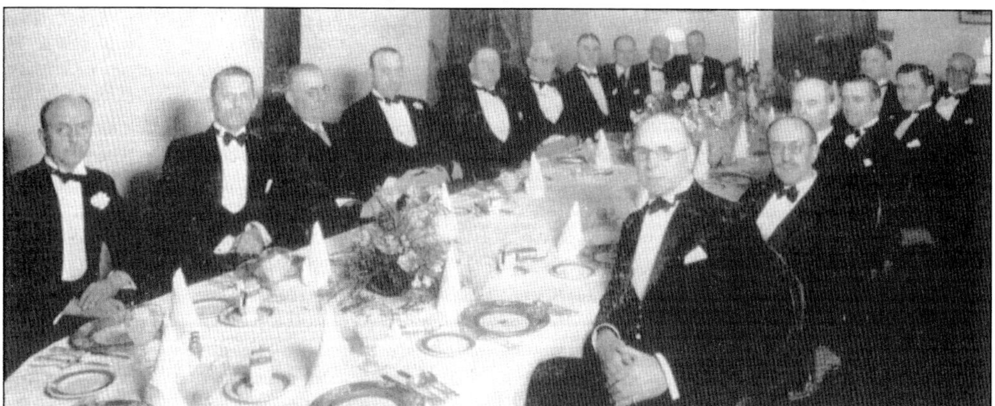

Directors Dinner. Faced with seemingly insurmountable problems, the club's board of directors took a break from its monthly business meetings for this special dinner in 1930. At the far side of the table are, from left to right, C. Howard Murphy, Charles E. Sorenson, John H. French, Mark R. Hanna, George W. Carter, William G. Fitzpatrick, Charles F. Becker, Herbert J. Woodall, Dr. George L. Renaud, and Arthur J. Scully. On the near side are, from left to right, Charles T. Bugh, George R. Osius, Conrad H. Smith, William C. Roney, William M. Mertz, and Joseph L. Hickey. (Courtesy of the Grosse Pointe Yacht Club.)

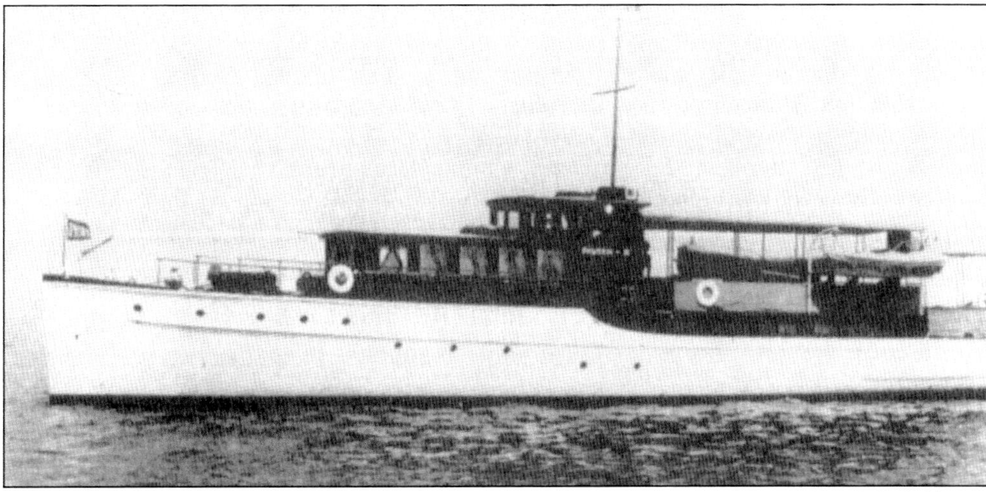

POWER YACHT *Phween* AND SAILING YACHT *Josephine II*. The Grosse Pointe Yacht Club clubhouse remained closed for two and a half years. Under the leadership of Commodore George Slocum and director Ward H. Peck, the club's finances were restructured and it reopened on July 1, 1938. By 1939, membership began to grow, a new swimming pool was opened, and a variety of new club social events were begun. The financial improvements, begun in 1939, included an increase in the number of boat slips from 23 to 56. Notable yachts like D.F. Broderick's power yacht *Phween* and William A. Pretsold's sailing yacht *Josephine II* once again filled the club's harbor. (Both, courtesy of the Grosse Pointe Yacht Club.)

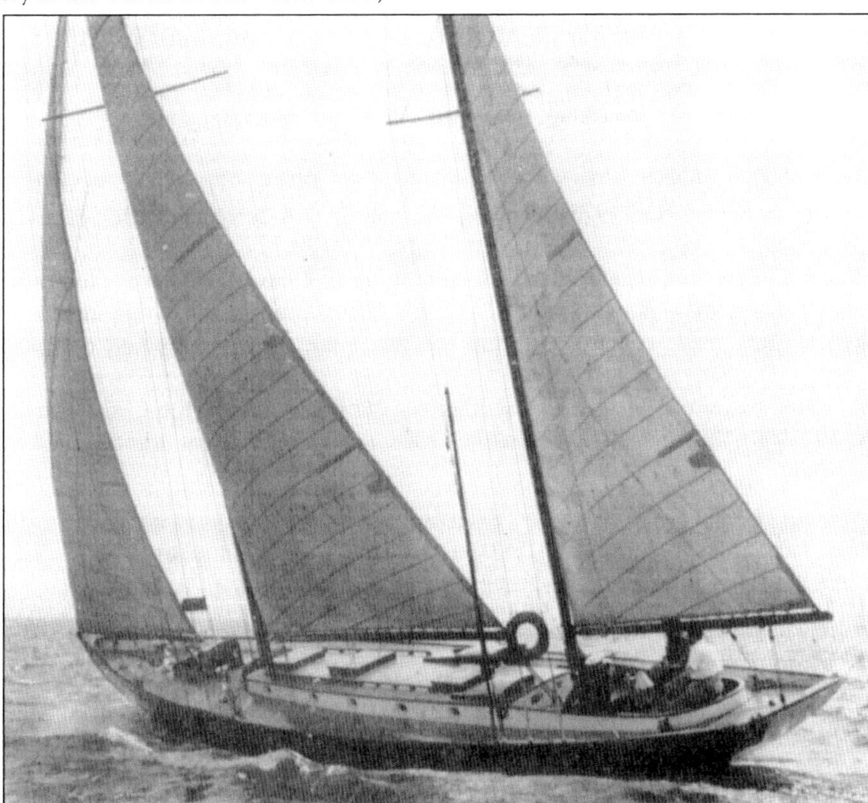

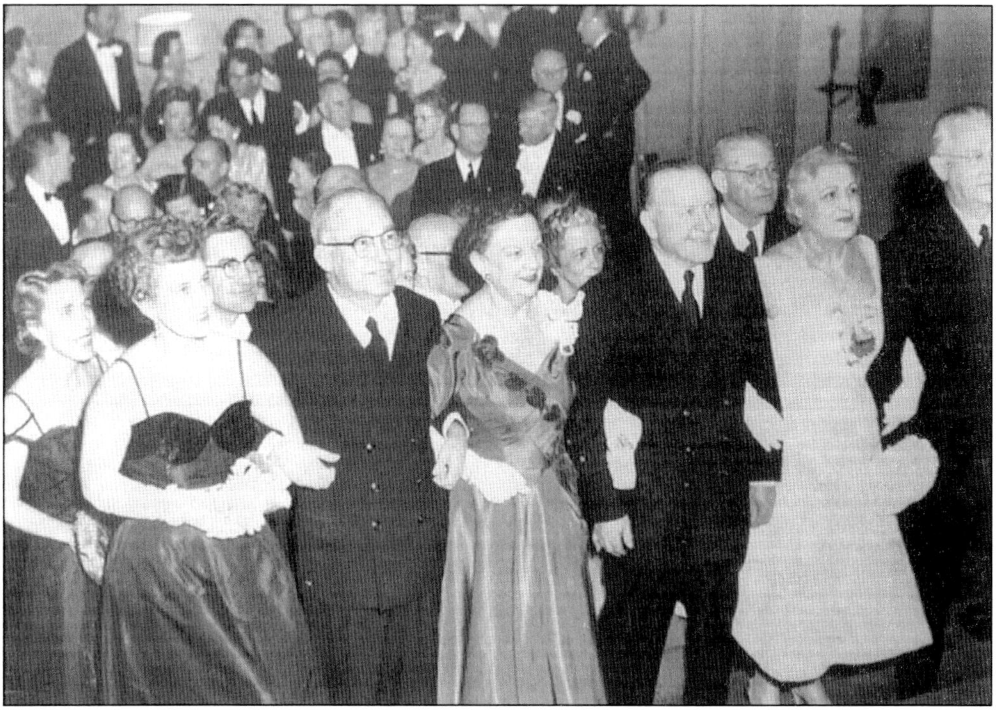

Commodore's Ball. With the end of World War II, life slowly returned to normal at the Grosse Pointe Yacht Club. Members who had gone off to war returned home; in 1944, forty-one members were in the armed forces. Members' attention returned to a range of boating, athletic, and of course, social events, like this Commodore's Ball of 1955. (Courtesy of the Grosse Pointe Yacht Club.)

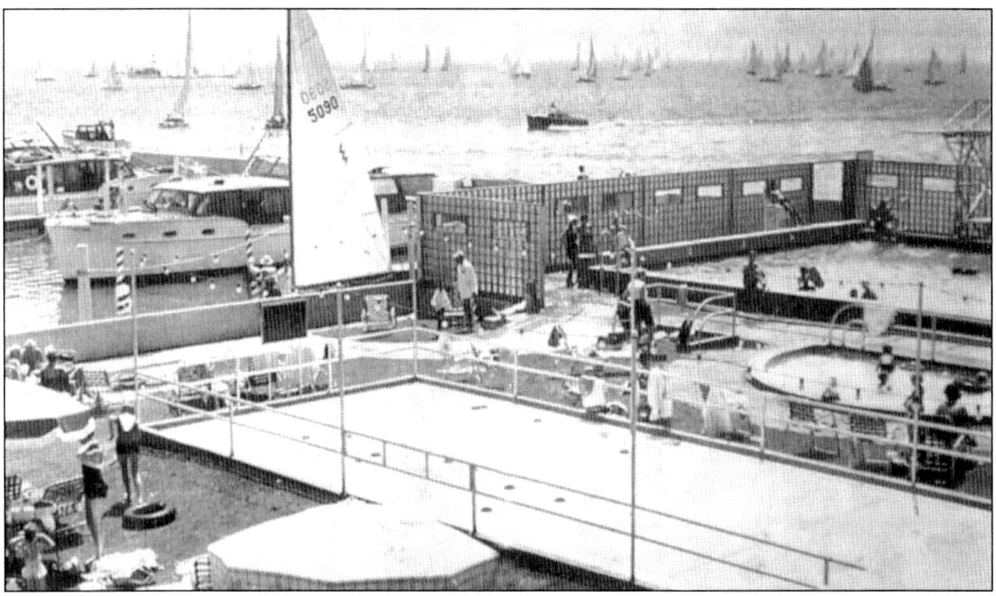

Time for a Swim and a Sail. Grosse Pointe Yacht Club regattas on Lake St. Clair, like the one seen here, attracted a growing number of participants during the 1950s and became one of the club's most popular events, as was a swim in the club's new pool, which had opened in 1939. (Courtesy of the Grosse Pointe Yacht Club.)

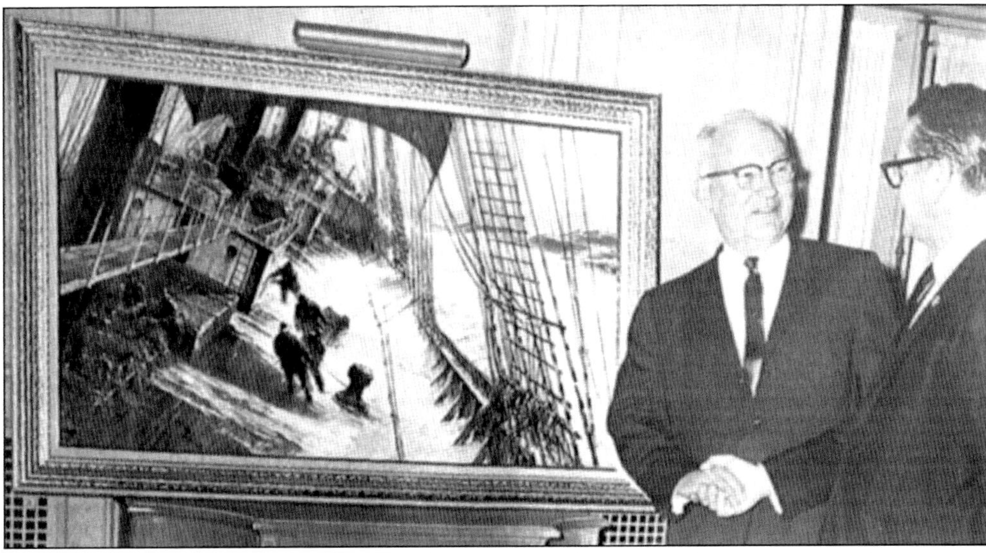

The Roaring Forties. In 1965, several past commodores graced the club with donations of original art. None, however, is as dramatic as past commodore Mervyn G. Gaskin's (left) gift of the painting *The Roaring Forties* to Commodore Harold E. Cross. Created by renowned Canadian nautical painter Jack Gray, this work became a treasured addition to the club's art collection. (Courtesy of the Grosse Pointe Yacht Club.)

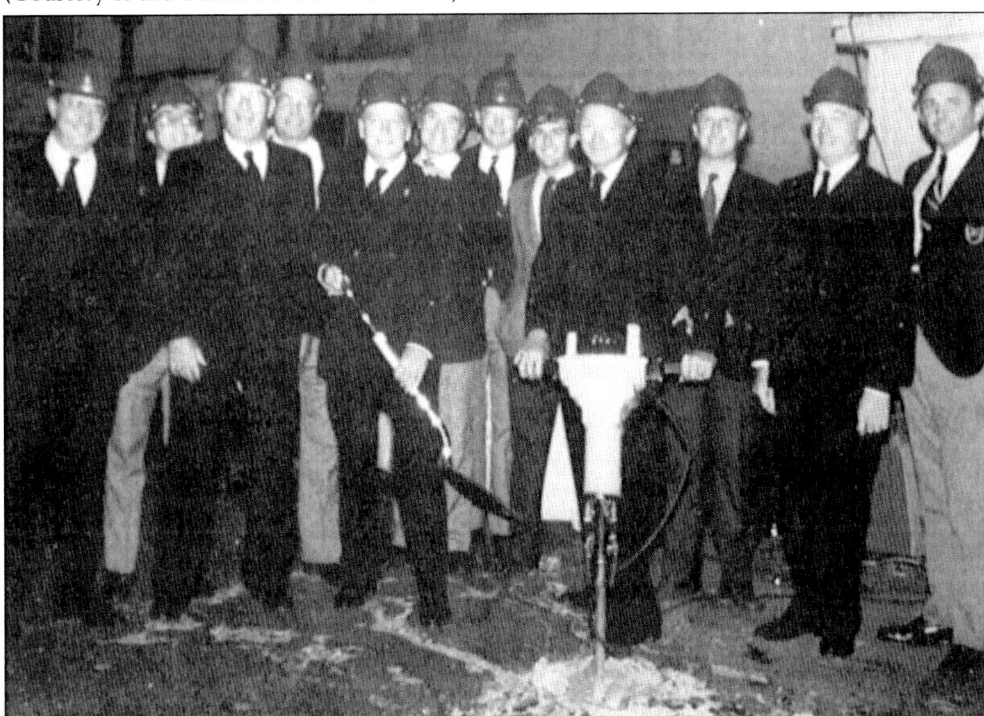

Construction. In 1984, the club achieved a major milestone. All debts, mortgages, and bonds were finally paid off. Then, in the fall of 1985, Commodore John Boll, seen here with the jackhammer at ground breaking ceremonies, oversaw the beginning of construction for the new North Wing of the clubhouse, which opened on March 30, 1986. (Courtesy of the Grosse Pointe Yacht Club.)

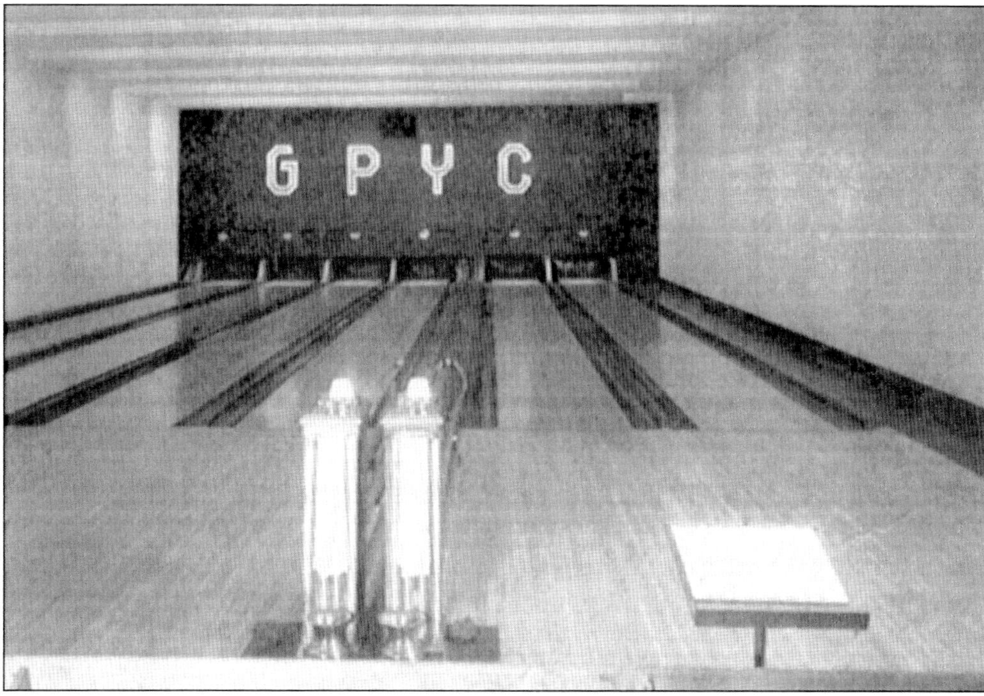

Bowling. Bowling has long been a popular pastime for club members, especially during the winter months. The club's first four bowling alleys were built in 1940. Bowling became such a success that two additional alleys were built two years later. The bowling alleys were constructed in a space originally envisioned for an indoor swimming pool that was built but never opened. (Courtesy of the Grosse Pointe Yacht Club.)

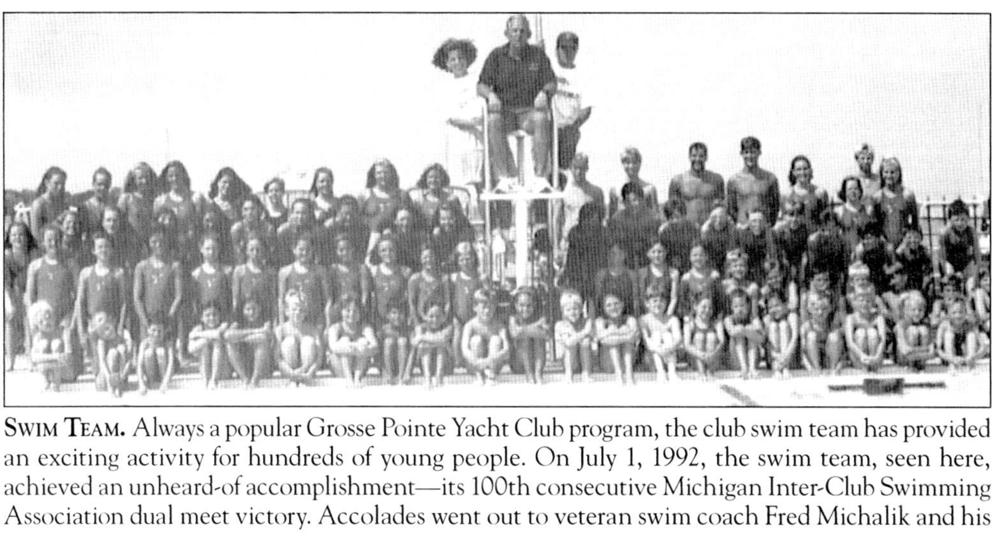

Swim Team. Always a popular Grosse Pointe Yacht Club program, the club swim team has provided an exciting activity for hundreds of young people. On July 1, 1992, the swim team, seen here, achieved an unheard-of accomplishment—its 100th consecutive Michigan Inter-Club Swimming Association dual meet victory. Accolades went out to veteran swim coach Fred Michalik and his staff and all the team members. (Courtesy of the Grosse Pointe Yacht Club.)

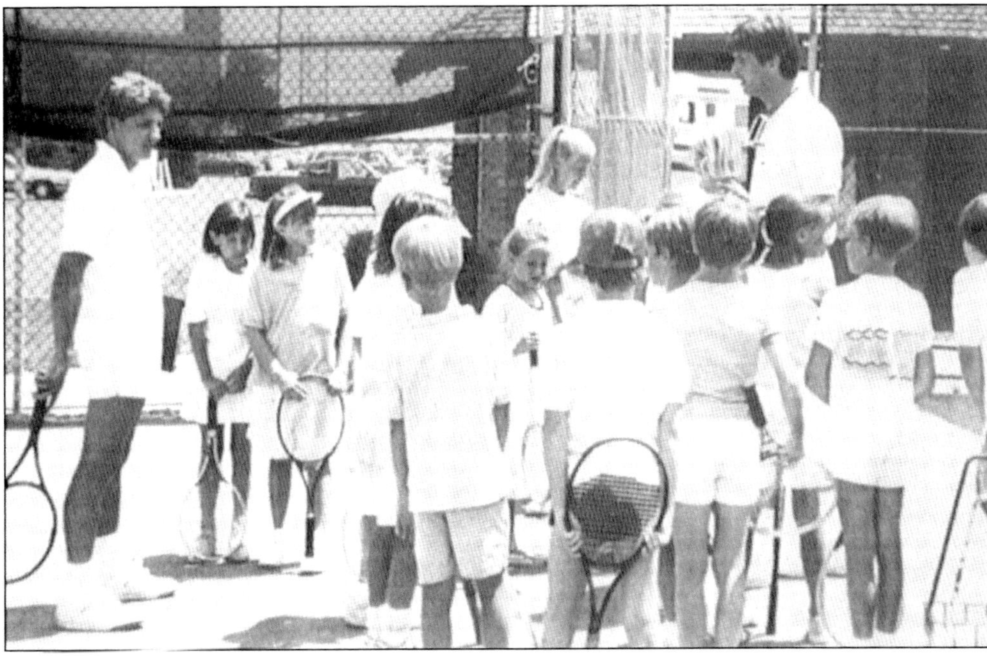

TENNIS. Tennis has long been an active sport at the Grosse Pointe Yacht Club. The first two courts were constructed in the 1960s. In 1978, six new professional clay courts replaced the original courts. Here, tennis pro Tom Cray gives instruction to youngsters as they get ready to head off to the new courts. (Courtesy of the Grosse Pointe Yacht Club.)

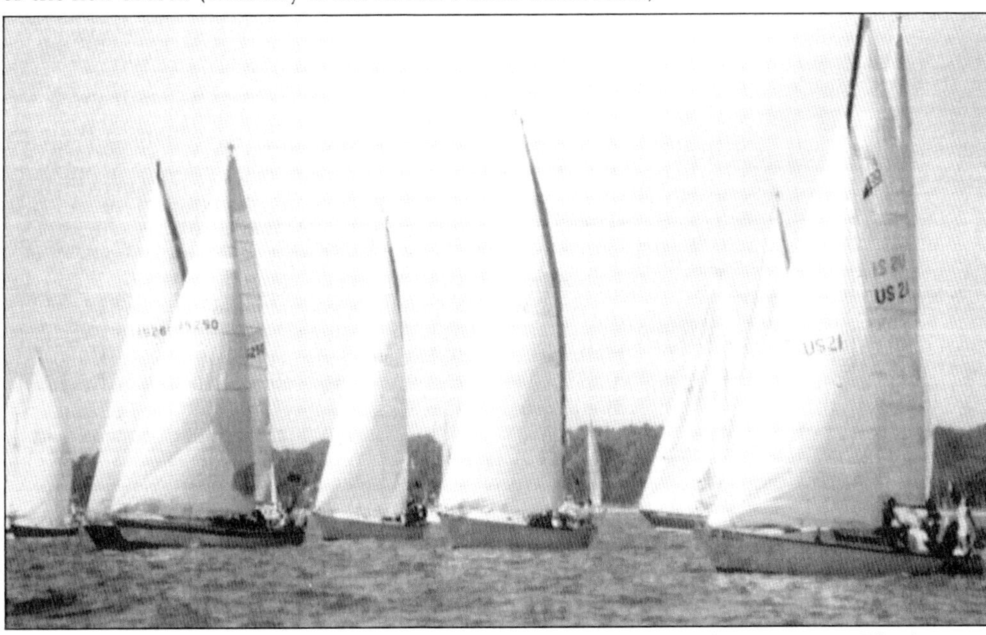

REGATTA. Of course, sailing has always been a mainstay of the club's activities. Whether part of the grand Port Huron–to–Mackinac Race, hosting national championships, teaching youths aboard one of the club boats, or participating in the annual Grosse Pointe Yacht Club Regatta on Lake St. Clair, sailing is key to the life of the Grosse Pointe Yacht Club. This 1988 photograph shows the 60th club regatta. (Courtesy of the Grosse Pointe Yacht Club.)

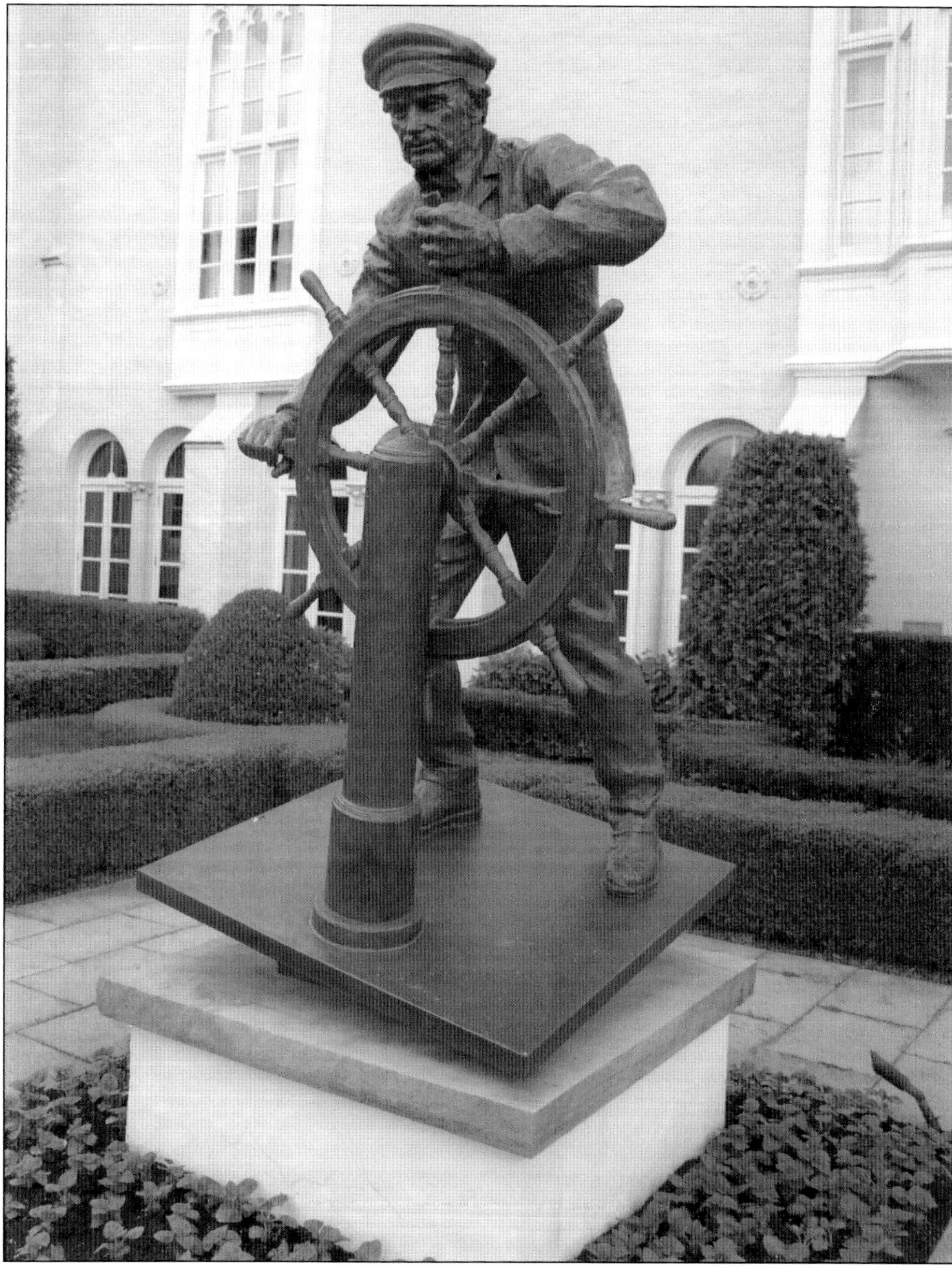

The Mariner. This outdoor bronze sculpture, cast by Norwegian artist Kirsten Kokkin, was a gift of past commodore John and Marlene Boll. It depicts a diligent helmsman steering his craft from a heeling deck. Placed in the club courtyard facing the flagpole and anchor, the sculpture honors past, present, and future commodores and signifies the importance of keeping the club on a steady course. Dedicated July 4, 2002, the sculpture sports an inscription that reads: "He works the sea from dawn to dusk and all the hours in between. He shows the toil of guiding the ship on all the miles yet not seen." Members celebrated the 100th anniversary of the club's founding in 2014. (Courtesy of Thomas P. Kliber.)

Five

The Edsel & Eleanor Ford House

The Edsel & Eleanor Ford House, the largest of the grand estates located in the Village of Grosse Pointe Shores, was built on the site known as Gaukler Point at the northern edge of the village where the Milk River flows into Lake St. Clair. This beautiful waterfront home became the residence of the Edsel Ford family in 1929. Edsel, the only child of Henry Ford and Clara Bryant, served first as secretary and then, beginning in 1919, as president of the Ford Motor Company. Eleanor Ford, the daughter of William Clay and Eliza Hudson, was also the niece of Joseph L. Hudson, founder of Detroit's leading department store. To design and build their home, the Fords engaged noted Detroit architect Albert Kahn. The Fords traveled to England with Kahn, where they were attracted to Cotswold-style architecture. Construction of the house began in 1926. While construction itself took only one year, two years were spent finishing the interior and fitting it with antique wood paneling and fireplaces brought from English manor houses. The decor and furnishings of the house reflect the Fords' lifelong love of art in its many forms. The house stands on grounds designed by renowned landscape architect Jens Jensen. Jensen's plan for the Ford House included the formation of a peninsula in order to create a cove, a lagoon, a large meadow, a formal rose garden, and various plantings to enhance the grounds in every season. Edsel died in 1943. Eleanor continued to live here for the next 33 years, and the estate continued to serve as the family's home until her death in 1976. Today, following Mrs. Ford's wishes, this beautiful estate is open to the public and is one of Michigan's premiere cultural attractions. The estate is now comprised of 87 acres. Mrs. Ford sold 43 acres of the original property in 1946 to Grosse Pointe Woods for that city's lakefront park. Visitors are able to tour the grounds and house, with its fine collection of antiques and paintings appearing much as they did when the Fords were in residence.

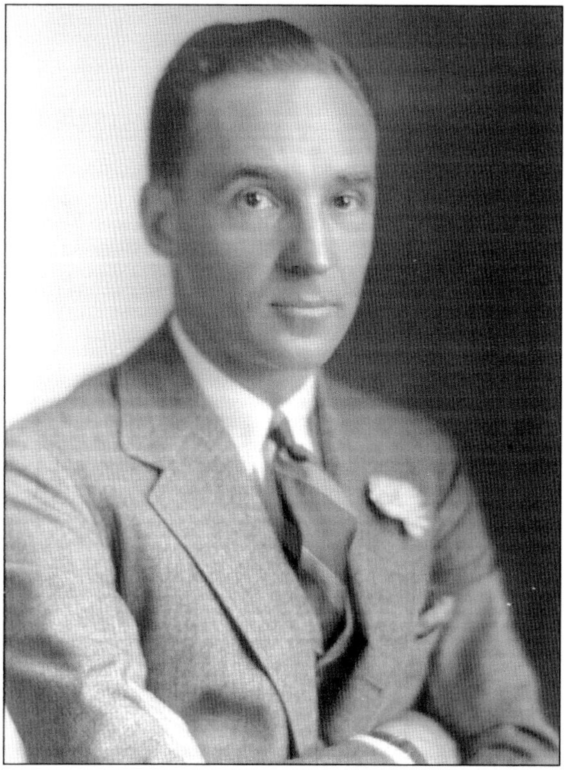

EDSEL B. FORD. Born in 1893, Edsel was the only child of Clara Bryant and Henry Ford, who founded the Ford Motor Company. Edsel, considered by his colleagues to be a talented automobile designer and a fine executive, served first as secretary of the Ford Motor Company and then as its president from 1919 until his death in 1943. (Courtesy of the Edsel & Eleanor Ford House.)

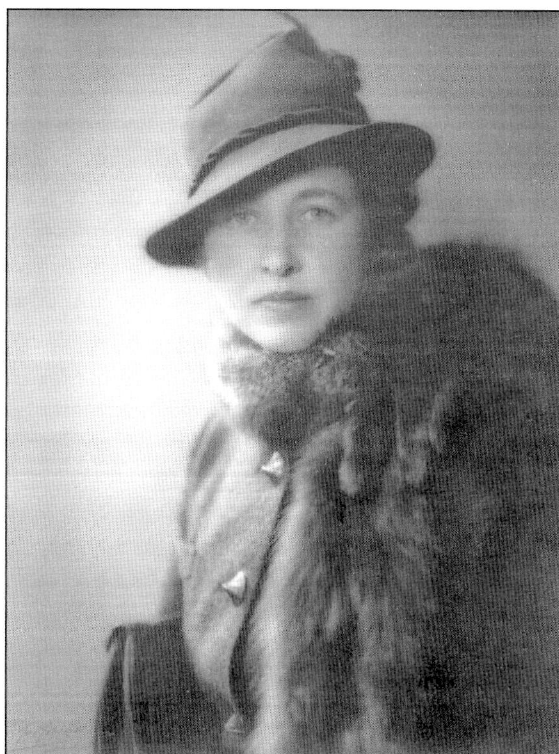

ELEANOR CLAY FORD. Eleanor, the daughter of Eliza Hudson and William Clay, was born in 1896. Married in 1916, newlyweds Edsel and Eleanor lived on Jefferson Avenue in the Indian Village section of Detroit, where they began their family. Their first child, Henry II, was born in 1917, followed by Benson in 1919, Josephine in 1923, and William in 1925. (Courtesy of the Edsel & Eleanor Ford House.)

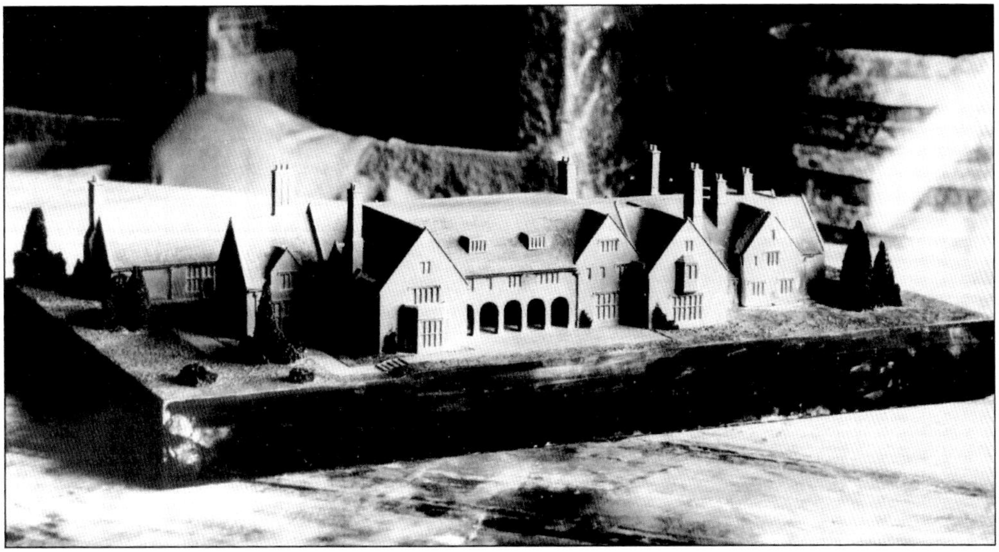

The House. The 1920s were an era of tremendous growth in Detroit, during which luxurious homes were being built, particularly on Lake St. Clair along Lake Shore Road in the Village of Grosse Pointe Shores. It was at this time that the Fords engaged one of the country's greatest architects, Albert Kahn of Detroit, to design their new home. A builder's model of the home is seen here. (Courtesy of the Edsel & Eleanor Ford House.)

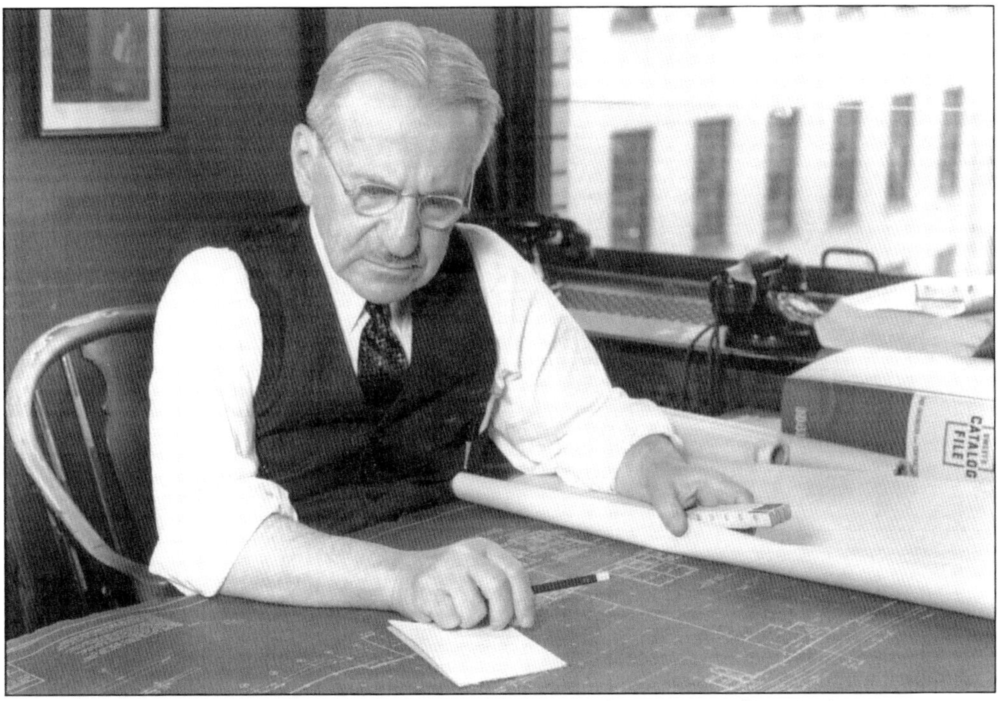

Albert Kahn. One of the greatest architects of the 20th century, Albert Kahn is sometimes called the "Architect of Detroit." His firm, Albert Kahn Associates, was founded in 1895. Kahn, noted for his industrial buildings, also designed a number of beautiful residential buildings, many along Lake Shore Road in the Village of Grosse Pointe Shores. One of the most remarkable of these fine homes is the Edsel & Eleanor Ford House. (Courtesy of Albert Kahn Associates.)

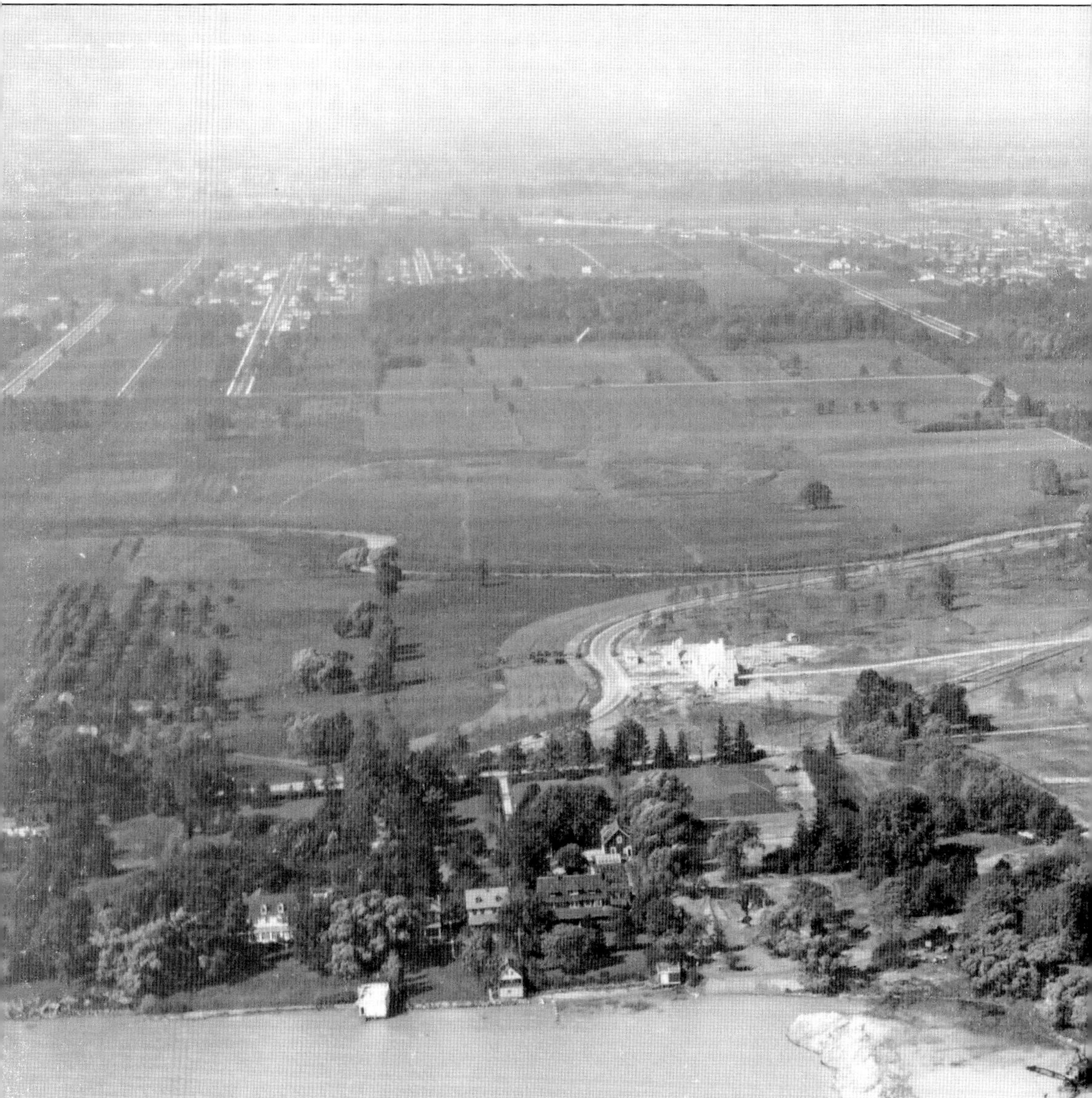

Ford House at Gaukler Point. Henry Ford originally purchased this property on Gaukler Point from Josephine Gaukler in 1914. He intended to build a great estate here but changed his mind and selected Dearborn for his new home—Fair Lane. Edsel purchased this property from his father, which included over 125 acres and over 3,000 feet of spectacular shoreline. Construction of the 30,000-square-foot house began in 1926. In this aerial view, photographed in 1927, the

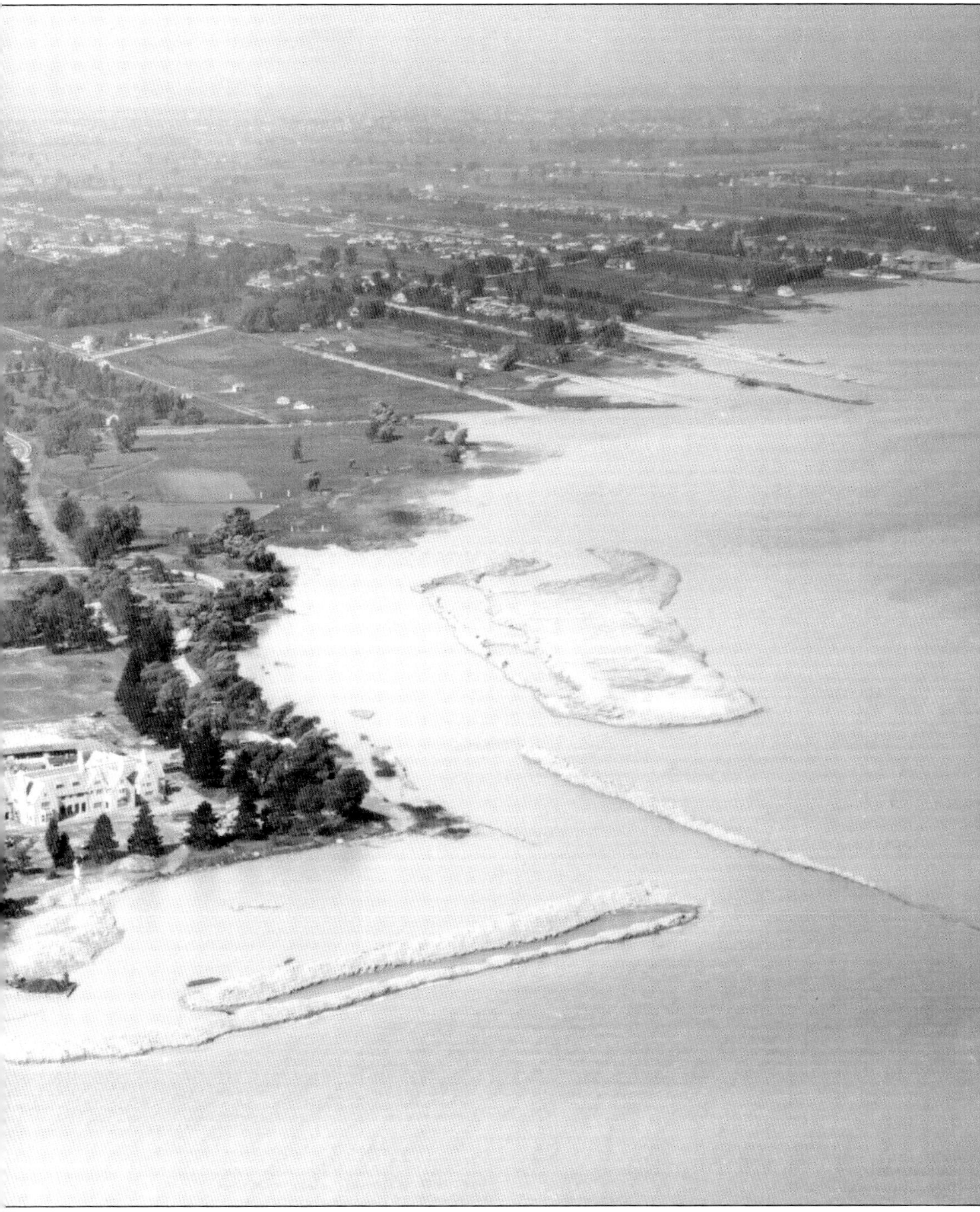

exterior of the house is nearly complete. At the center can be seen the Milk River, flowing into Lake St. Clair. To the right is the peninsula named Bird Island under construction. In the distance at right center is the neighboring village of St. Clair Shores. (Courtesy of the Edsel & Eleanor Ford House.)

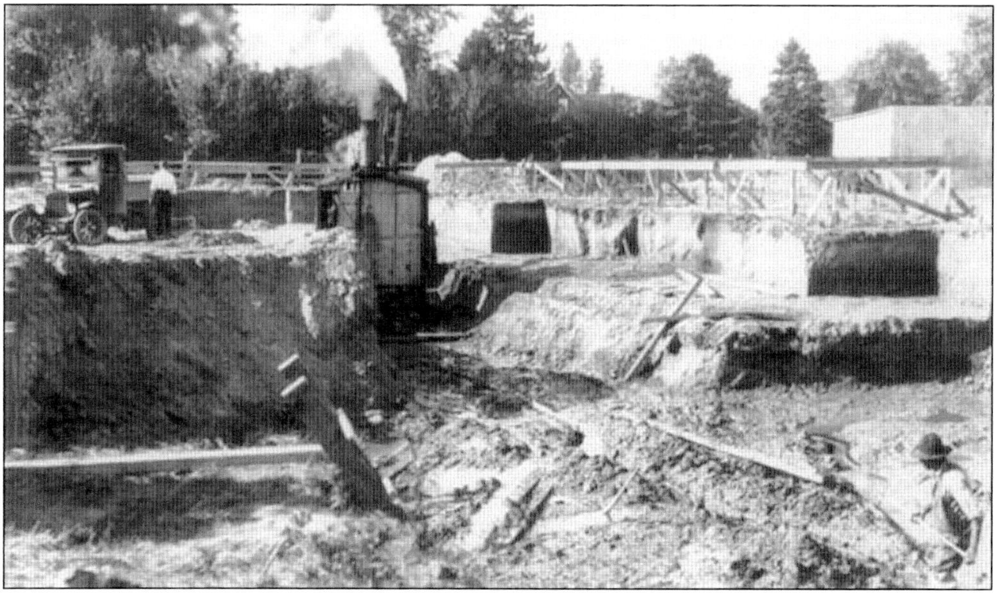

Construction Begins on Main House. Attracted to the architecture of the Cotswolds, the Fords traveled to England with Albert Kahn to gather ideas for the design of their new home. They asked Kahn to design a house that would resemble the closely assembled village cottages typical of that region of the English countryside. Construction of the 60-room home, which has three stories and a basement, began in 1926 and took three years to complete: one year to build the house itself and two years to complete the interior. The exterior of the house was faced with Briar Hill sandstone from Indiana. The stone for the shingles was imported from England and was split and laid by English craftsmen. (Both, courtesy of the Edsel & Eleanor Ford House.)

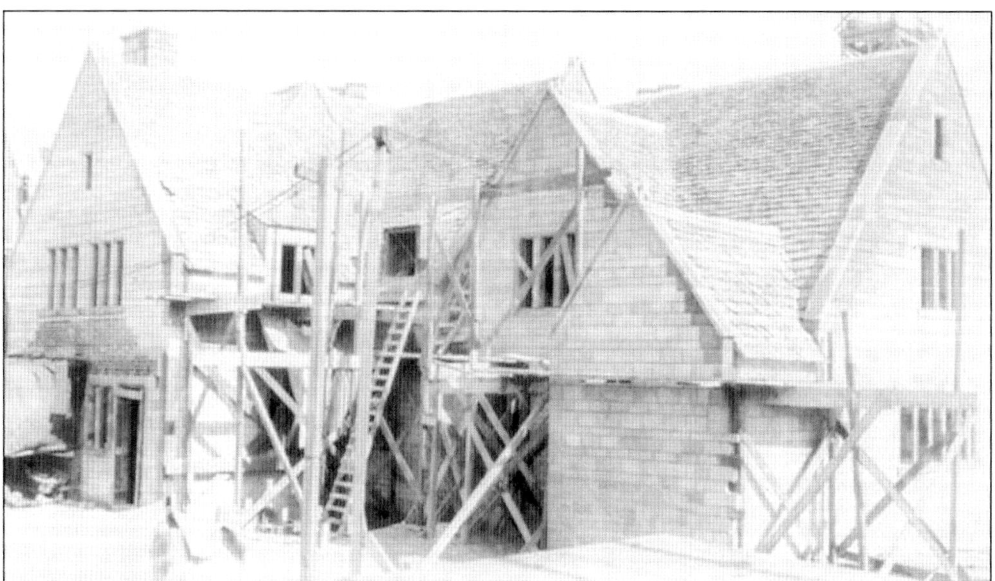

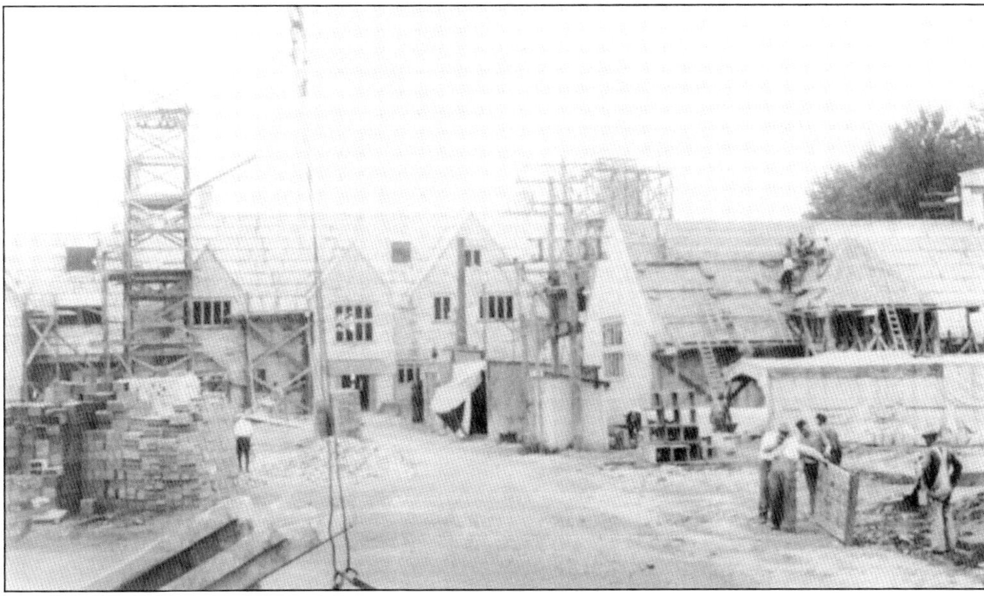

Construction and the Main Entrance. The exacting detail on the exterior of the house was continued inside. The interior fittings were completed under the direction of Charles Roberson, an expert in adapting old European paneling and fittings to American interiors. This included a variety of antique architectural elements, such as wood paneling and carved fireplaces, brought over from England. Also true to the Cotswold style, the walls were either of stone or paneled in wood. The ceilings were plastered with decorative motifs, a different pattern for each room. The decor and furnishings of the house reflected the Fords' lifelong love of art in its many forms. The wood or stone floors were covered with Oriental rugs. Porcelain vases were mounted as lamps. There were stone, bronze, and ivory sculptures; decorative metal chandeliers; and sconces throughout the house. When it was finally completed in late 1929, the Fords took up residence in their new home. (Both, courtesy of the Edsel & Eleanor Ford House.)

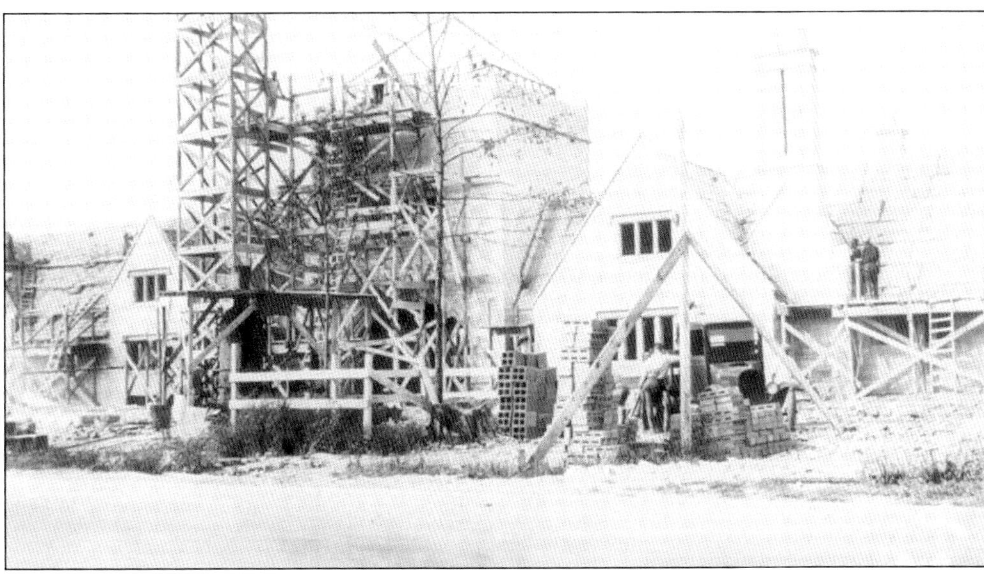

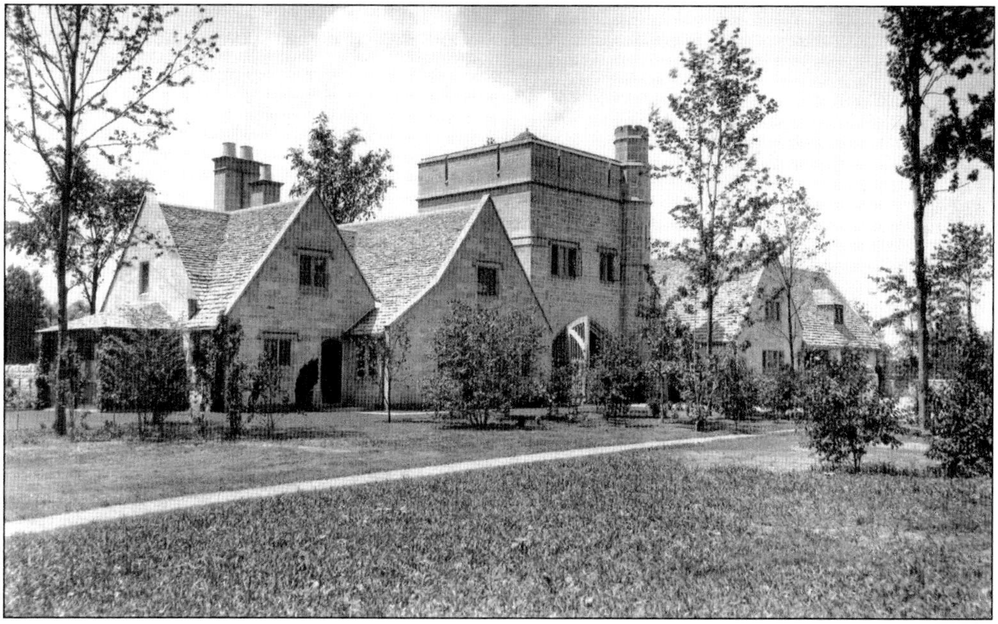

Gate Lodge. The Gate Lodge, often mistaken for the Ford House itself, fronts onto Lake Shore Road and is the entranceway to the grand estate. It has the same sandstone exterior and split-shingled roof as the main house. The Gate Lodge was designed with two large cottages for staff members and their families and a third smaller apartment in the archway over the drive. (Courtesy of the Edsel & Eleanor Ford House.)

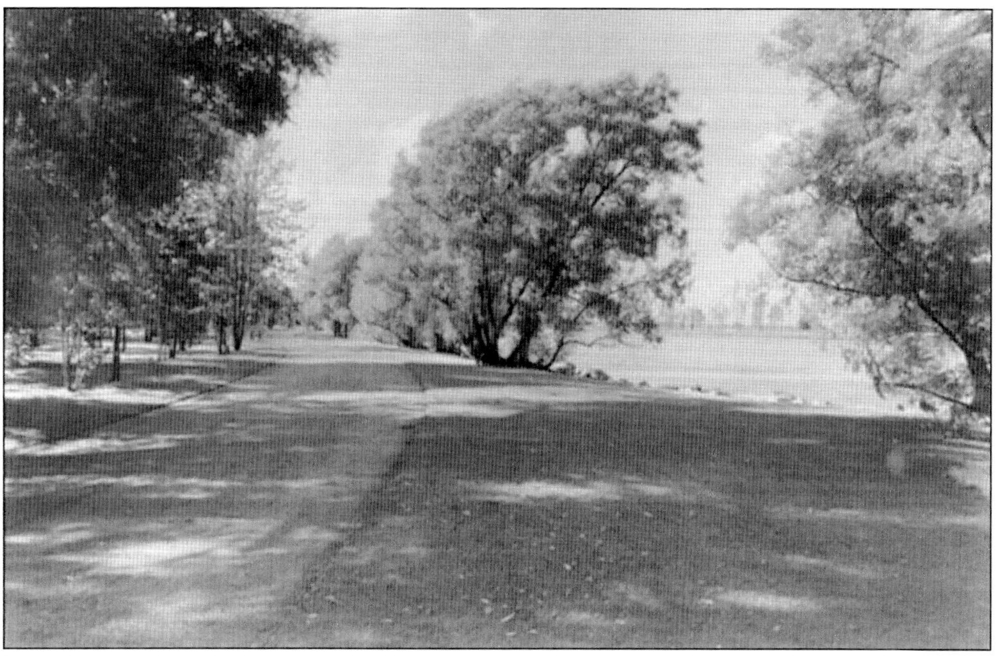

Main Drive. Danish American landscape architect Jens Jensen designed the estate's grounds. Using his traditional "long view" plan, visitors are given a glimpse of the long meadow as they proceed up this main drive and past the cove. Only at the end does the visitor see the entire house. (Courtesy of the Edsel & Eleanor Ford House.)

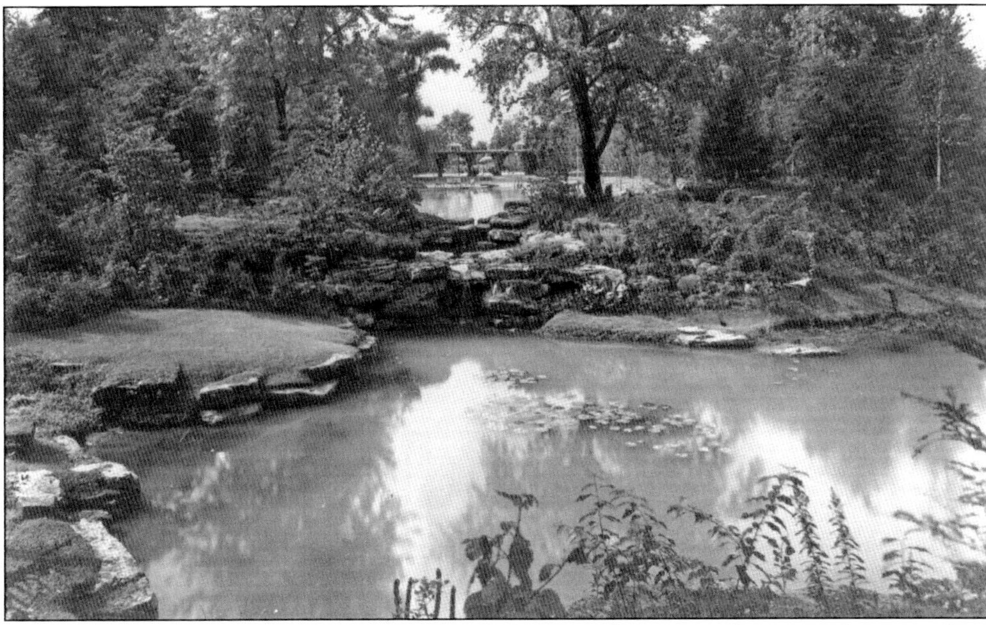

Lagoon and Pool. Jensen's plan was to design the grounds using Michigan's indigenous plants and trees. The area of the lagoon and pool, seen here, was designed to offer a quiet, woody feeling with its grove of birch trees, plantings of trillium, flowering dogwood, brilliant azaleas, and a small rock garden. This area was designed particularly to provide a relaxed and informal setting for the Fords. (Courtesy of the Edsel & Eleanor Ford House.)

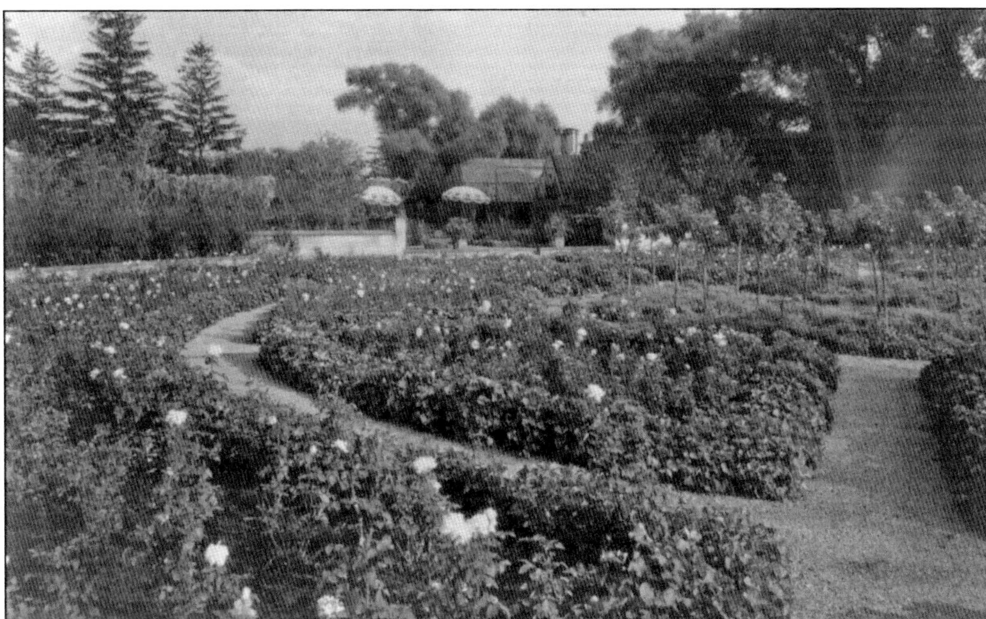

Rose Garden. Originally the only formal aspect of the grounds was this rose garden, a special request of Mrs. Ford's. It was built in a traditional English wagon-wheel design, and the garden was planted with over 2,000 white and yellow tea roses, Mrs. Ford's favorite flowers. (Courtesy of the Edsel & Eleanor Ford House.)

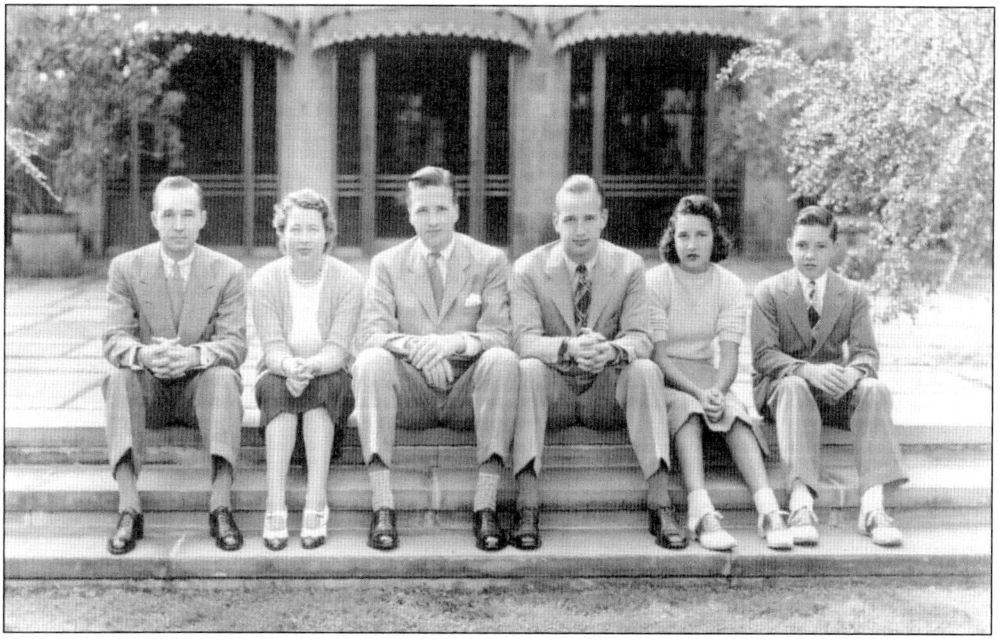

THE FAMILY. The Fords built the home for themselves and their family, first and foremost. Pictured here in 1938 on the terrace steps at their Gaukler Point home, the Fords pose with their four children. From left to right are Edsel, Eleanor, Henry II, Benson, Josephine, and William Clay. (Courtesy of the Edsel & Eleanor Ford House.)

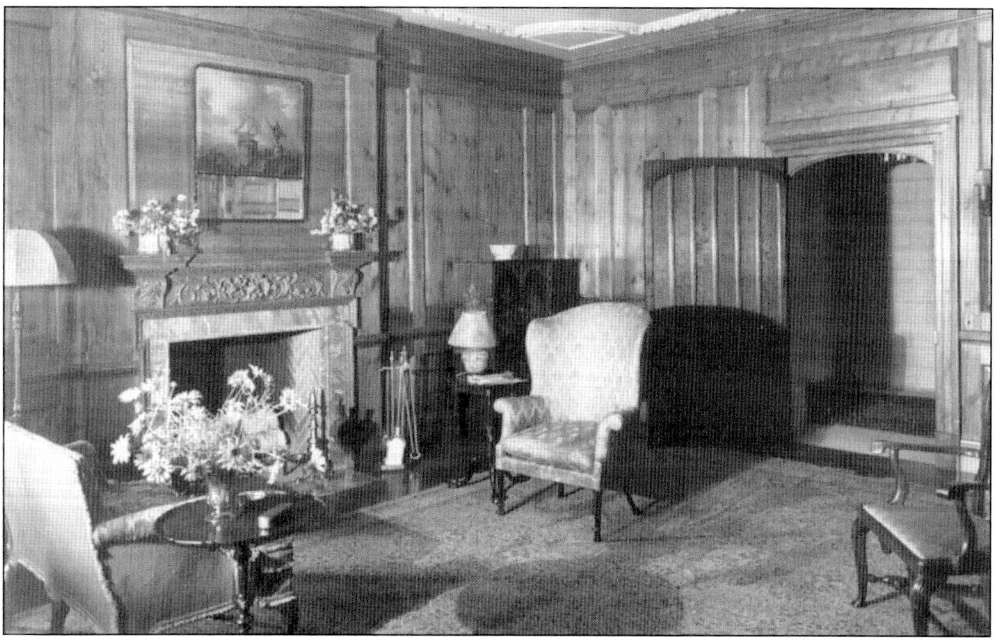

MORNING ROOM. This room received the soft morning light and functioned primarily as Mrs. Ford's morning sitting room or as the room to which ladies retired following dinner in the adjoining dining room. The light pine paneling is from an 18th-century house in Spitalfields, England. Carved leaves, shells, and scrolls decorate the mantel and were repeated in the plaster decoration of the ceiling. (Courtesy of the Edsel & Eleanor Ford House.)

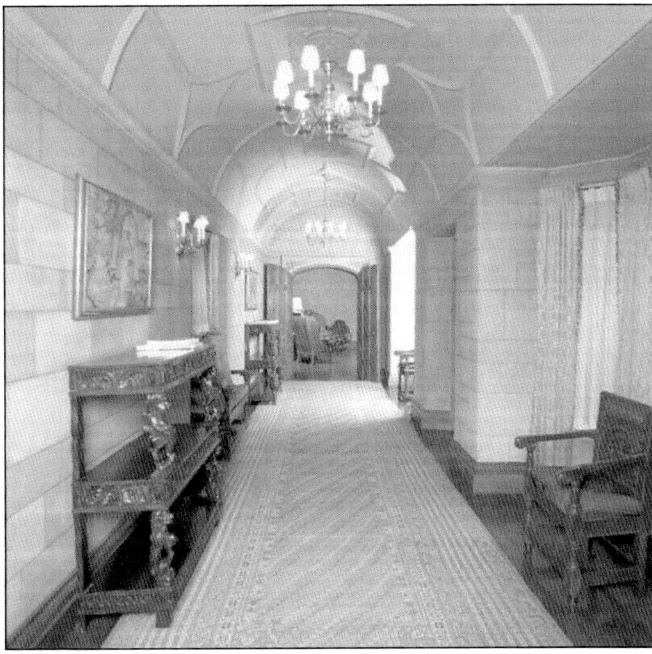

Cloister. Connecting the drawing room to the gallery is this long hallway, known as the cloister. The stone walls, barrel-vault ceiling with ornamental plaster decorations, stained glass, and 18th-century brass chandeliers foreshadow the architectural style found in the gallery. Lining this hall are various pieces of Elizabethan and Jacobean furniture. (Courtesy of the Edsel & Eleanor Ford House.)

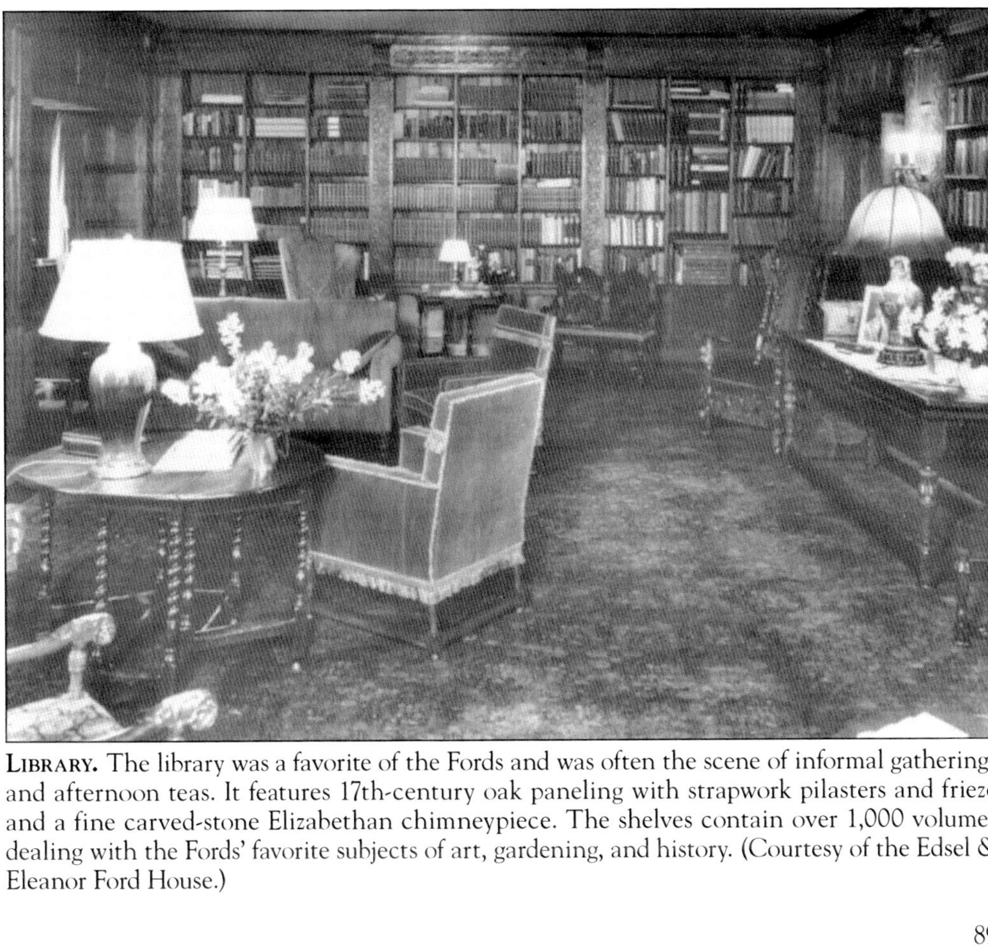

Library. The library was a favorite of the Fords and was often the scene of informal gatherings and afternoon teas. It features 17th-century oak paneling with strapwork pilasters and frieze and a fine carved-stone Elizabethan chimneypiece. The shelves contain over 1,000 volumes dealing with the Fords' favorite subjects of art, gardening, and history. (Courtesy of the Edsel & Eleanor Ford House.)

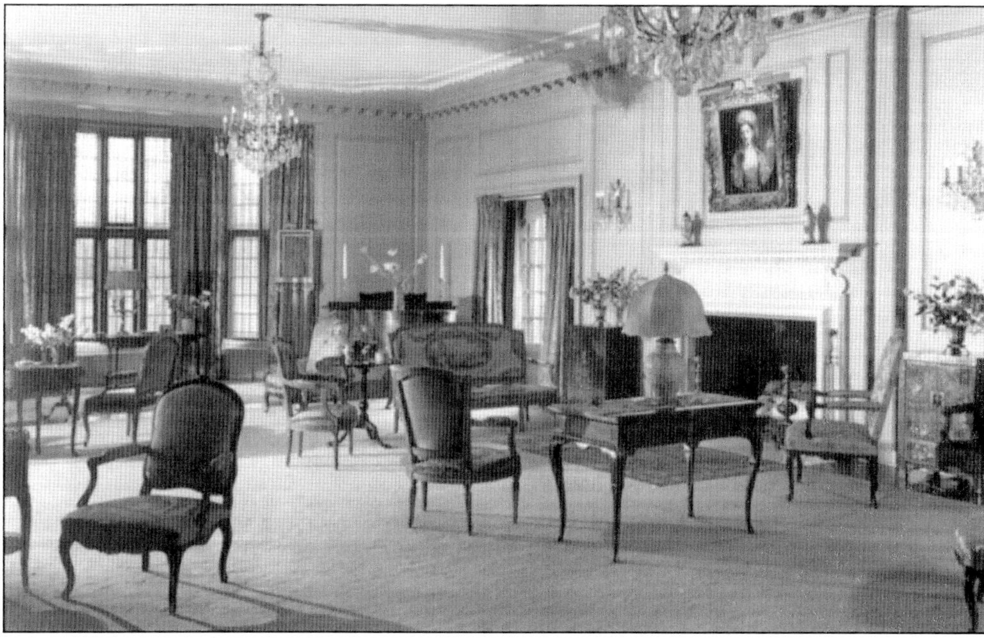

DRAWING ROOM. The most formal room in the house is the drawing room. The Fords often entertained guests here before dinner and also hosted meetings here of the cultural and charitable organizations they supported. The room was originally English, but in 1956, Mrs. Ford redecorated in a French mode to complement her collections of French Impressionist and Post-Impressionist paintings and 18th-century French furniture. (Courtesy of the Edsel & Eleanor Ford House.)

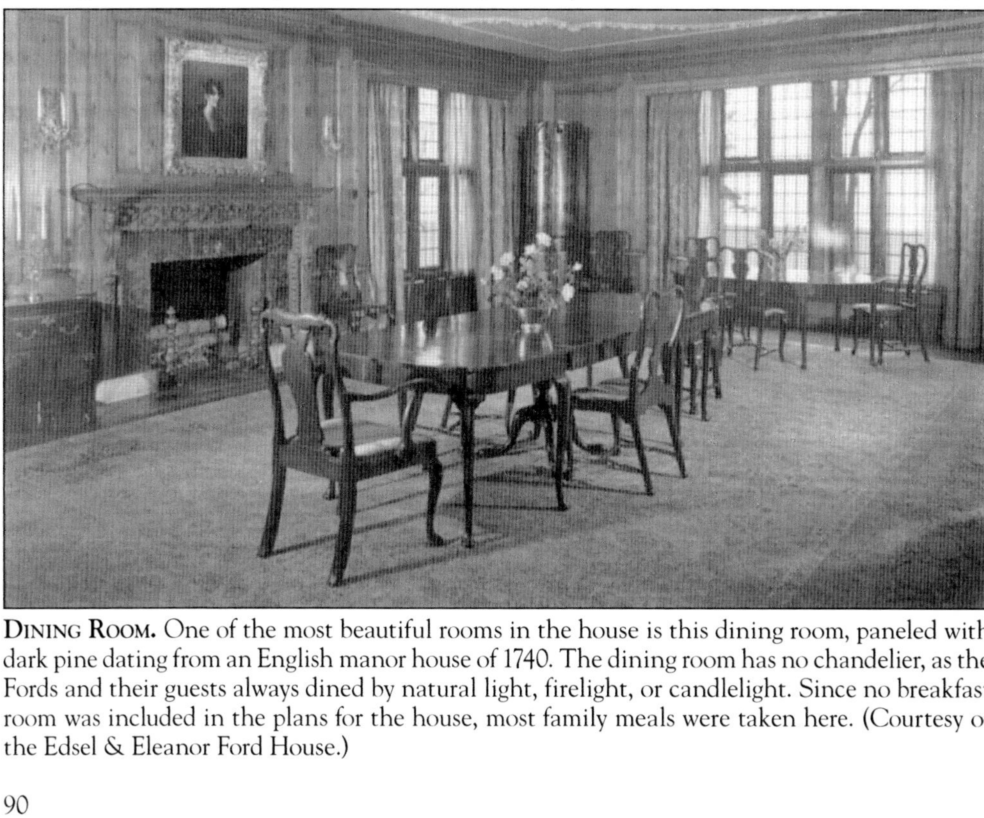

DINING ROOM. One of the most beautiful rooms in the house is this dining room, paneled with dark pine dating from an English manor house of 1740. The dining room has no chandelier, as the Fords and their guests always dined by natural light, firelight, or candlelight. Since no breakfast room was included in the plans for the house, most family meals were taken here. (Courtesy of the Edsel & Eleanor Ford House.)

Gallery. The largest room in the house is the gallery, which resembles an English baronial hall with its architectural details and furnishings. The Fords used this room for family parties, especially at Christmastime, a favorite holiday of Mrs. Ford's, and when the family would play games or watch first-run movies. The barrel-vault ceiling of ornamental plaster, with its Tudor rose and French fleur-de-lis emblems, is reminiscent of a ceiling from a 17th-century English manor. (Courtesy of the Edsel & Eleanor Ford House.)

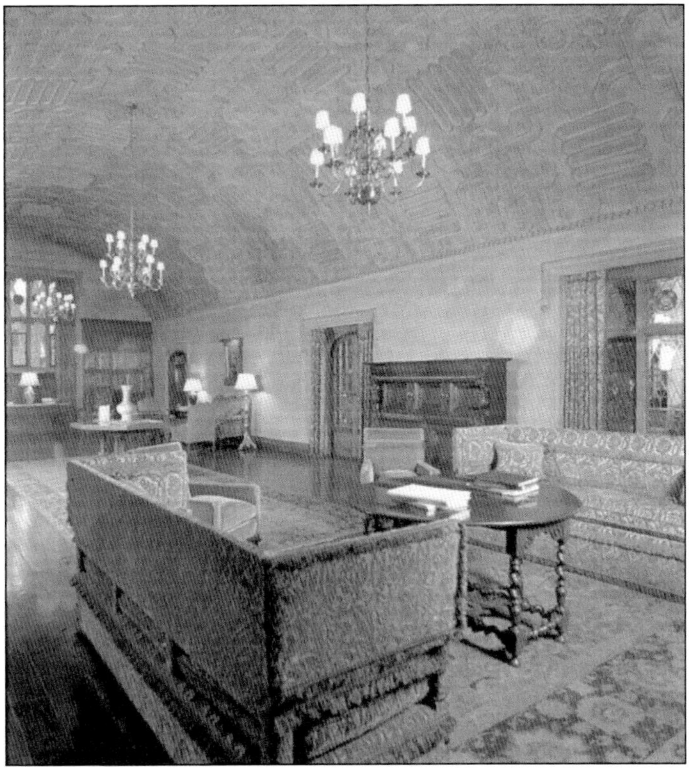

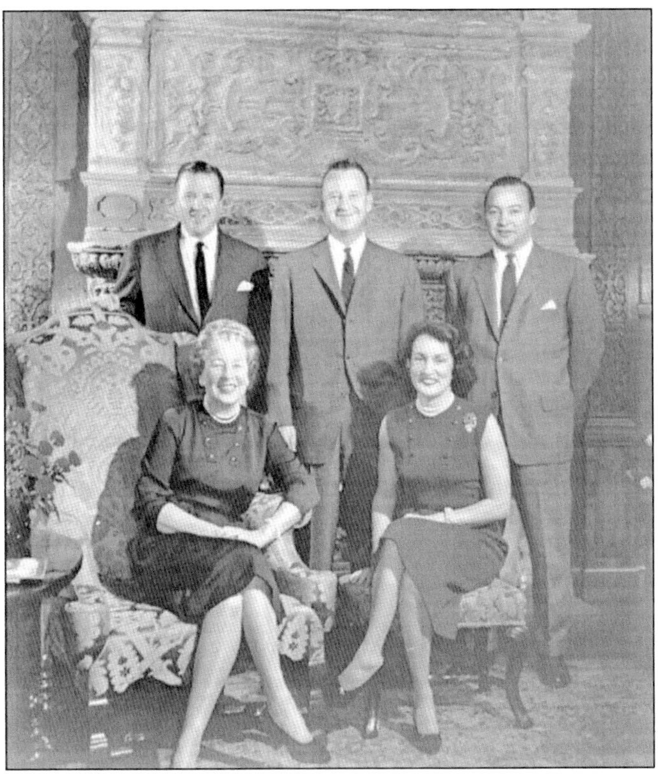

Mrs. Ford and Her Family. Mrs. Ford chose the library, the family's favorite gathering place, as the setting for this mid-1950s portrait of herself and her children. Standing from left to right are Henry, Benson, and William, while Josephine is seated next to her mother. Mrs. Ford always felt the library presented an aura of warmth and leisure. (Courtesy of the Edsel & Eleanor Ford House.)

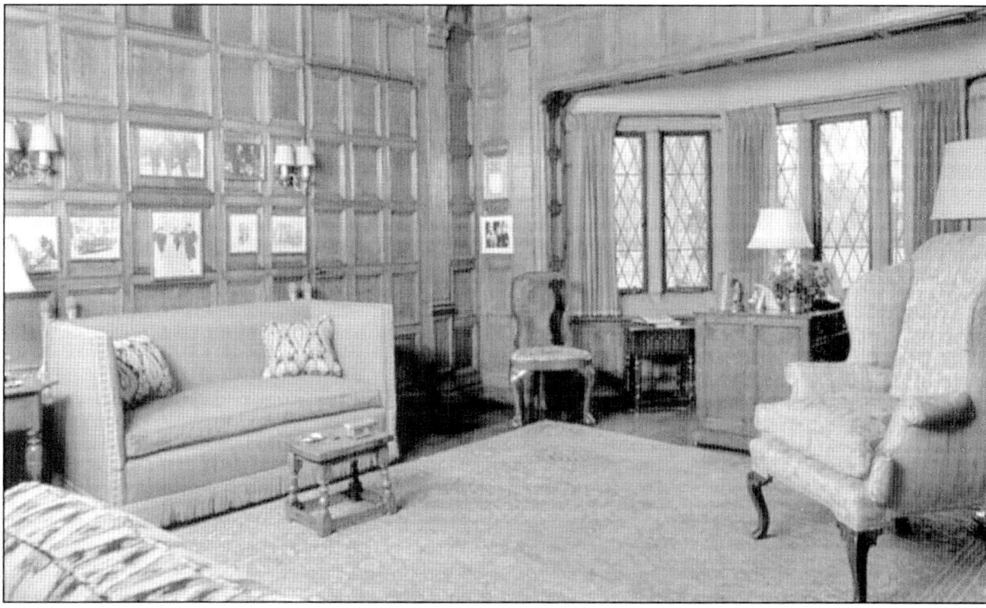

Mr. Ford's Study. This study was the personal retreat of Edsel Ford and the room to which gentlemen retired after dinner across the hall. The room's Elizabethan oak paneling conceals two doors: one led to a private washroom and the other to a photographic darkroom. As seen by the many pictures in the room, photography rivaled sailing as Edsel's favorite hobby. From 1926 to 1927, Edsel served as commodore of the Grosse Pointe Yacht Club. (Courtesy of the Edsel & Eleanor Ford House.)

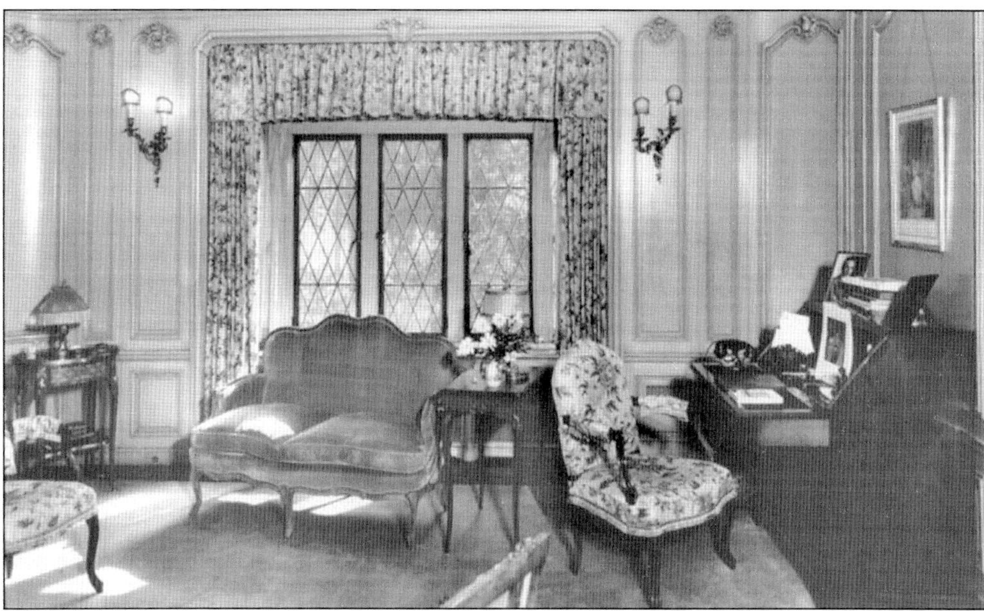

Mrs. Ford's Sitting Room. One of the most interesting rooms in the house is Mrs. Ford's sitting room. It was here that she conducted most of her daily business, read books, wrote letters, and sometimes took her meals. The room exudes a subtle femininity with its color scheme, fine furnishings, paintings, and personal mementos. This photograph dates from the early 1930s. Note the rotary dial telephone on her desk. (Courtesy of the Edsel & Eleanor Ford House.)

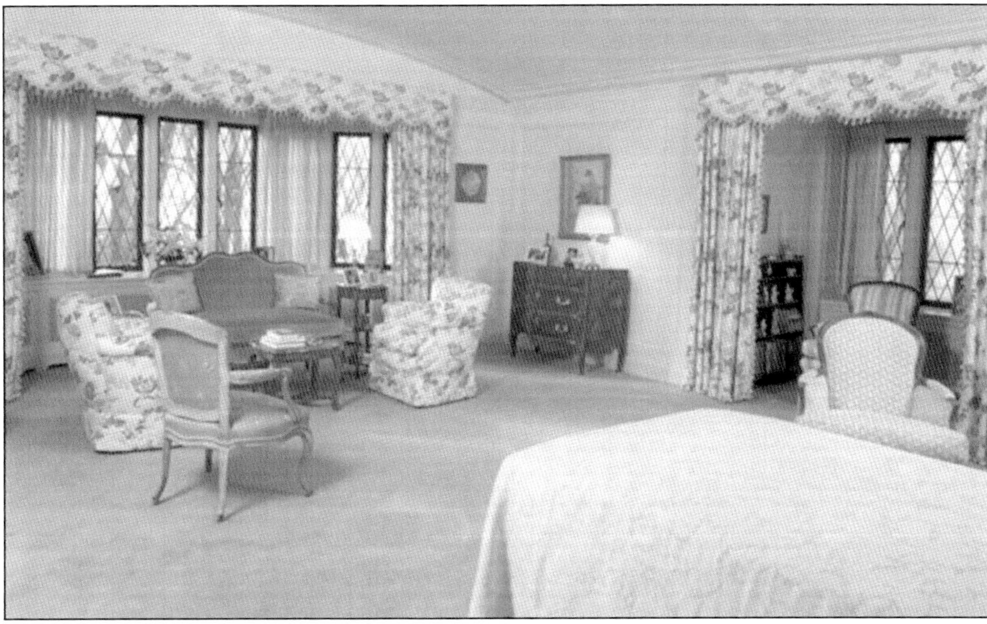

Master Bedroom. Mr. and Mrs. Ford's bedroom featured spectacular views on three sides. Toward the east are Gaukler Point and the lake beyond, to the south are the lagoon and the swimming pool, and to the west, below a small balcony, is the Apple Court. Around the room are various prints and drawings, both antique and modern. As in many of the rooms in their home, photographs of family and friends are visible everywhere. (Courtesy of the Edsel & Eleanor Ford House.)

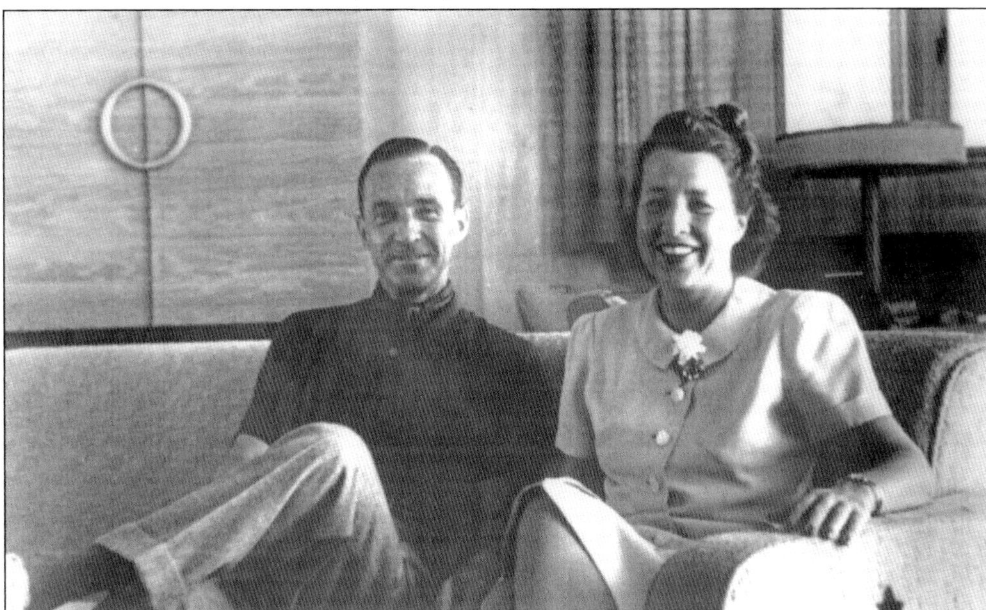

Edsel and Eleanor. Here is a wonderful informal photograph of Edsel and Eleanor, taken around 1940. They had a lifelong love of art and art collecting that is evident particularly in the furnishings of their home and in their association with the Detroit Institute of Arts (DIA). Edsel served on the DIA Arts Commission from 1925 to 1943, and Eleanor served from 1943 to 1976. (Courtesy of the Edsel & Eleanor Ford House.)

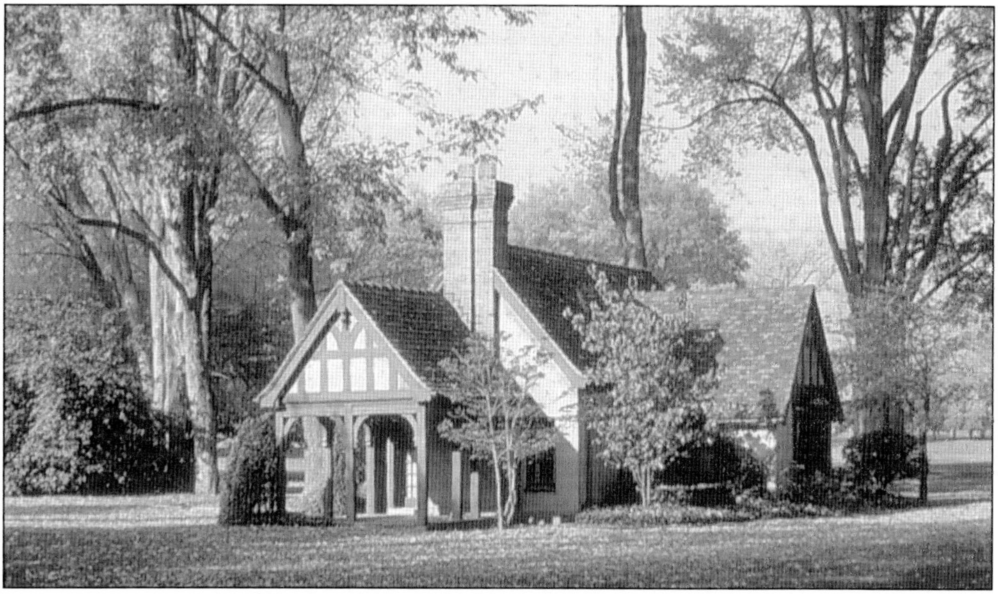

The Playhouse. One of the most unique buildings to be found on the grounds of the estate is the two-third-scale Tudor-style playhouse. Built in 1930, it was a gift from Mrs. Henry Ford to Josephine, her only granddaughter, who was then seven. The gable ends of the playhouse were decorated in high-relief stucco with characters from well-known nursery rhymes, including Old King Cole, the Cow that Jumped Over the Moon, and Little Miss Muffet. (Courtesy of the Edsel & Eleanor Ford House.)

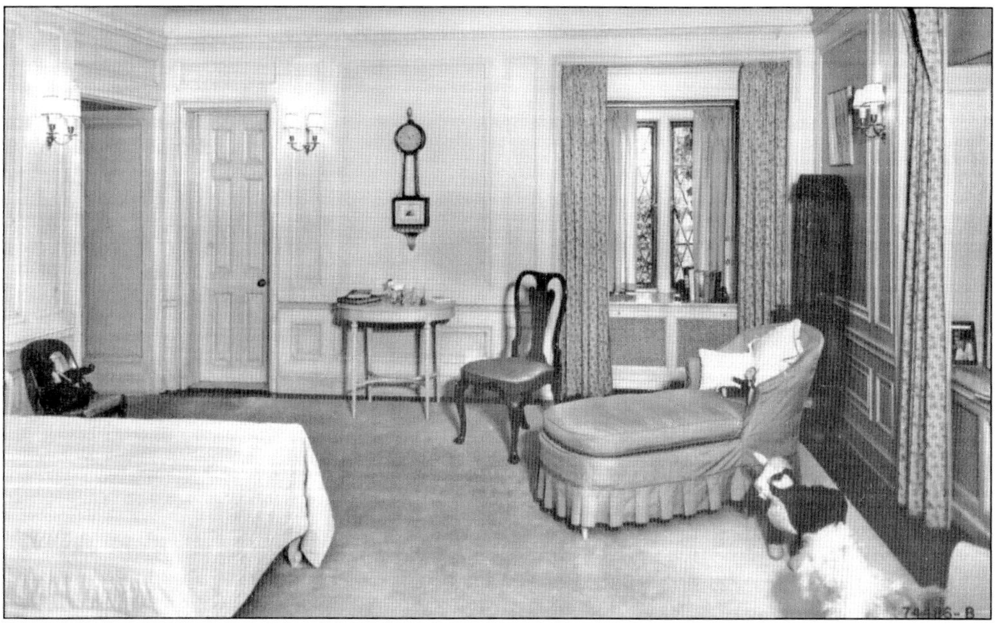

Josephine's Bedroom. This view of Josephine's bedroom dates from the early 1930s, and like any little girl's bedroom, there are a number of stuffed animals. Note there is not one piece of the 18th-century furniture for which the rest of the house is famous. The room has wonderful views of the surrounding lawns, trees, and water from the windows on three sides. (Courtesy of the Edsel & Eleanor Ford House.)

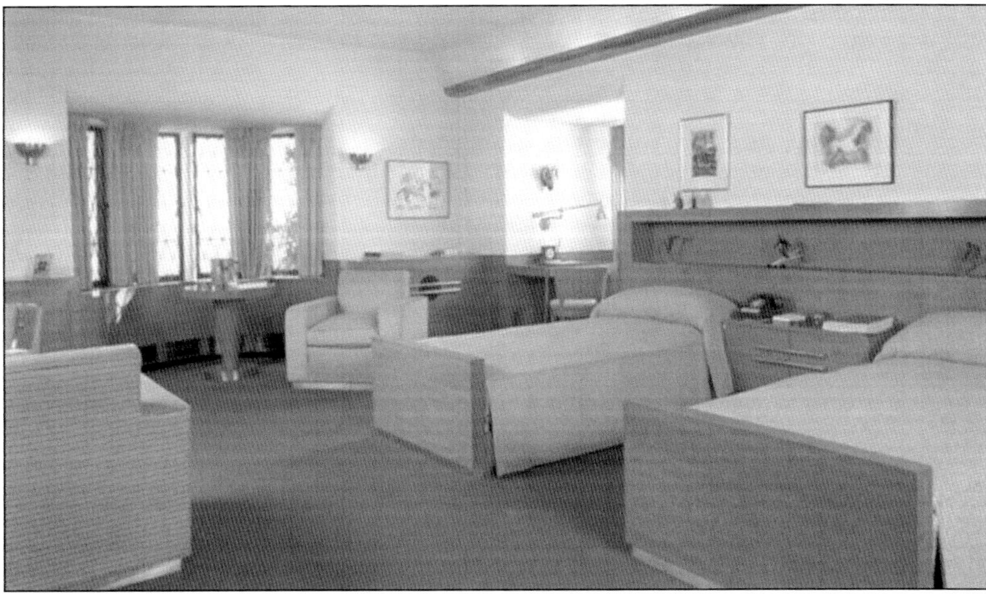

The Boys' Bedroom. At various times, each of the Ford boys occupied this bedroom. Henry and Benson shared this room from 1929 until about 1935, when 17-year-old Henry moved across the hall into his own room. When Henry married in 1940, Benson moved across the hall, and this became William's room. Most of the furniture was built in. For entertainment, a record player and speakers were built into the wall and two tables contained built-in radios. (Courtesy of the Edsel & Eleanor Ford House.)

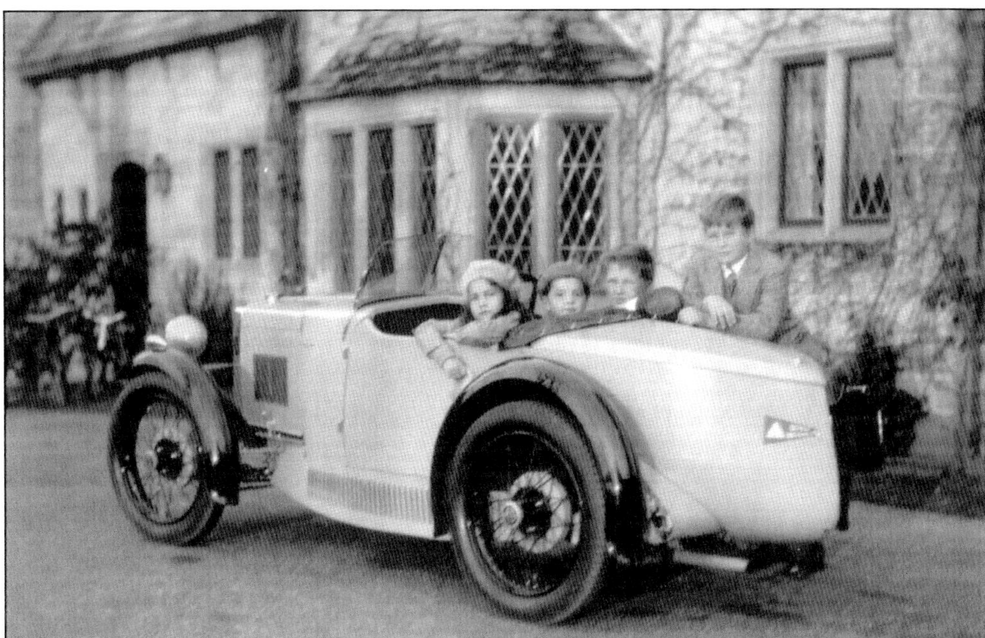

The Children and a Car. What could be more appropriate for a photograph of the children of the president of an automobile company than a car? Seen here in front of the Ford House around 1930 with an MG Midget, one of Edsel's personal favorite cars, are, from left to right, Josephine, William Clay, Henry, and Benson. (Courtesy of the Edsel & Eleanor Ford House.)

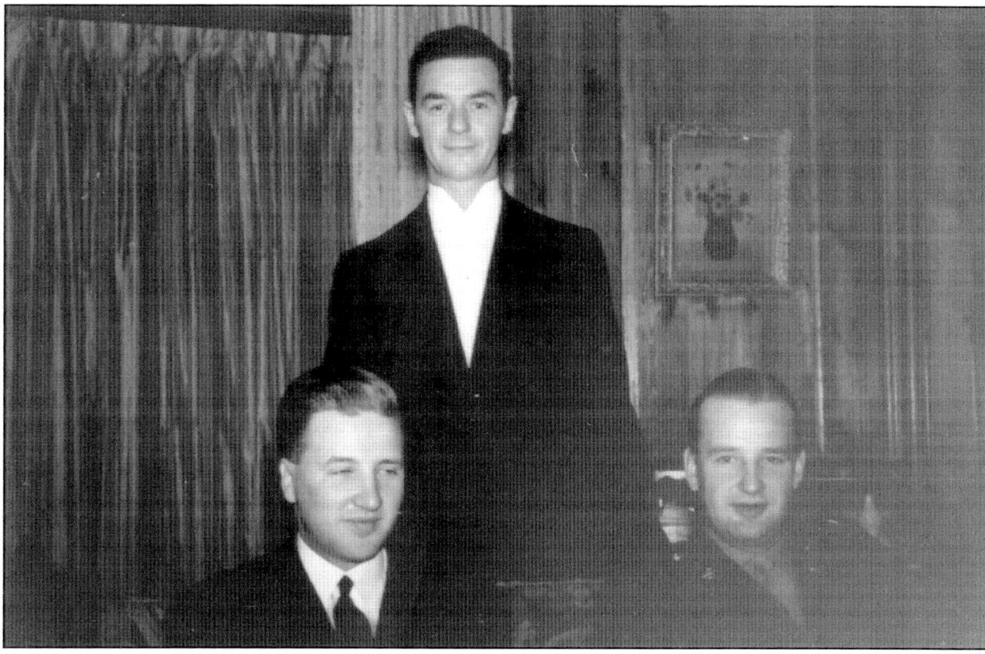

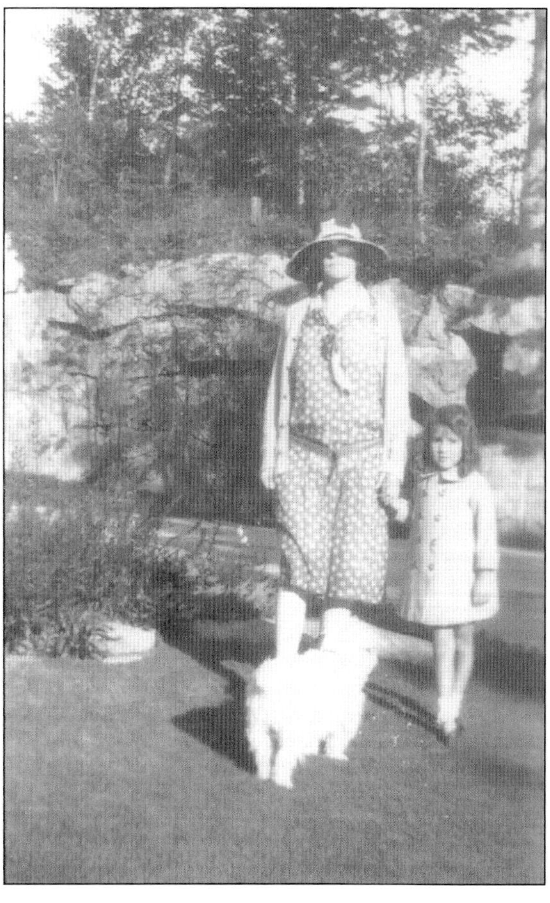

The Butler. Tomas Sellars, seen here with Henry II (left) and Benson (right), served as butler to the Ford family for nearly 30 years. Tom worked from 7:00 a.m. until 7:00 p.m., with a three-hour lunch break. If the Fords were entertaining, he stayed later. Each day, he changed clothes twice. He wore gray in the morning, changed for lunch if there were visitors, and donned a tuxedo for dinner. (Courtesy of the Edsel & Eleanor Ford House.)

The Governess. Judith Tagand, seen here with Josephine, served for many years as the Ford family governess. Affectionately known as Mademoiselle, she spoke only French to William and Josephine. Mademoiselle was the only staff person to live within the family portion of the house, as it offered easy access to the young children. After Josephine married, Mademoiselle came to work for her young family. (Courtesy of the Edsel & Eleanor Ford House.)

THE WATCHMAN. Thomas Laughlin, seen here at the entrance to the Gate Lodge, served the Ford family as head of security. Laughlin began working for Edsel and Eleanor Ford soon after they were married. He continued to work for the Fords and moved with his family to Gaukler Point, taking up residence in one of the cottages in the Gate Lodge. Laughlin served the Ford family until his death in 1972, an incredible 66 years. (Courtesy of the Edsel & Eleanor Ford House.)

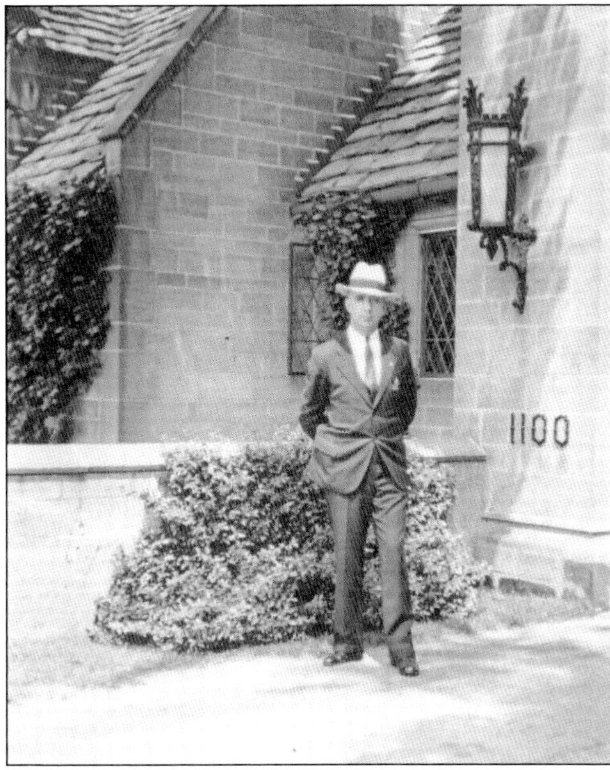

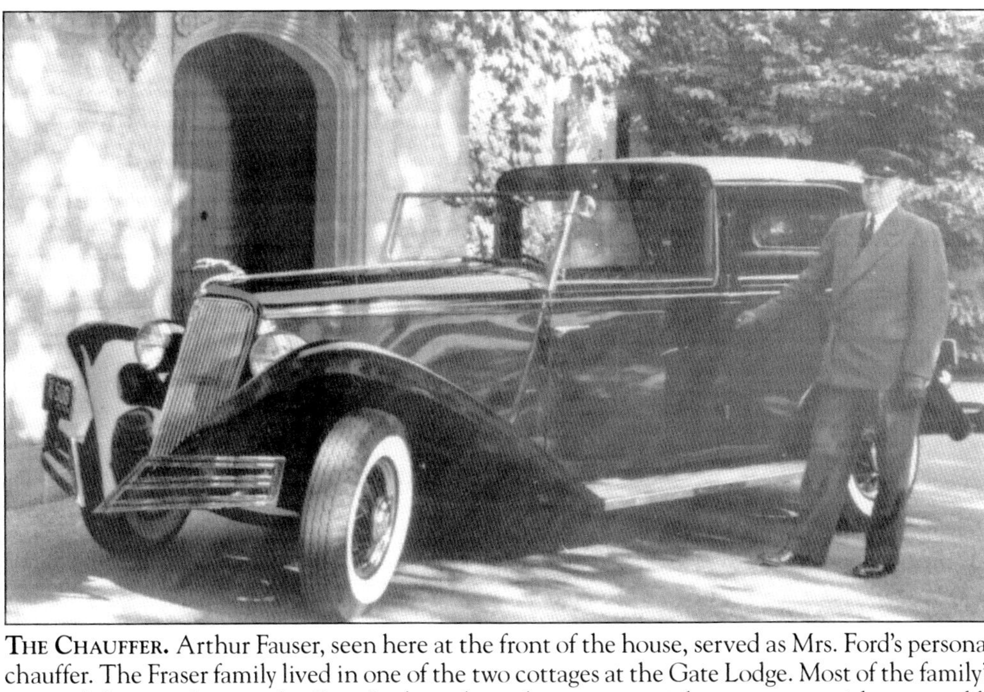

THE CHAUFFER. Arthur Fauser, seen here at the front of the house, served as Mrs. Ford's personal chauffer. The Fraser family lived in one of the two cottages at the Gate Lodge. Most of the family's automobiles were kept at the Gate Lodge, where there was an eight-car garage with a turntable that was used to turn the automobiles around to face outward, eliminating the need to back out of the garage. (Courtesy of the Edsel & Eleanor Ford House.)

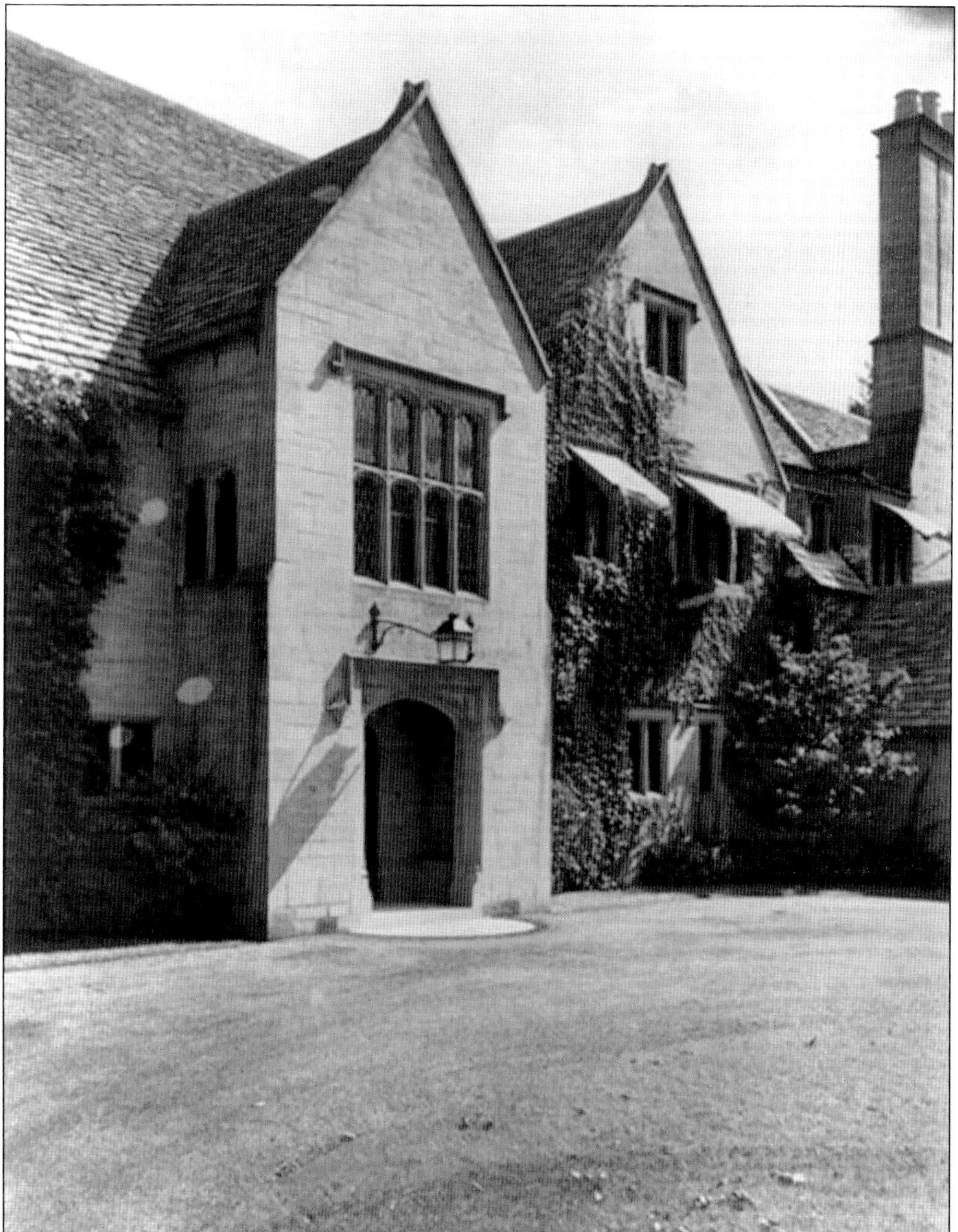

The Front Door. This view of the main entrance to the Edsel & Eleanor Ford House was taken shortly after the family moved in at Christmastime 1929. Edsel died here in 1943. Eleanor continued to live here until her death in 1976. Today, following Mrs. Ford's wishes, this beautiful estate is open to the public and is one of Michigan's premiere cultural attractions. The estate is now comprised of 87 acres. Mrs. Ford sold 43 acres of the original property in 1946 to Grosse Pointe Woods for that city's lakefront park. Visitors are welcome to tour the grounds and house, with its fine collection of antique furniture and paintings looking much as they did when the Fords were in residence. (Courtesy of the Edsel & Eleanor Ford House.)

Six

Points Nearby

Many Grosse Pointe Shores residents were business, industrial, and professional leaders in the city of Detroit. This fostered active support, and often leadership positions, in that city's cultural, arts, professional sports, and civic affairs. Closer to home, village residents also enjoyed the convenience of a variety of social, shopping, religious, health, and educational opportunities in the neighboring Grosse Pointe communities. Founded in 1897, the Country Club of Detroit moved in 1923 from its original site on Lake St. Clair to its new clubhouse where its golf course was located. Preferring to remain on the water, the club's yachtsmen formed the Grosse Pointe Club. Horsemen and polo players created the Hunt Club in 1911, while golfers formed the Lochmoor Club in 1917. Though residents frequently shopped in downtown Detroit, they looked to neighborhood groceries, confectioneries, and clothiers for occasional purchases, particularly in the two shopping areas known as "the Village" and "the Hill," both located on Kercheval Avenue. For church, residents at first had only the choice of either St. Paul's Catholic Church or the Protestant church. St. Paul's parishioners moved into their new church in 1899. The Protestant church, reorganized as a Presbyterian church in 1920, moved into its present building, Grosse Pointe Memorial Church, in 1927. Other denominations were soon to follow. Sensing a need for community recreation and social services, a group of Grosse Pointers created the Mutual Aid and Neighborhood Club in 1911–1912. During the 1918 influenza epidemic, Cottage Hospital opened. Grosse Pointe's second hospital, Bon Secours, opened in 1945. The Grosse Pointe War Memorial, formed to honor those who had served in our country's wars, opened in 1949 as a community center for educational and charitable activities. Of the many schools nearby is the Grosse Pointe Academy, with roots dating to 1885, and St. Paul's Catholic School. Once ready for high school, many Grosse Pointe Shores residents sent their children to the Grosse Pointe High School, later renamed South High, built in 1927. Then, due to a population boom, Grosse Pointe North High School opened in 1968. The first branch library was opened in the Grosse Pointe Shores Village Hall in 1922. The Central Library on Fisher Road and Kercheval Avenue opened in 1953. The Provencal-Weir House, the museum of the Grosse Pointe Historical Society, opened in 1996. Social, cultural, religious, and educational opportunities were all found nearby.

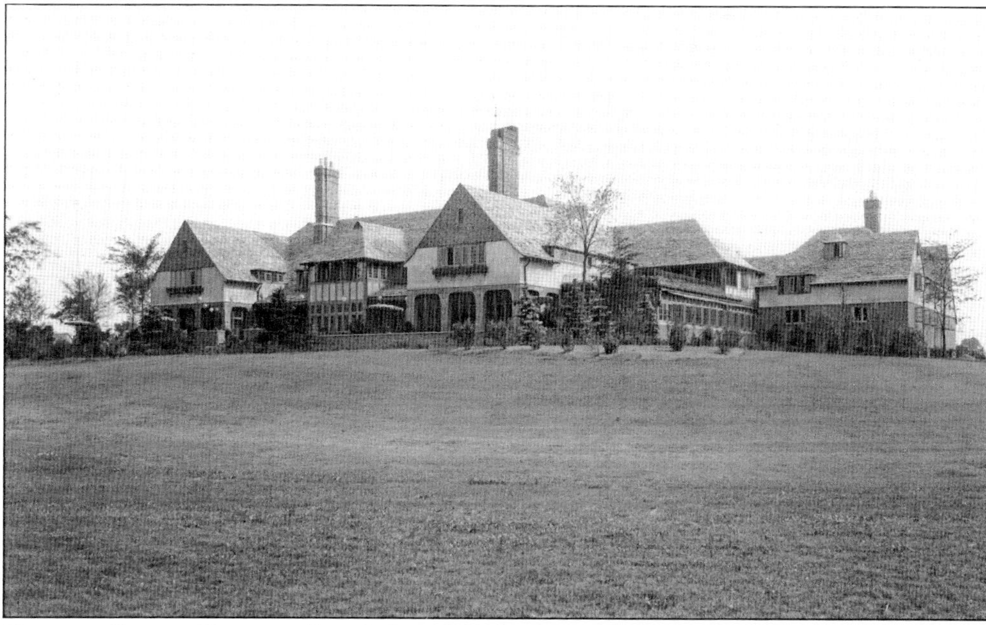

COUNTRY CLUB OF DETROIT. Founded in 1897, the venerable Country Club of Detroit moved in 1923 from its original site on Lake St. Clair to its new clubhouse on the old Weir farm where the golf course was located. Members had just two years to enjoy their new clubhouse. Early in the morning of October 18, 1925, it was destroyed by fire. The clubhouse was rebuilt and reopened in the fall of 1927. (Courtesy of the Manning Brothers.)

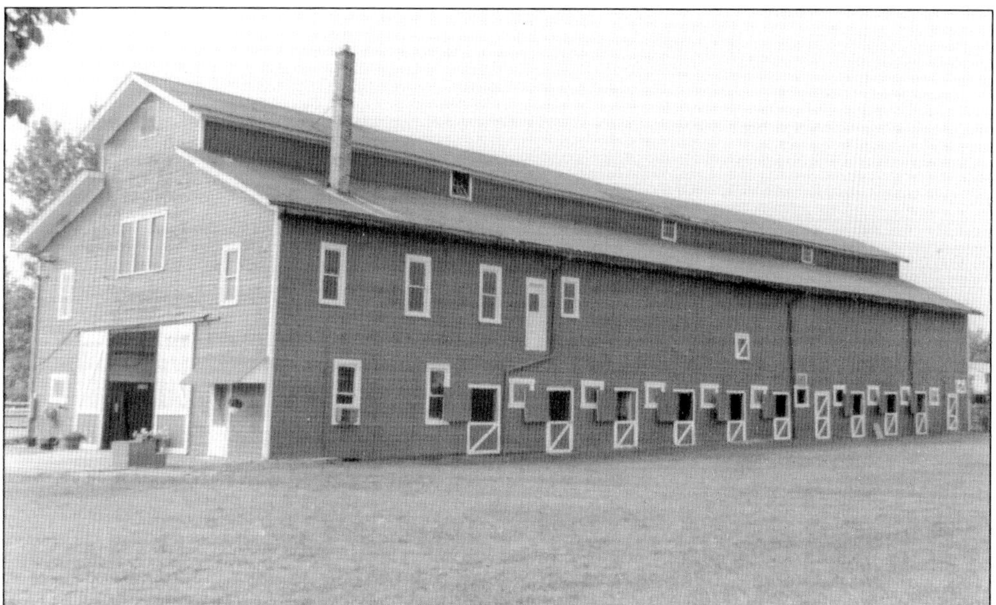

HUNT CLUB. The Grosse Pointe Hunt Club was established in 1911 as Grosse Pointe's major location for horseback riding and polo. In 1911, Dr. Harry Torrey moved this horse barn from his property, the former Claireview Stock Farm on Lake Shore Road. Sadly, because of fireworks, this barn caught fire in July 2001, killing 19 horses and destroying the barn. A new barn was built, and the Hunt Club is active today. (Courtesy of the Grosse Pointe Historical Society.)

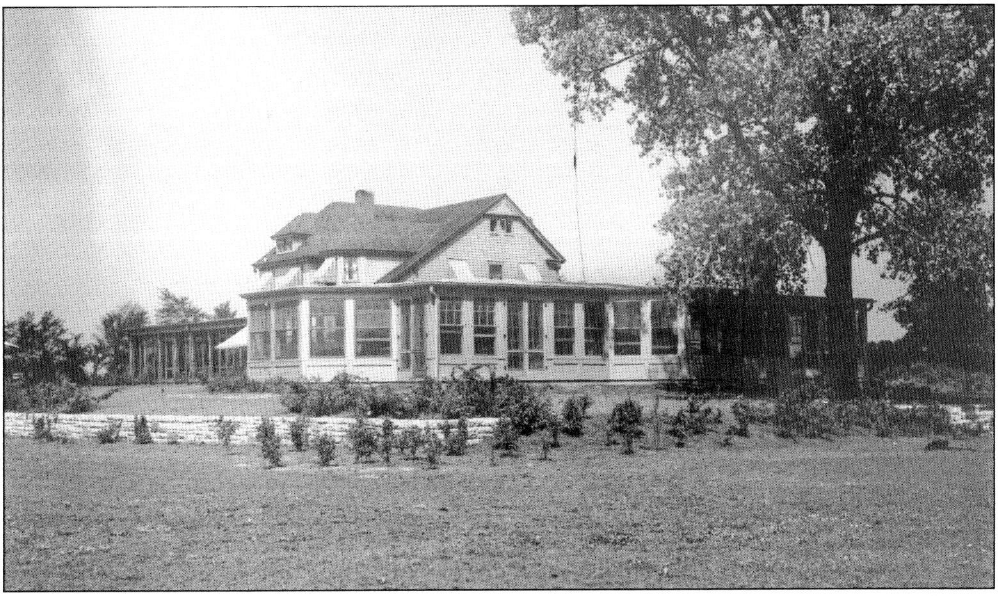

Lochmoor Club. In February 1917, prominent area golfers including A.J. Buhl, Roy D. Chapin, Horace Dodge, John Dodge, Edsel Ford, and Oscar Webber purchased 136 acres of farmland off Vernier Road and began building the Lochmoor Club. After a day on the greens, golfers gathered in this farmhouse. The structure was destroyed by fire in February 1924, and a new clubhouse was built. The current clubhouse dates from 1969. (Courtesy of the Walter P. Reuther Archives, Wayne State University.)

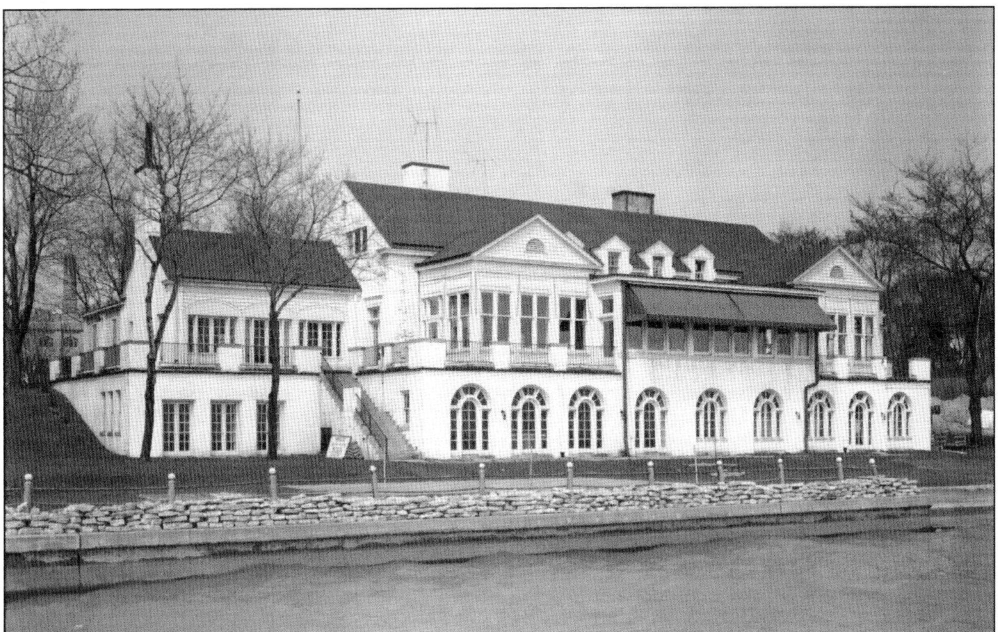

Grosse Pointe Club. When the Country Club of Detroit moved to its new location in 1923, the club's yachtsmen preferred to remain on the waterfront and founded the Grosse Pointe Club, known affectionately as the "Little Club." The new clubhouse, seen here, was designed by Robert O. Derrick and opened in 1927. (Courtesy of the Manning Brothers Historic Photograph Collection.)

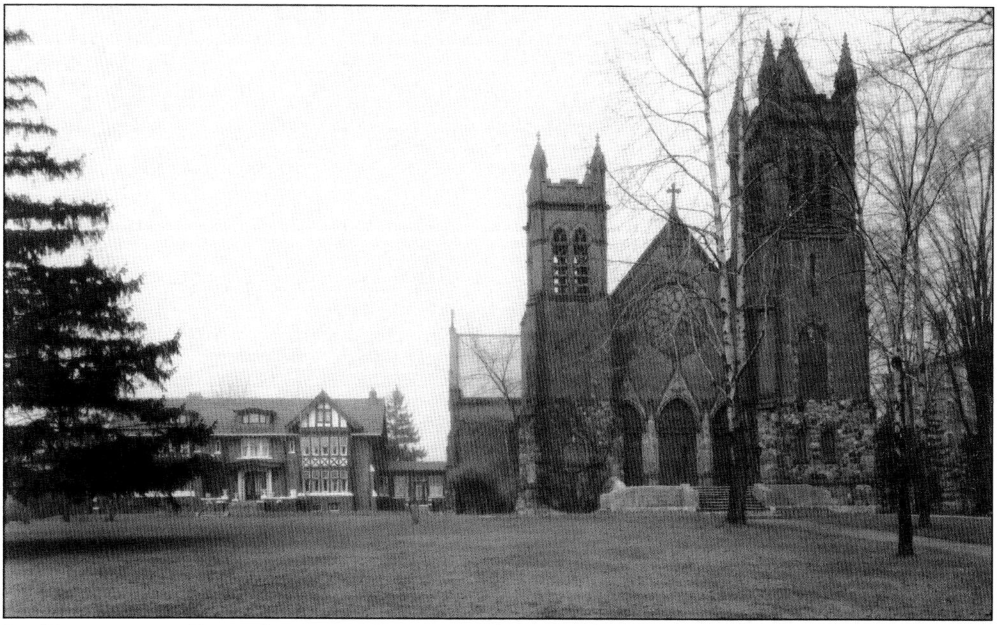

St. Paul on the Lake Catholic Church. This French Gothic–style church building dates to 1899 and the parish heritage dates to the 1820s. The church was built under the guidance of Fr. John Elsen, whose funeral was the first service in the new church. It replaced an 1848 frame building. The first church building, dating from 1825, was located on Lake Shore Road just north of Vernier Road. (Courtesy of the Manning Brothers Historic Photograph Collection.)

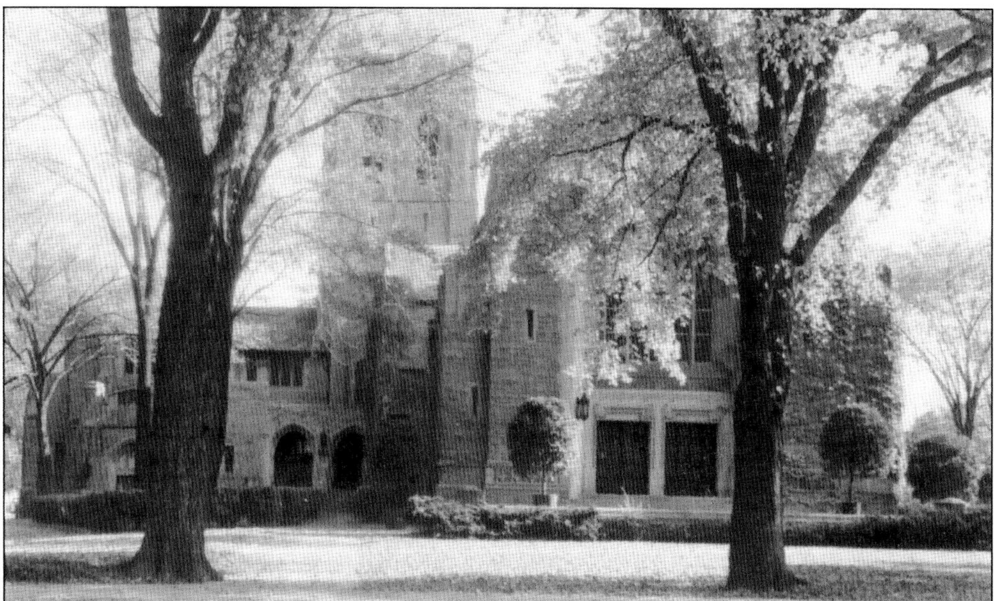

Grosse Pointe Memorial Church. The present Neo-Gothic church, built of ashlar limestone, was dedicated on May 15, 1927, honoring the founders who organized the Grosse Pointe Protestant Church in 1865 and built their first church in 1867. This was followed by a new building, known as the "Ivy-Covered Church," built on this site in 1894. In 1920, the congregation reorganized as a Presbyterian church. (Courtesy of the Grosse Pointe Historical Society.)

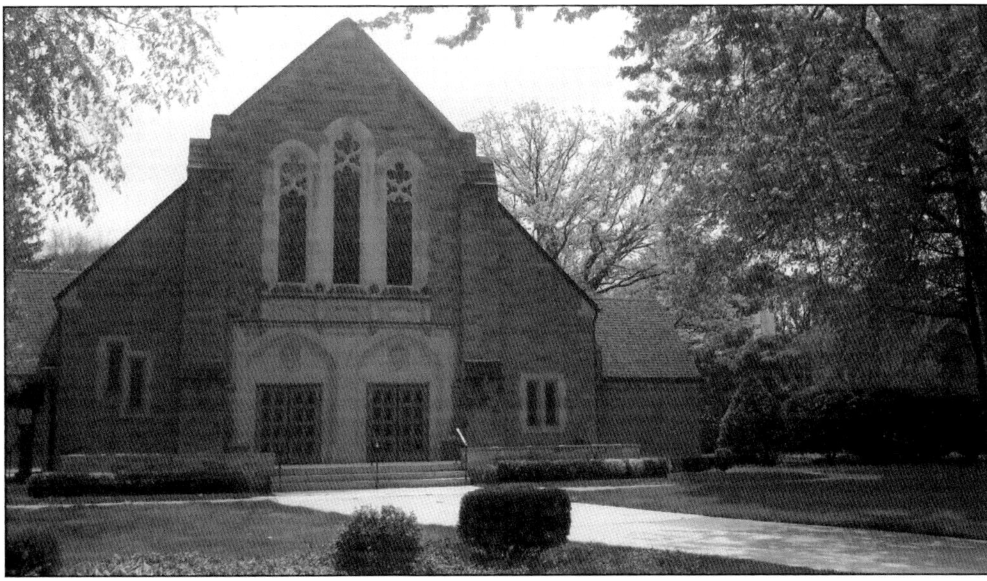

Grosse Pointe Woods Presbyterian Church. On October 2, 1939, the Presbytery of Detroit officially commissioned this church as a satellite of Grosse Pointe Memorial Church. Two of its members, Dr. and Mrs. Harry H. Torrey, donated the land for the new church from their Grosse Pointe Shores estate Claireview. The dedication service for the present church was held May 23, 1948. (Courtesy of the Village of Grosse Pointe Shores.)

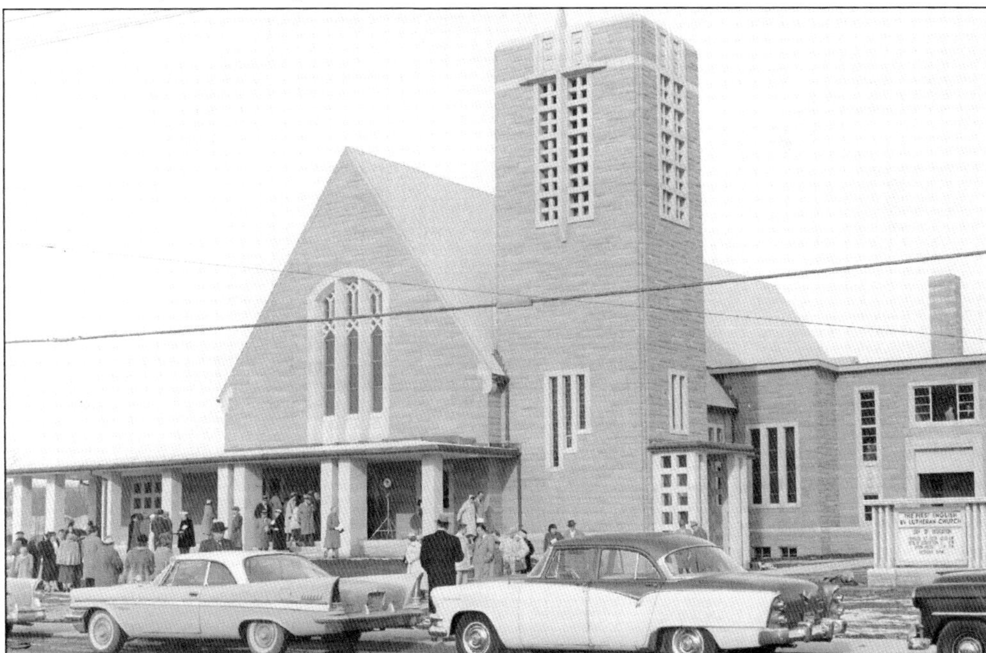

First English Lutheran Church. First English Lutheran Church was founded in Detroit in 1896. First English received its name because it was the first congregation in Detroit to use the English language exclusively in worship. In the 1950s, the decision was made to move to Grosse Pointe. Land from the old Vernier Farm was purchased, and the new church was dedicated on December 15, 1957. (Courtesy of First English Lutheran Church.)

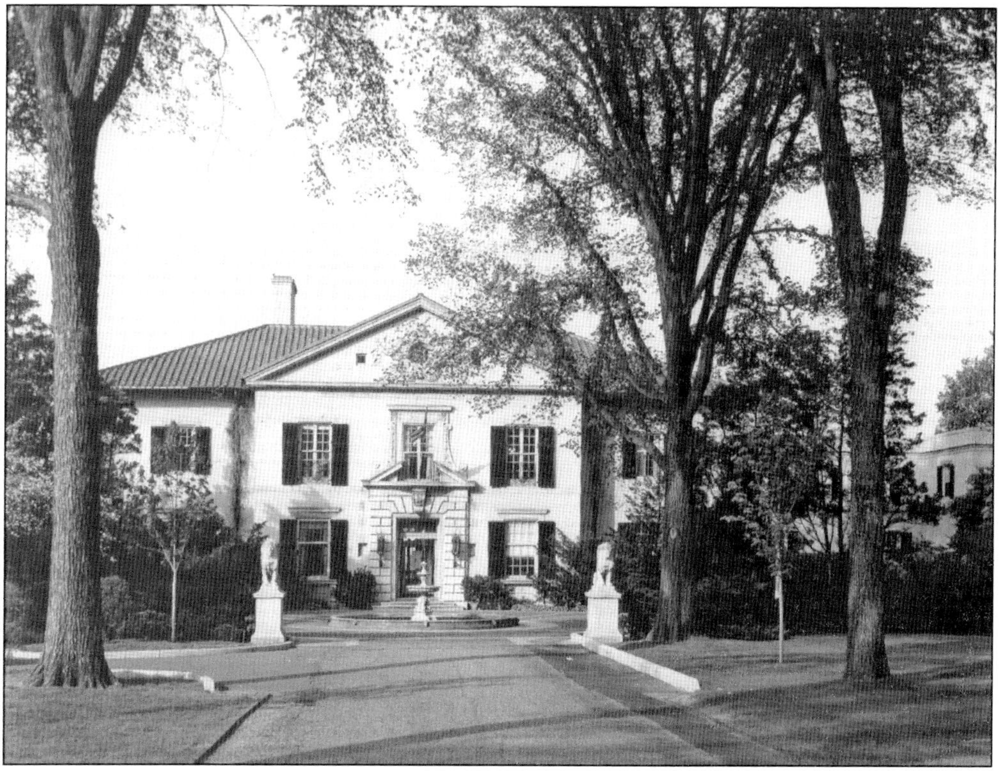

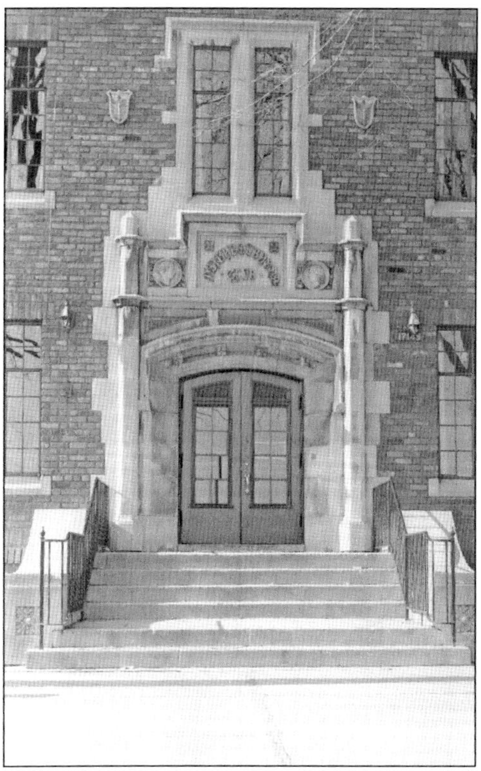

Grosse Pointe War Memorial. This impressive residence was built in 1910 for Russell A. Alger Jr., one of the founders of the Packard Motor Car Company. Designed by Charles A. Platt in Italian Renaissance style with extensive gardens, the estate was called the Moorings. Following Alger's death, it was used as a branch of the Detroit Institute of Arts (1936–1948). Later renamed the War Memorial, the building now serves as a community center for all five of the Grosse Pointes. (Courtesy of the Grosse Pointe Historical Society.)

Neighborhood Club. Sensing a need for community recreation and social services, a group of Grosse Pointers founded the National Aid and Neighborhood Club in 1911 and opened a clubhouse on Oak Street (now Muir Road). A second clubhouse, seen here, was built in the 1920s. A new clubhouse replaced this building in 1968. The present clubhouse was dedicated on January 7, 2013, and the Neighborhood Club continues "to provide enriching activities that bring families together." (Courtesy of the Grosse Pointe Historical Society.)

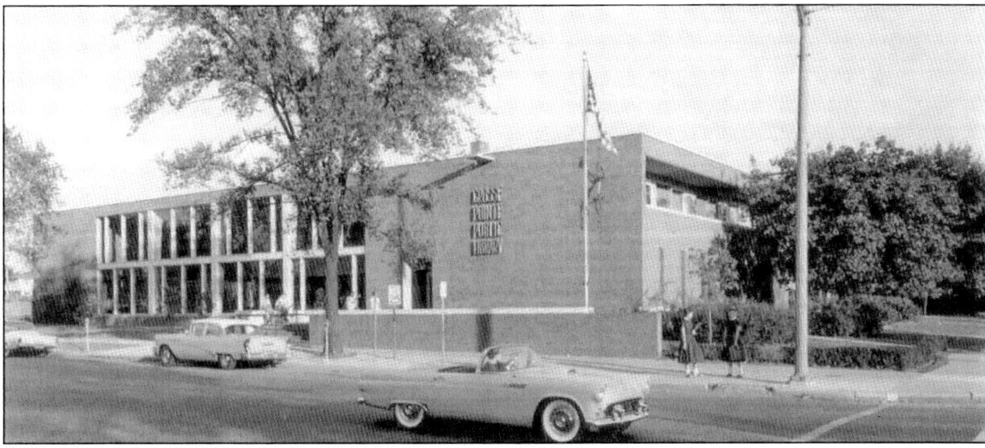

Grosse Pointe Central Library. Public library service in Grosse Pointe dates from 1922. In June 1929, the Grosse Pointe Public Library was finally established by the school district. In 1953, the Central Library, seen here, was built at Kercheval Avenue and Fisher Road. The library was reorganized as a district library in 1989 and continues its mission of service to all five Grosse Pointe communities. (Courtesy of the Grosse Pointe Public Library.)

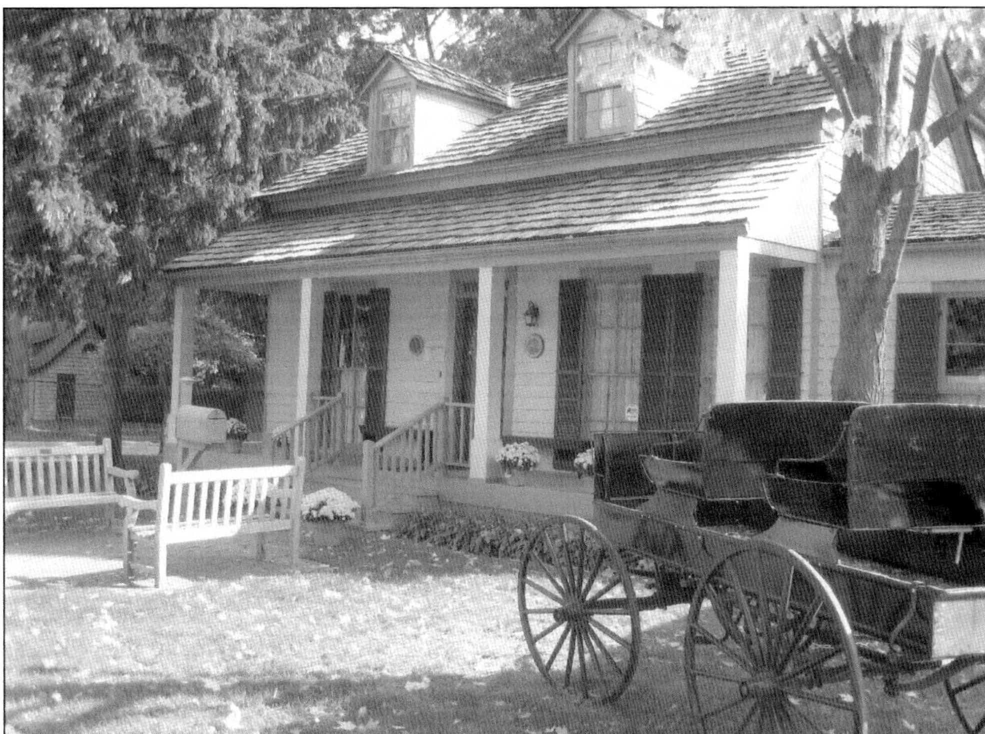

Provencal-Weir House. This landmark Greek Revival farmhouse is believed to be Grosse Pointe's oldest surviving residence. Built around 1823 by Detroiter Pierre Provencal on a site near Provencal and Lake Shore Roads, it was later owned by the Weir family. It was moved to its present location on Kercheval Avenue in 1914. Beautifully restored by the Grosse Pointe Historical Society, the house serves as the community's historical museum. (Courtesy of the Grosse Pointe Historical Society.)

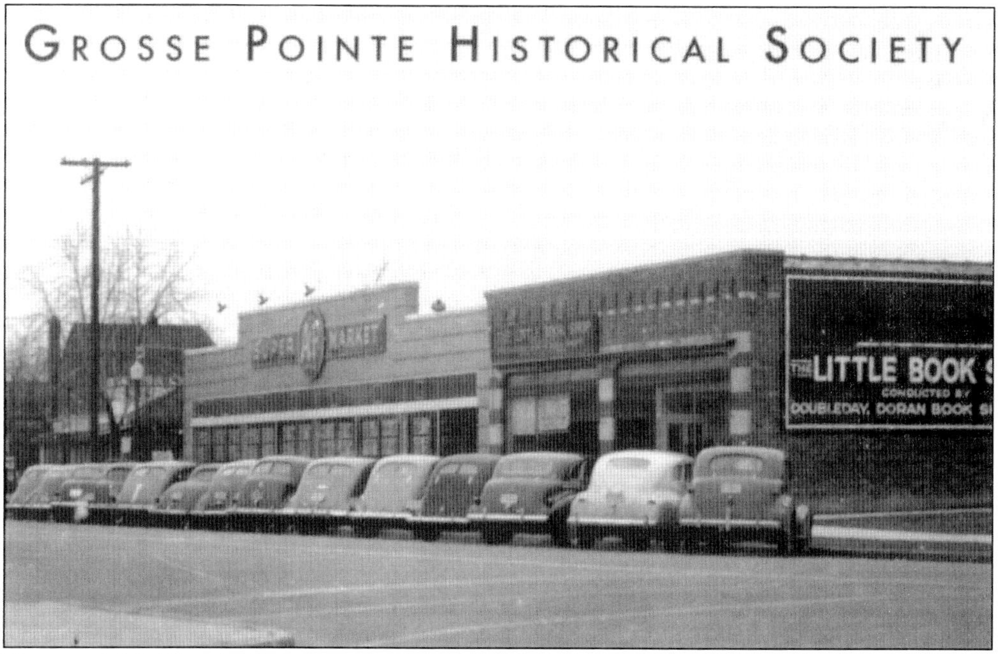

VILLAGE A&P. This A&P Supermarket anchored the three-block shopping district known locally as the Village. This shopping area, developed in the 1920s, was built on the Robert and James Abbot farm on Kercheval Avenue and what was originally called Field Street. (Courtesy of the Grosse Pointe Historical Society.)

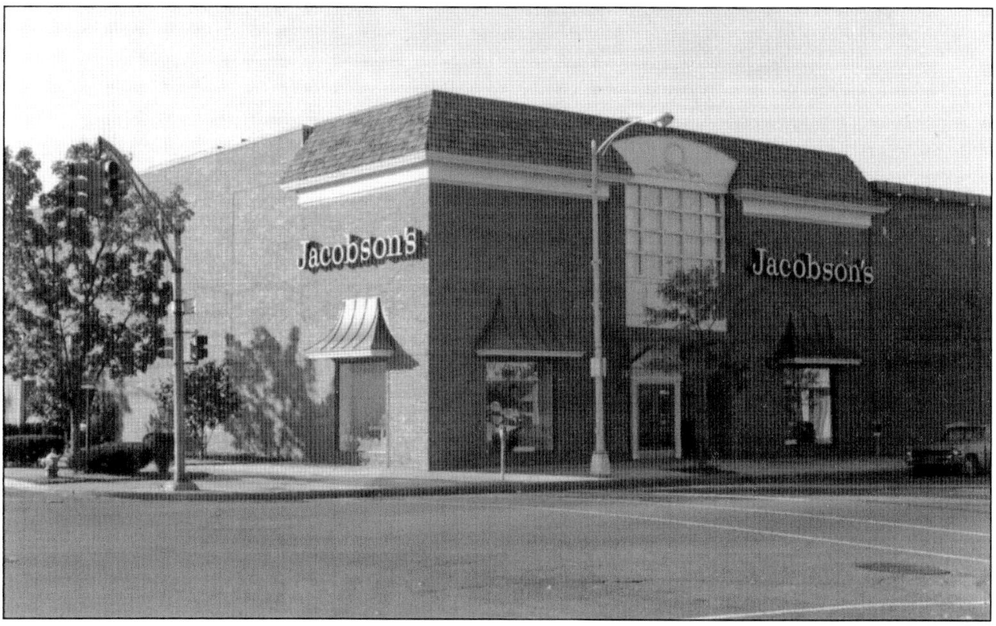

JACOBSON'S DEPARTMENT STORE. Jacobson's opened on Kercheval Avenue in the Village in 1944. Affectionately known as "Jacs," the store was known for its posh atmosphere, designer apparel, jewelry, home furnishings, personalized customer service, and fashion shows. It was also the place to meet for lunch in the Village. For nearly 60 years, Jacobson's was a Grosse Pointe landmark. The store closed in 2002. (Courtesy of the Grosse Pointe Historical Society.)

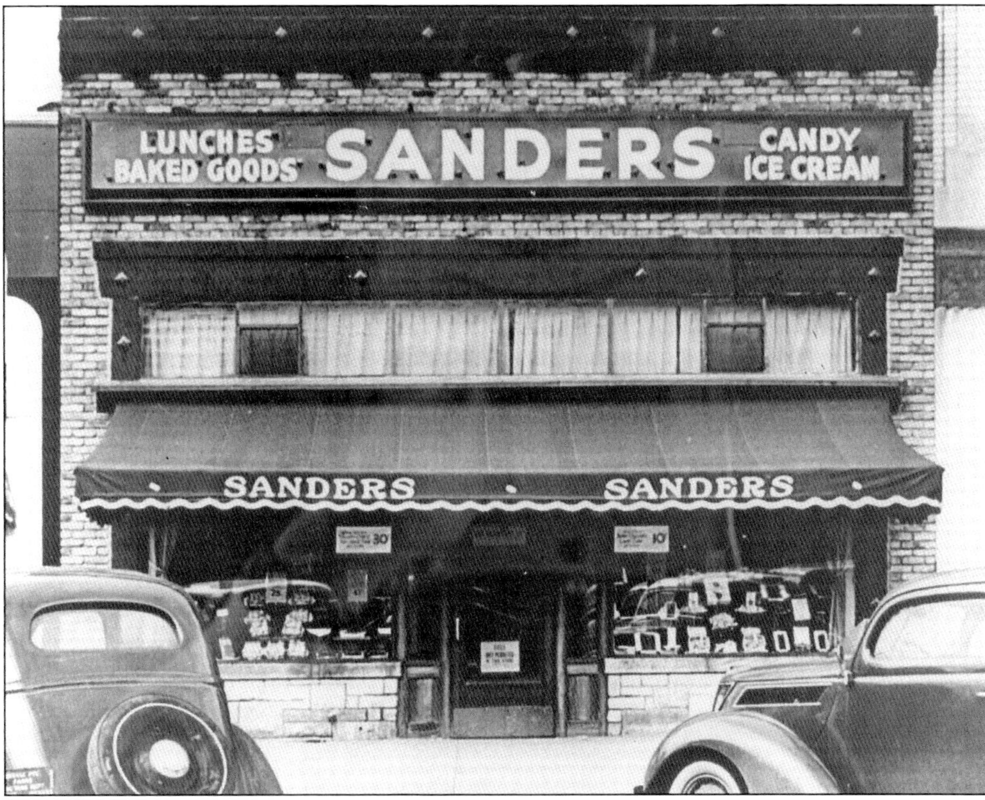

SANDERS IN THE VILLAGE. Sanders was first opened in downtown Detroit in 1875. The company grew to more than 57 stores like this one, which opened in the Village in 1934. The shop sold candy, fudge toppings, and baked goods, as well as light lunches and an assortment of desserts at its fountain counter, including ice cream sodas, sundaes, hot fudge cream puffs, and of course, its iconic bumpy cake, which is still popular today. (Courtesy of the Grosse Pointe Historical Society.)

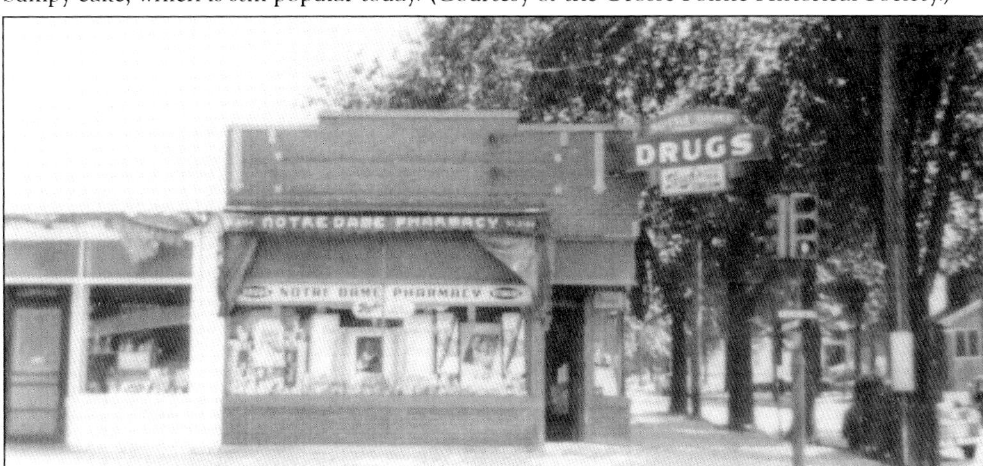

NOTRE DAME PHARMACY. This small-town drugstore has been an integral part of the Village since the 1920s. In 1944, this location was closed when the block was purchased for the new Jacobson's department store. Notre Dame Pharmacy moved down the street, reopened, and is still a favorite of Grosse Pointers. (Courtesy of the Grosse Pointe Historical Society.)

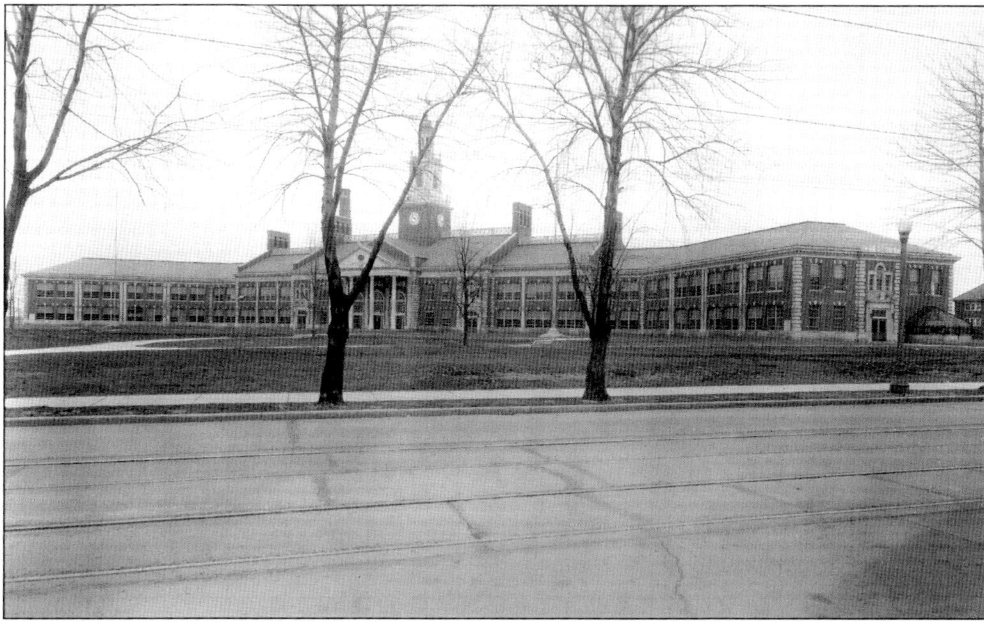

South High School. Grosse Pointe High School, as it was originally named, was built in 1927 at the corner of Fisher Road and Grosse Pointe Boulevard. This photograph shows the school shortly after it opened in 1928. Note the interurban railway tracks. The school became Grosse Pointe South High School in 1967, when a second high school, Grosse Pointe North, opened. (Courtesy of the Manning Brothers Historic Photograph Collection.)

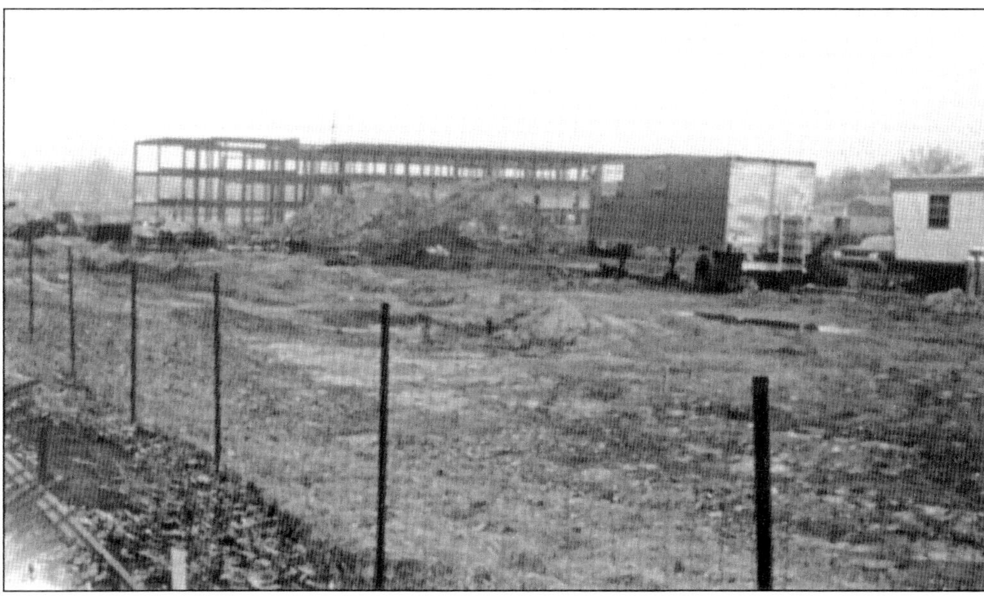

North High School. In the 1940s and 1950s, increased school enrollment prompted the construction of new middle and elementary schools in Grosse Pointe. With an additional 400 students enrolled each year in the 1960s, the community soon needed a second high school. Built on the Old Vanderbusch farm, Grosse Pointe North High School, seen here under construction, opened in 1968. Its first senior class graduated in 1970. (Courtesy of the Grosse Pointe Historical Society.)

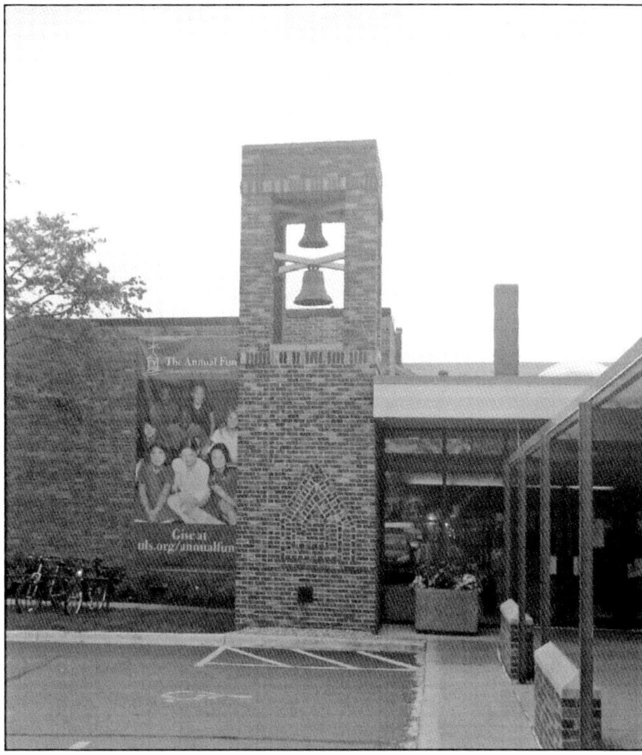

University Liggett School. Changes also occurred at local private schools. In 1954, Grosse Pointe Country Day and Detroit University Schools combined to form the coeducational Grosse Pointe University School (GPUS). Meanwhile, Liggett School, founded in 1878, moved from Detroit to a new campus in Grosse Pointe Woods in 1964. In 1969, it merged with GPUS to form University Liggett School. (Courtesy of the Village of Grosse Pointe Shores.)

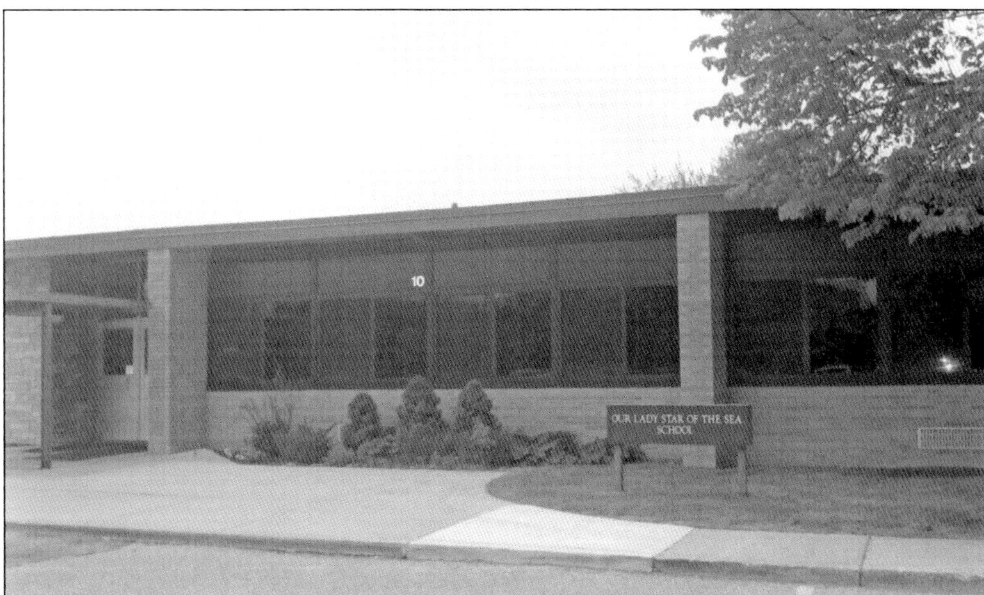

Our Lady Star of the Sea School. In 1955, Our Lady Star of the Sea Catholic Church was built on vacant farmland adjacent to the Village of Grosse Pointe Shores. An elementary school opened in the fall of 1958, which was followed by a high school in 1959. The high school flourished as an all-girls school until its closing in 1993. From that point, the high school building became the middle school. Today, Star of the Sea serves 350 students. (Courtesy of the Village of Grosse Pointe Shores.)

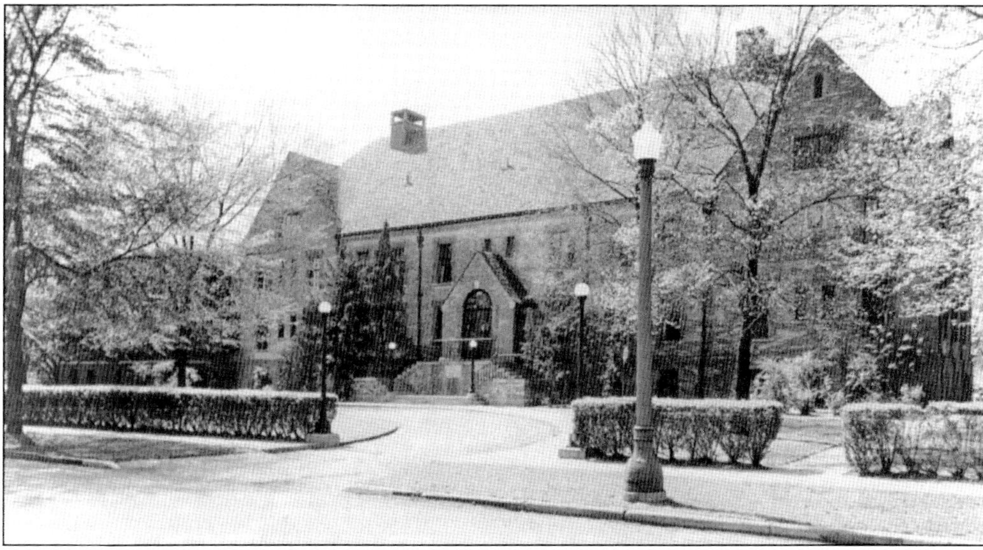

Cottage Hospital. During the 1918 influenza epidemic, the Neighborhood Club opened Cottage Hospital in a village home across the street from the club. The two institutions separated amicably in 1927, and a new building was constructed for Cottage Hospital on Kercheval Avenue in 1928. The hospital was expanded and enlarged several times over the years. In 1986, Cottage Hospital became affiliated with Detroit's Henry Ford Health System. (Courtesy of the Grosse Pointe Historical Society.)

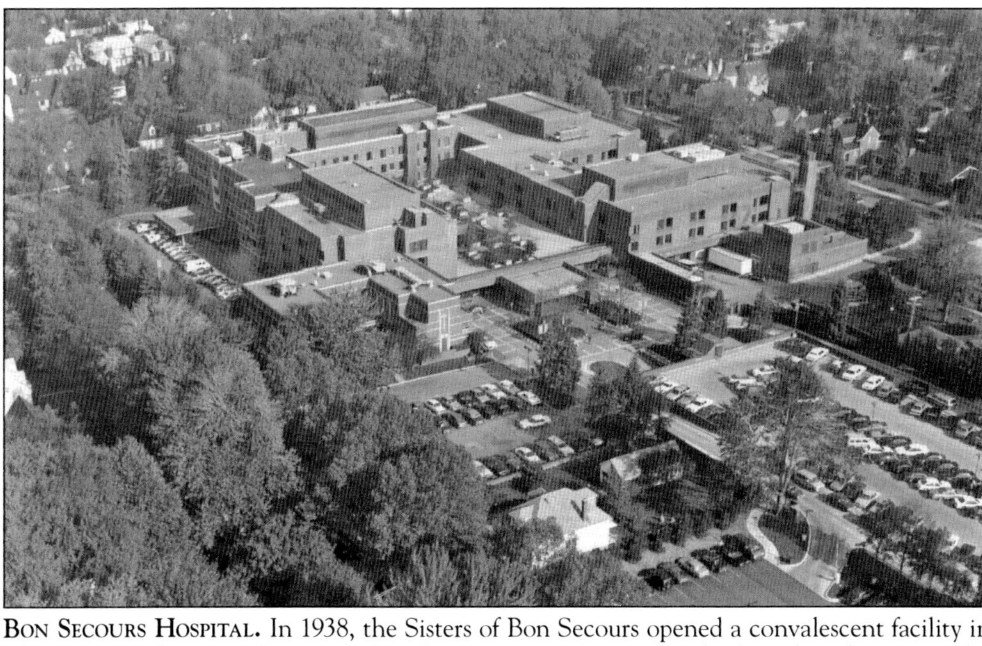

Bon Secours Hospital. In 1938, the Sisters of Bon Secours opened a convalescent facility in a house on Cadieux Road near Kercheval Avenue on property they had purchased in 1924. The need for another hospital in Grosse Pointe was recognized, and the facility became a full-service hospital in 1945. Over the years, the hospital was enlarged and expanded, as can be seen in this aerial photograph from 1975. In 2007, Bon Secours Hospital became part of the Beaumont Health System and was renamed Beaumont Hospital–Grosse Pointe. (Courtesy of the Grosse Pointe Historical Society.)

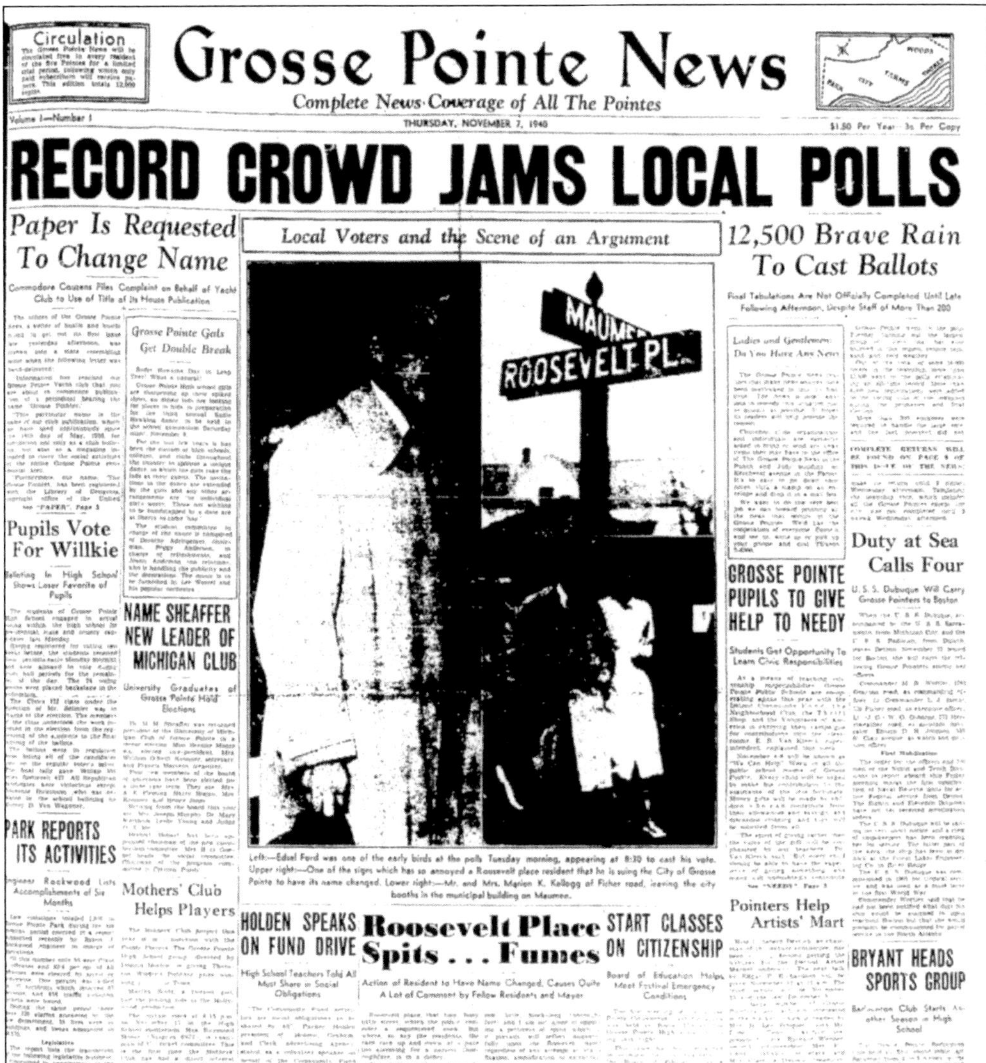
Circulation

Grosse Pointe News

Complete News Coverage of All The Pointes

Volume I—Number 1 THURSDAY, NOVEMBER 7, 1940 $1.50 Per Year—3c Per Copy

RECORD CROWD JAMS LOCAL POLLS

Paper Is Requested To Change Name

Commodore Couzens Files Complaint on Behalf of Yacht Club to Use of Title of Its House Publication

Local Voters and the Scene of an Argument

Left:—Edsel Ford was one of the early birds at the polls Tuesday morning, appearing at 8:30 to cast his vote. Upper right:—One of the signs which has so annoyed a Roosevelt place resident that he is suing the City of Grosse Pointe to have its name changed. Lower right:—Mr. and Mrs. Marion K. Kellogg of Fisher road, leaving the city booths in the municipal building on Maumee.

12,500 Brave Rain To Cast Ballots

Final Tabulations Are Not Officially Completed Until Late Following Afternoon, Despite Staff of More Than 200

Grosse Pointe Gals Get Double Break

Ladies and Gentlemen: Do You Have Any News

Pupils Vote For Willkie

NAME SHEAFFER NEW LEADER OF MICHIGAN CLUB

University Graduates of Grosse Pointe Hold Elections

GROSSE POINTE PUPILS TO GIVE HELP TO NEEDY

Students Get Opportunity To Learn Civic Responsibilities

Duty at Sea Calls Four

U. S. S. Dubuque Will Carry Grosse Pointers to Boston

PARK REPORTS ITS ACTIVITIES

Mothers' Club Helps Players

HOLDEN SPEAKS ON FUND DRIVE

High School Teachers Told All Must Share in Social Obligations

Roosevelt Place Spits . . . Fumes

Action of Resident to Have Name Changed, Causes Quite A Lot of Comment by Fellow Residents and Mayor

START CLASSES ON CITIZENSHIP

Pointers Help Artists' Mart

BRYANT HEADS SPORTS GROUP

ART ASSOCIATIONS TO SPONSOR NEW CLASSES

PARENT-TEACHERS BOOK ADDRESS BY MARSHALL

ONE KILLED, ONE INJURED IN AUTO ACCIDENT HERE

ROTARY CLUB WILL HOLD ANNUAL FEATHER PARTY

MUSKOKA THREESOME CELEBRATES AGAIN

ALGER HOUSE SHOWS NEW ARTIST'S WORK

Grosse Exaggerations

SCOUT LEADERS' COURSE HELD IN DEFER SCHOOL

Grosse Pointe News. With their offices and businesses located in downtown Detroit, many Grosse Pointe Shores residents regularly read the big city's major daily newspapers. For their local news, however, they turned to their local newspaper—the *Grosse Pointe News.* Its first issue, seen here, hit the newsstands on November 7, 1940. For many years, the paper's offices were on Kercheval Avenue. In October 2012, the paper moved to new offices on Mack Avenue, where it continues its fine job of reporting the local news. (Courtesy of the Grosse Pointe Public Library.)

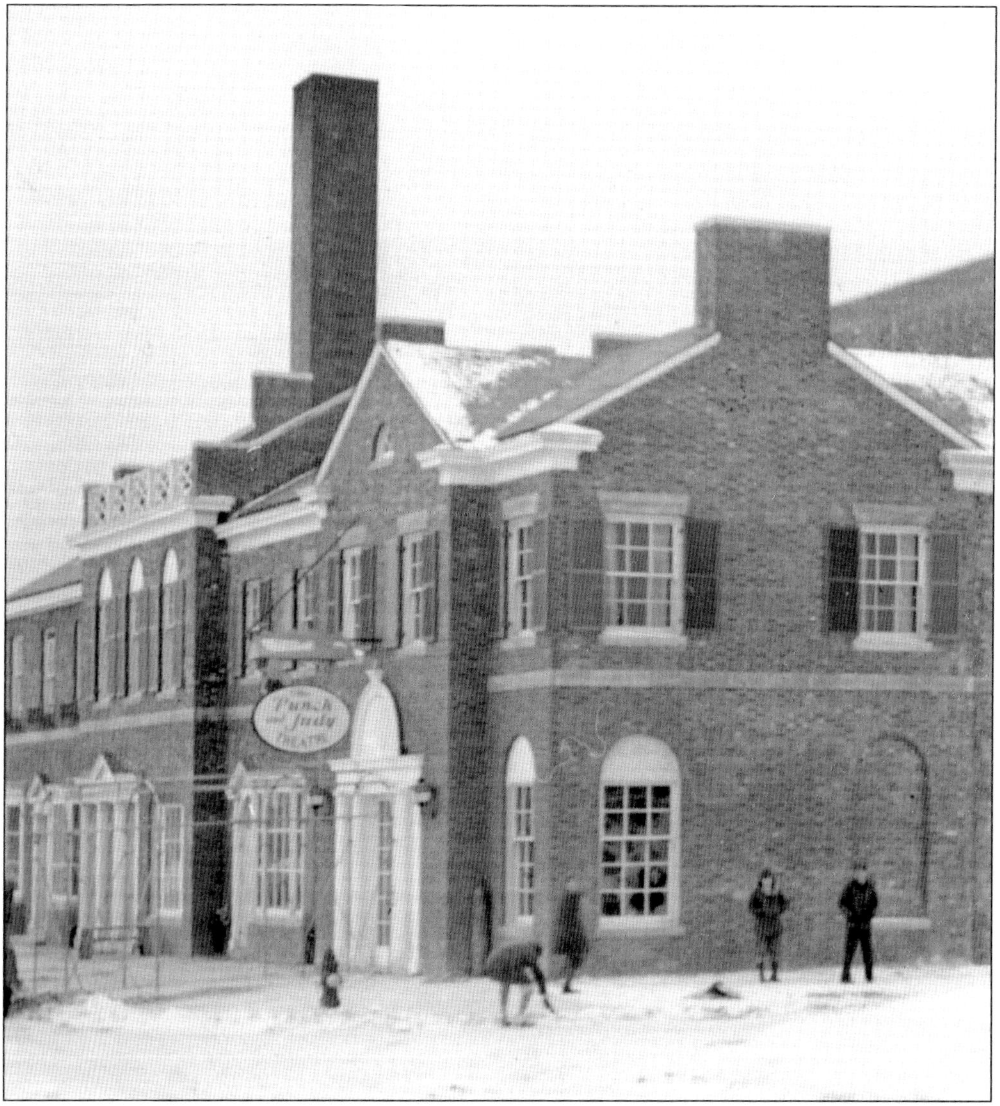

PUNCH AND JUDY THEATER. The Punch and Judy Theater, opened in 1930, was designed by Robert O. Derrick in Colonial Revival style, looking more like an 18th-century Boston manor than a movie house. Located on Kercheval Avenue in Grosse Pointe Farms, the theater seated around 740 and contained an organ and a balcony, which originally had a higher ticket price than the orchestra seats. After it was closed as a movie theater in 1977, the Punch and Judy was almost purchased by a church, which ended up being turned down by the city. Later that same year, plans were made to turn the theater into a venue for live stage shows and concerts. But the city again said no. In 1978, the Punch and Judy turned to repertory films, but it did not last, and the theater closed in 1984. Finally, in 1985, the beloved theater was gutted and converted into offices; the quaint Colonial American exterior remains relatively unaltered. (Courtesy of the Grosse Pointe Historical Society.)

Seven

The Village Becomes a City

During the 1960s and 1970s, the population of the Village of Grosse Pointe Shores grew dramatically. In 1950, the population stood at just over 1,000. By 1960, it had grown to 2,301, and by 1970, it was up to 3,042. As the population changed, so did the structure of the community. This change brought about a desire by residents to further enhance their community. This was seen especially in the formation of the Grosse Pointe Shores Beautification Committee in 1983 and the creation of the nonprofit Grosse Pointe Shores Improvement Foundation in 1984. It was at this time that change also came to the village hall, now known as the Municipal Building. Early in 1980, plans were begun for the complete renovation of the building interior while maintaining the integrity of Albert Kahn's 1915 design. This renovation, which won a variety of architectural awards, was dedicated on September 9, 1984. Further enhancement to the community occurred with the redevelopment of the municipal park and pool followed by the renovation and enlargement of the municipal marina and harbor. While all of these changes were indeed important, the most significant change came on February 24, 2009, when village residents voted to incorporate as a city with a new name, the Village of Grosse Pointe Shores, A Michigan City. This incorporation signified a simplification of governmental structure and the streamlining of municipal operations. Grosse Pointe Shores was the last of the five Grosse Pointe communities to incorporate as a city. This incorporation formally marked the end of the Grosse Pointe Township of Wayne County, formed in 1848, and the end of Lake Township, that small portion of the village that extended into Macomb County. Two years later, in the summer of 2011, the residents celebrated the 100th anniversary of their community. The festivities lasted for three days in July with fireworks, a concert by the Detroit Symphony Orchestra on the Ford House grounds, an ice cream social with birthday cake in Osius Park, and a grand parade down Lake Shore Road.

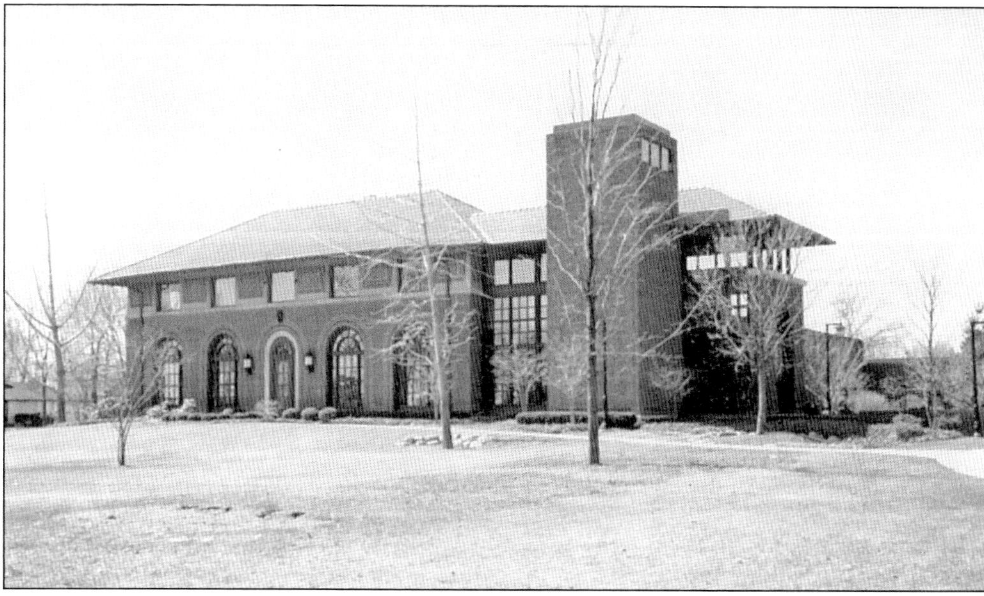

"NEW" MUNICIPAL BUILDING. By the early 1980s, it had become obvious that the Municipal Building was badly in need of repairs. The decision was made to completely renovate the interior, build an addition for an elevator, and expand the garage area for public safely vehicles. The work was completed in the fall of 1984, and the village received a number of awards for this work while preserving the integrity of the exterior of the original Albert Kahn–designed building. (Courtesy of Albert Kahn Associates.)

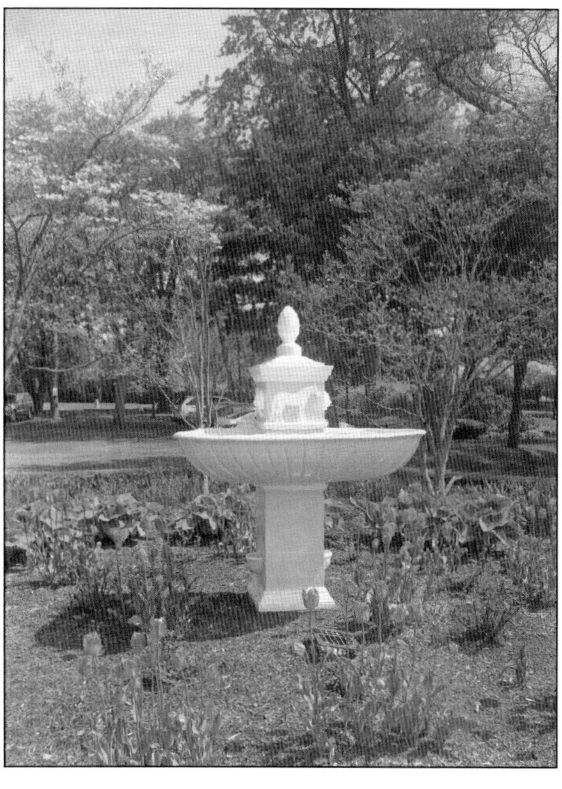

"NEW" FOUNTAIN. The renovation of the village hall in 1984 included moving the old horse and dog fountain from Osius Park to a newly landscaped area at the building's main entrance. Eventually, however, the fountain began to show its age. In honor of the fountain's 100th anniversary in 2014, it was completely refurbished and painted the original pale blue, and now proudly stands as a true village landmark. (Courtesy of the Village of Grosse Pointe Shores.)

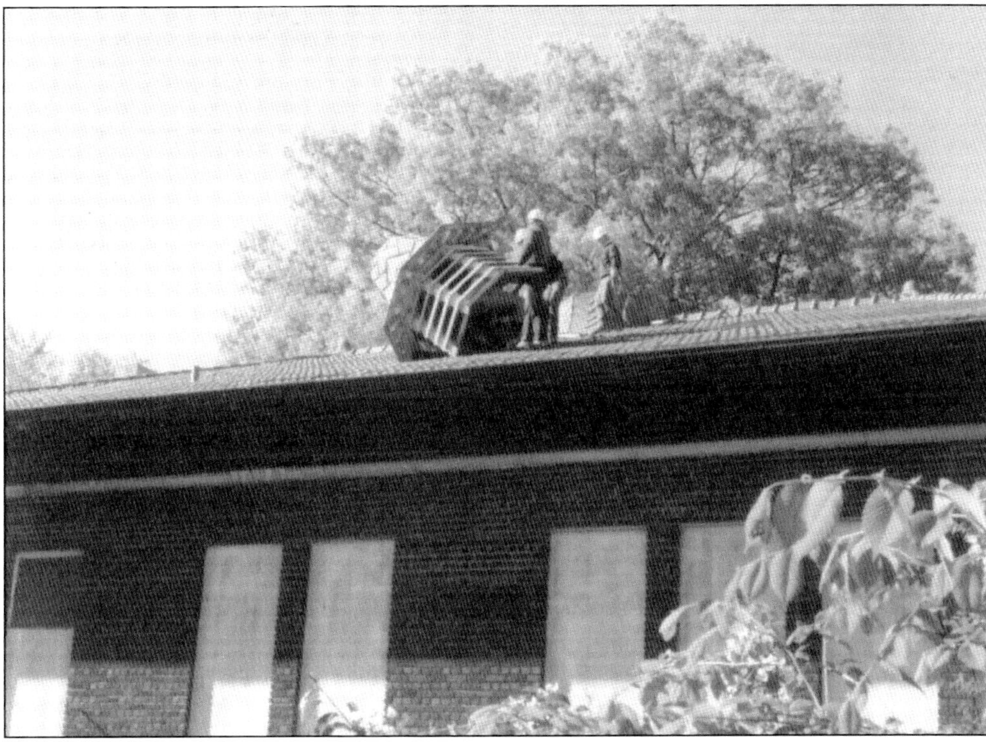

School Demolition. The Vernier School, vacant for several years, was badly in need of restoration. The village polled its citizens, and almost two thirds responded that it should be demolished rather than spend the $1.5 to $2 million to restore it, and so the old schoolhouse was torn down in 1994. (Courtesy of the Grosse Pointe Historical Society.)

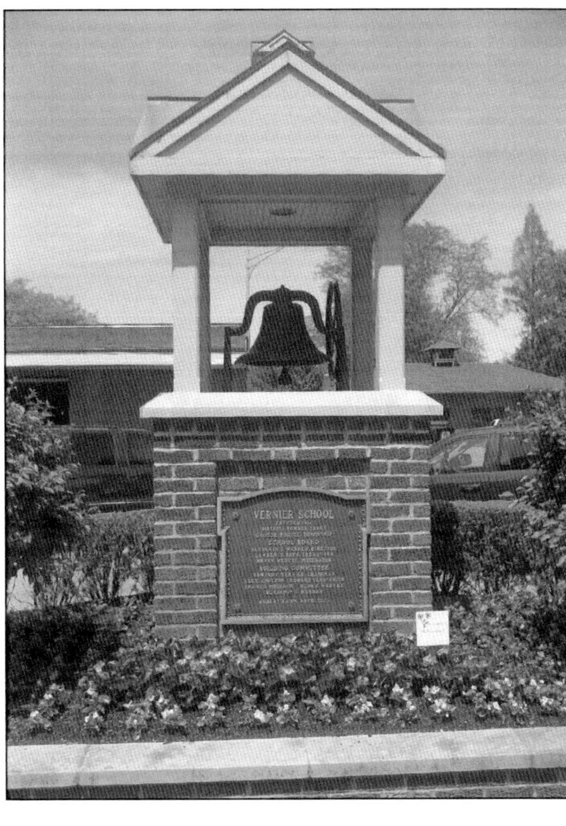

School Bell. Although demolished in 1994, there are remaining vestiges of the old Vernier School. The school's bell was salvaged and is on display with an accompanying plaque on the building's former site on Vernier Road adjacent to the Municipal Building. Also, bricks from the school adorn the welcome signs to the village. (Courtesy of the Village of Grosse Pointe Shores.)

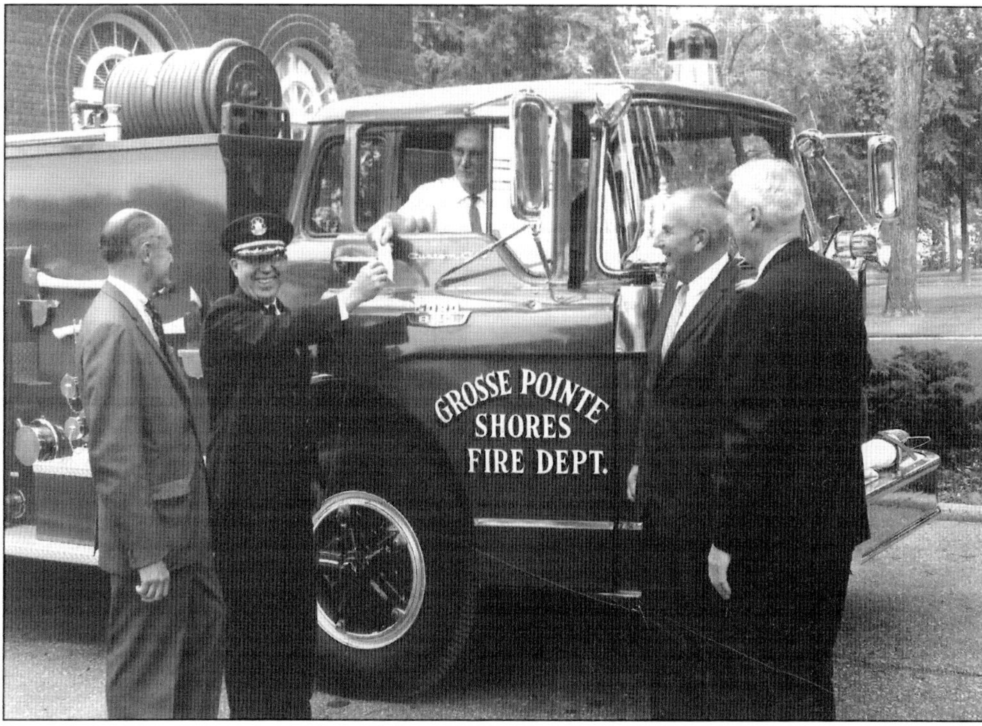

NEW FIRE TRUCKS. In 1962, the village purchased two new fire trucks to replace the vintage 1920s Seagram Pumper fire truck that had served the community so well. These new fire trucks required the installation of new doors at the Municipal Building garage. Upon its retirement, the old truck was placed on display at The Henry Ford Museum in Dearborn. (Courtesy of the Village of Grosse Pointe Shores.)

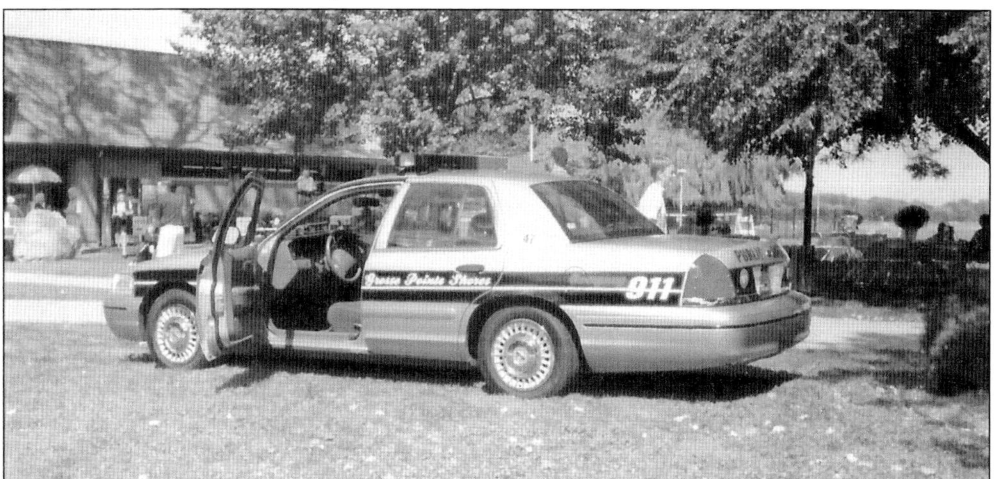

POLICE CAR. The Village of Grosse Pointe Shores Department of Public Safety, established in 1911, is the oldest public safety department in the nation. The Municipal Building has always been the home of the department and remains so to this day. Originally, the department of public safety was housed on the second floor with an apartment for firemen. When the building was remodeled in 1984, public safety offices were moved to the first floor. (Courtesy of the Village of Grosse Pointe Shores.)

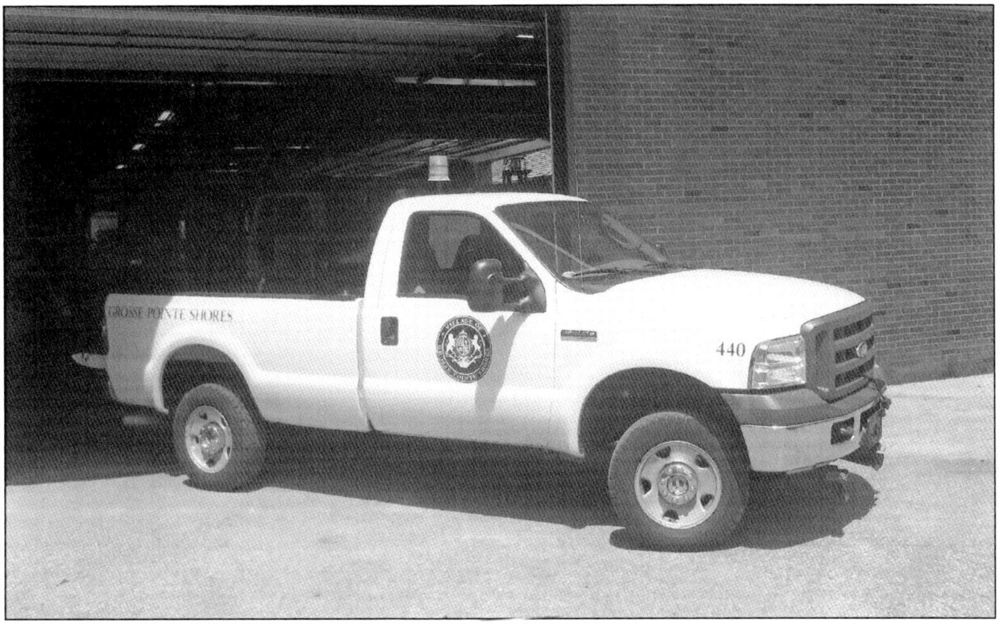

DEPARTMENT OF PUBLIC WORKS. The Village of Grosse Pointe Shores Department of Public Works was established in 1911 and has continued to care for the village. The department is responsible for rubbish pickup; maintenance of village grounds, buildings, water mains, and sewers; and maintaining the village fleet, such as the truck seen here at the municipal garage located behind the Municipal Building. (Courtesy of the Village of Grosse Pointe Shores.)

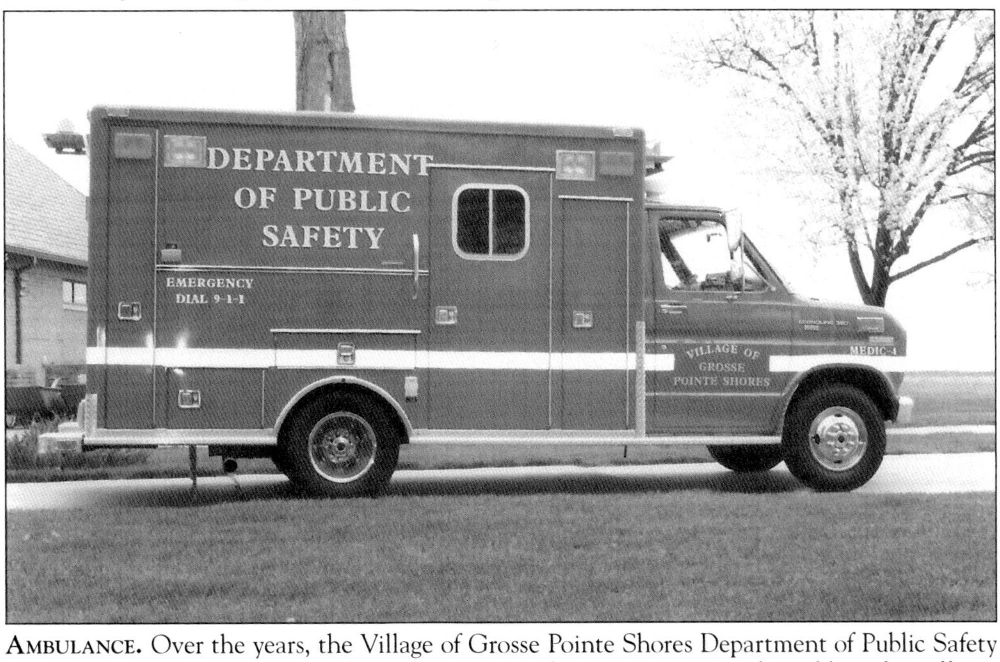

AMBULANCE. Over the years, the Village of Grosse Pointe Shores Department of Public Safety continued to improve and upgrade its equipment and training. In 2001, the public safety officers were the first triple-trained (police/fire/paramedic) officers in the nation. By 2011, the department included 17 officers, 6 scout cars, 2 fire trucks, a motorcycle and patrol bike, and this ambulance. (Courtesy of the Village of Grosse Pointe Shores.)

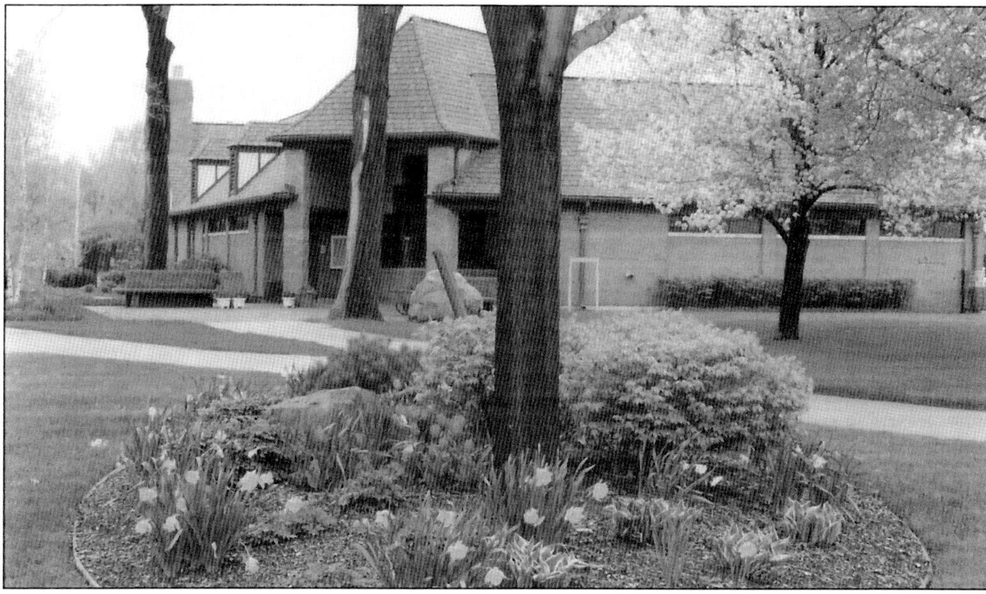

The Bathhouse. Following its expansion and renaming in 1932, a range of improvements were made to Osius Park. To better coordinate the work and to plan for future enhancements, the decision was made in 2000 to prepare a long-range park plan. In 2001, Albert Kahn Associates were selected to prepare a park master plan. This plan, which is still being updated and followed to this day, included the construction of this new bathhouse. (Courtesy of the Village of Grosse Pointe Shores.)

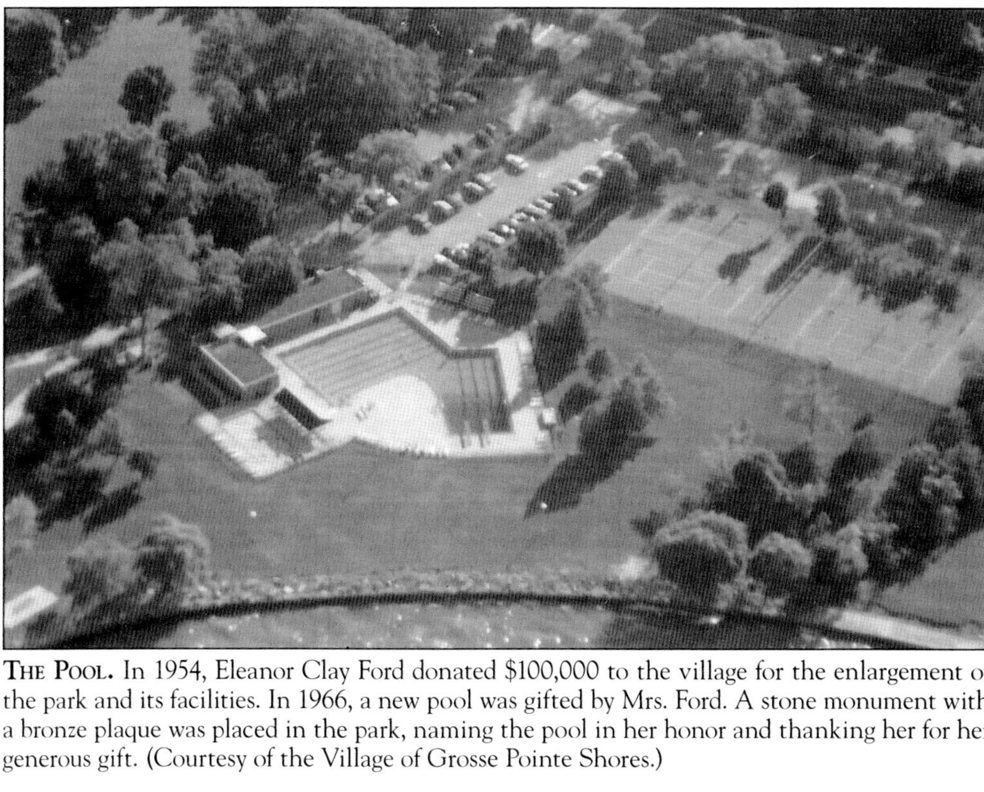

The Pool. In 1954, Eleanor Clay Ford donated $100,000 to the village for the enlargement of the park and its facilities. In 1966, a new pool was gifted by Mrs. Ford. A stone monument with a bronze plaque was placed in the park, naming the pool in her honor and thanking her for her generous gift. (Courtesy of the Village of Grosse Pointe Shores.)

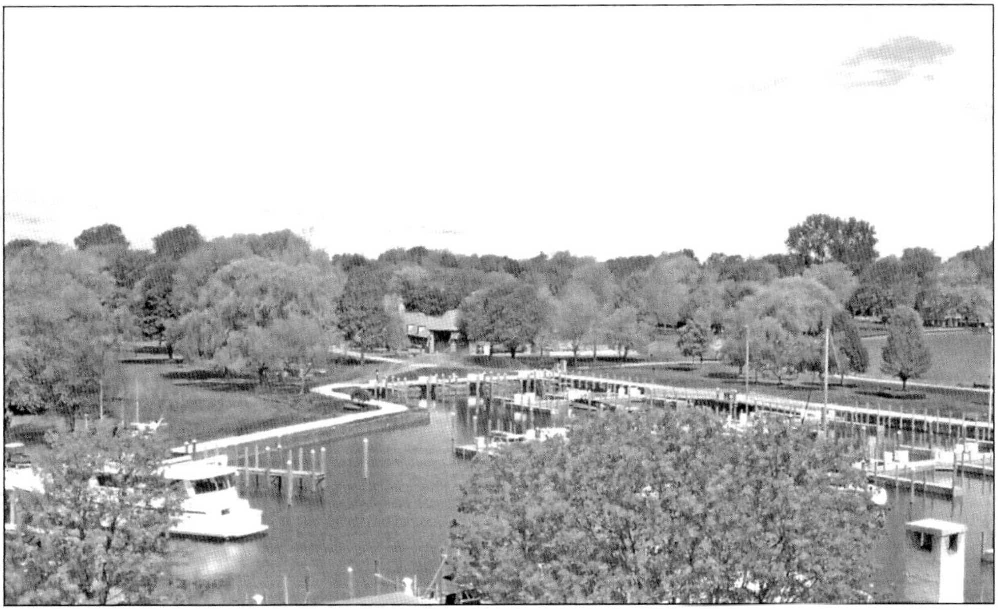

Marina Harbor. Renovations to the Village Marina at Osius Park were begun in October 2007 and were completed in April the following year in time for the opening of the 2008 boating season. The new harbor was expanded to 137 boat wells with floating docks and included new electrical and water service, new dock boxes, new lighting, and a new walkway to the outer harbor. (Courtesy of the Village of Grosse Pointe Shores.)

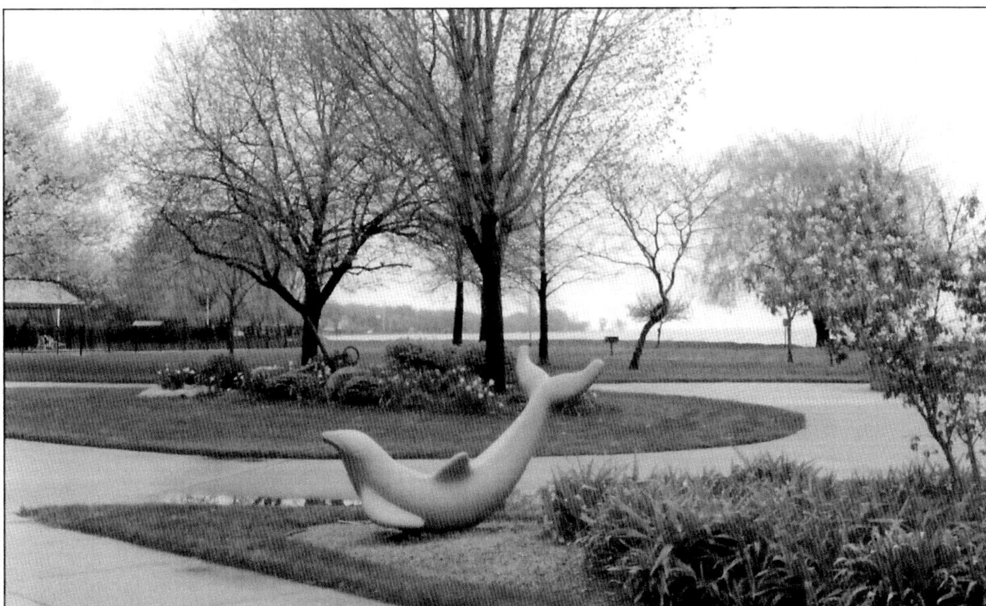

The Park Today. Today, George Osius Park has grown to more than eight acres. In addition to the new bathhouse, pool, and updated marina, park amenities include tennis courts, volleyball pit, basketball courts, playscapes, wading pool, pavilion, splash pad, extensive picnic areas, and concession stand. The park landscaping is stunningly attractive and impeccably maintained. (Courtesy of the Village of Grosse Pointe Shores.)

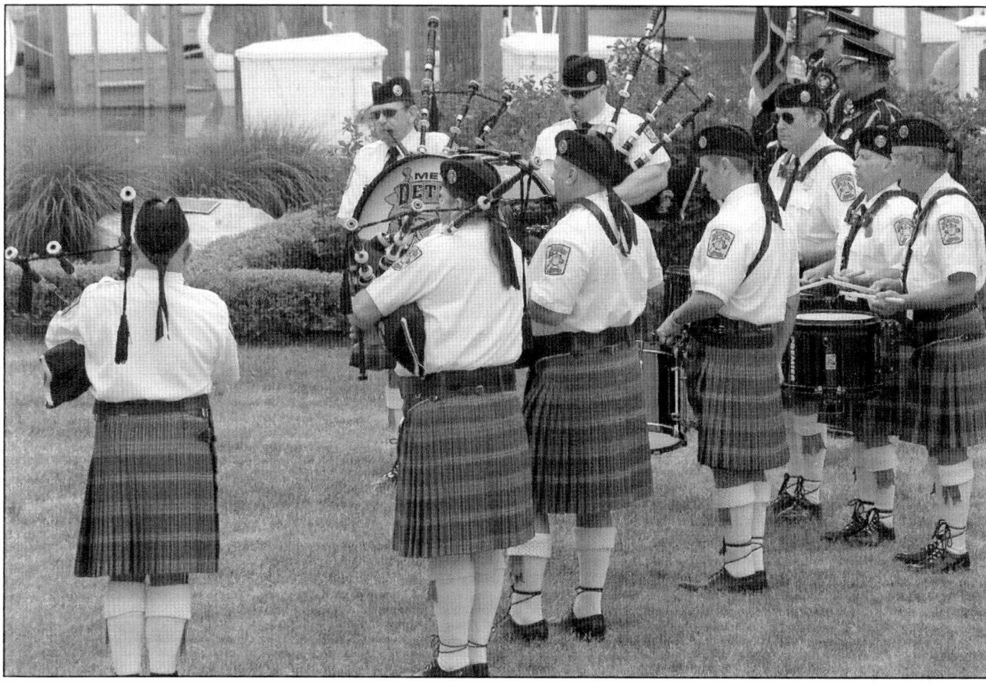

Centennial Ceremony at Osius Park and Centennial Parade. In the summer of 2011, the residents of the Village of Grosse Pointe Shores joined together to celebrate the 100th anniversary of their community. The festivities lasted for three days in July beginning with A Night at The Ford House, which included an evening reception, concert by the Detroit Symphony Orchestra, and fireworks display on the grounds of The Ford House. The next day, A Look Back in Time, held at Schroeder Park behind the village hall, included the dedication and ribbon cutting for the Schroeder Field House, ice cream sundaes, and buggy and wagon decorating for the children. (Both, courtesy of the Village of Grosse Pointe Shores.)

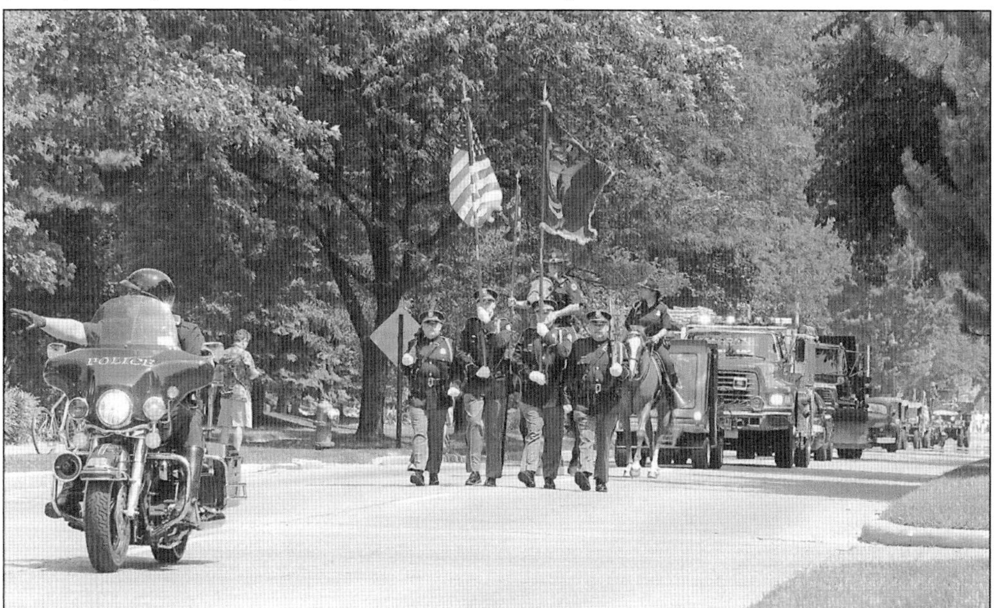

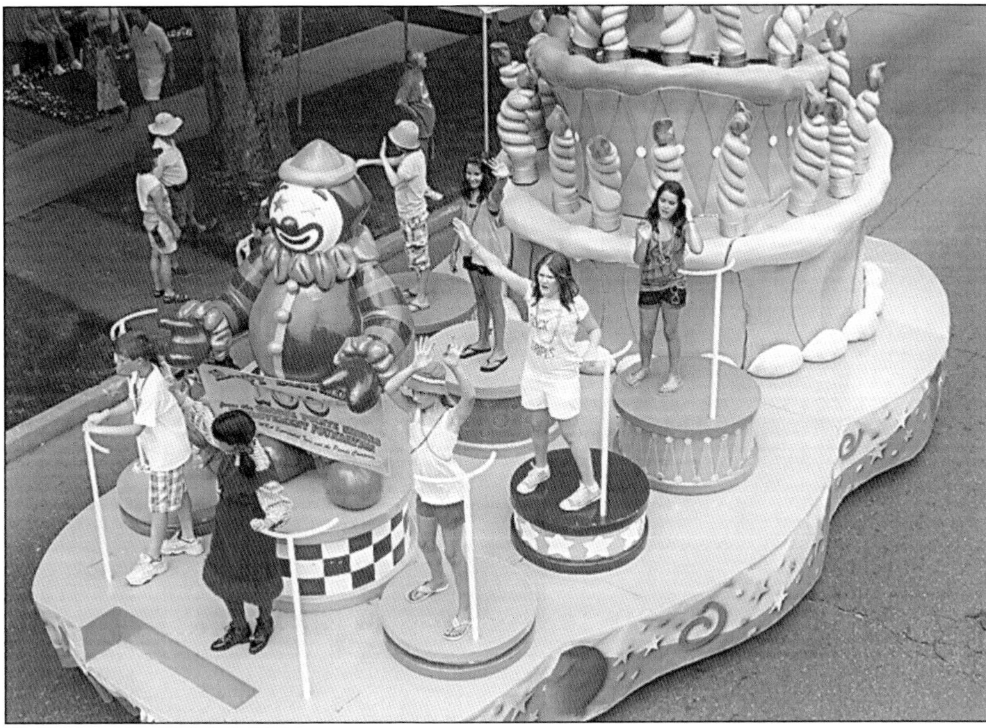

CENTENNIAL FLOAT AND SINGING THE NATIONAL ANTHEM. The final day of the celebration began with the Happy 100 Years Centennial Parade. The parade began on the grounds of The Ford House and continued down Lake Shore Road to Osius Park. Following the parade, the festivities continued at the park with a flag raising, singing of the national anthem, and presentation ceremony to village veterans. Then there was the viewing of a time capsule and village history display, the singing of "Happy Birthday" with birthday cake, a vintage auto display, a variety of family events and pool games, and finally, the serving of Little Caesers pizza and National Coney Island hot dogs. (Both, courtesy of the Village of Grosse Pointe Shores.)

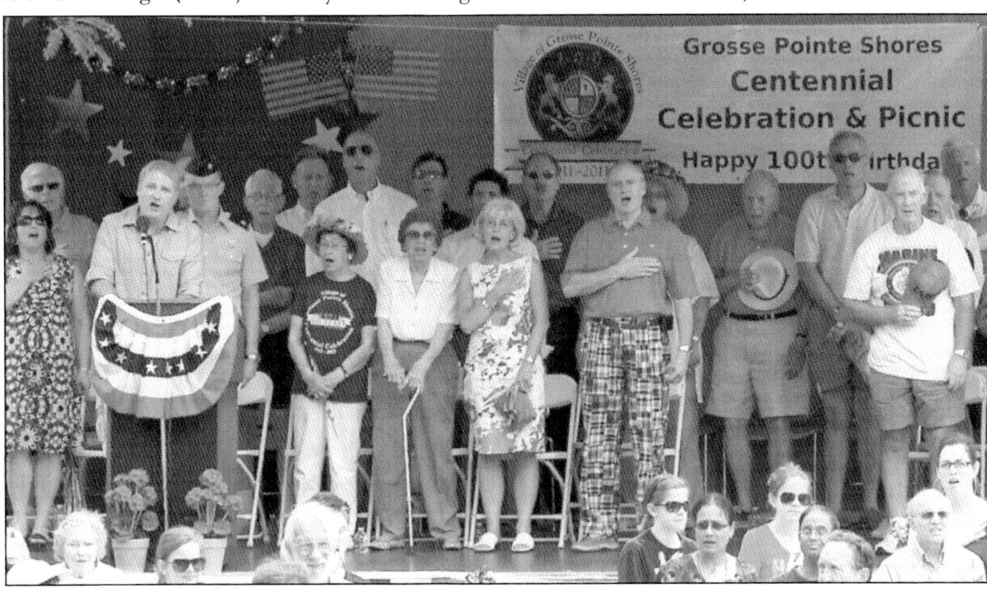

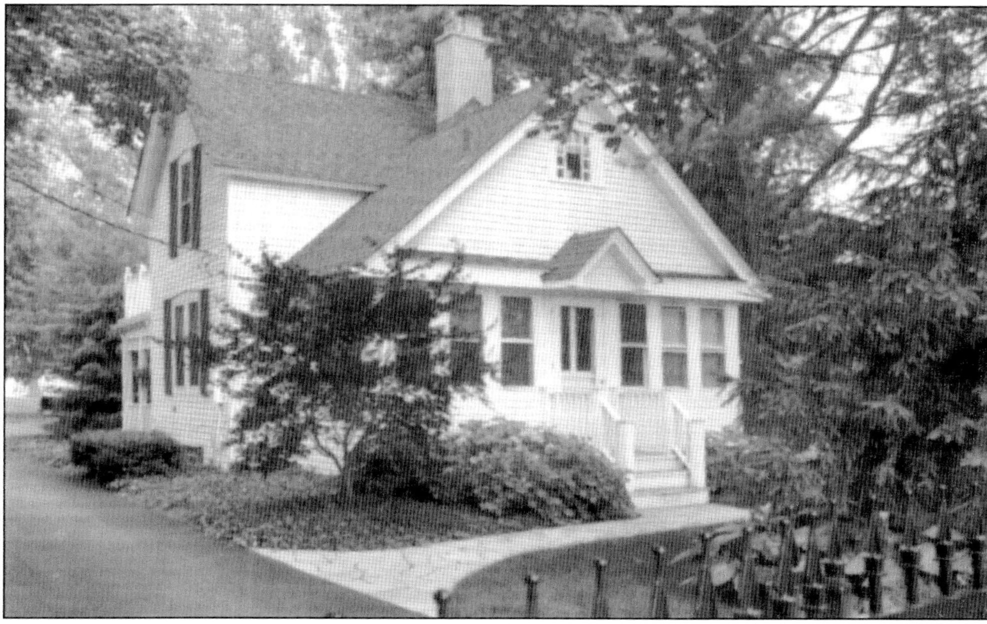

830 Lake Shore Road and 888 Lake Shore Road. The centennial celebration of the Village of Grosse Pointe Shores included a formal recognition of homes in the village that were built before 1911. In all, more than a dozen of these homes were honored. Four of them are shown on this page and the following page. These beautiful homes are still standing, but what was life like here 100 years ago? Lake Shore Road was unpaved. To reach downtown Detroit, a village resident had to travel by either horse and buggy, boat, interurban, or possibly by motorcar. The community was still largely one of rural farms, a handful of summer cottages, and a few permanent year-round houses. (Both, courtesy of the Village of Grosse Pointe Shores.)

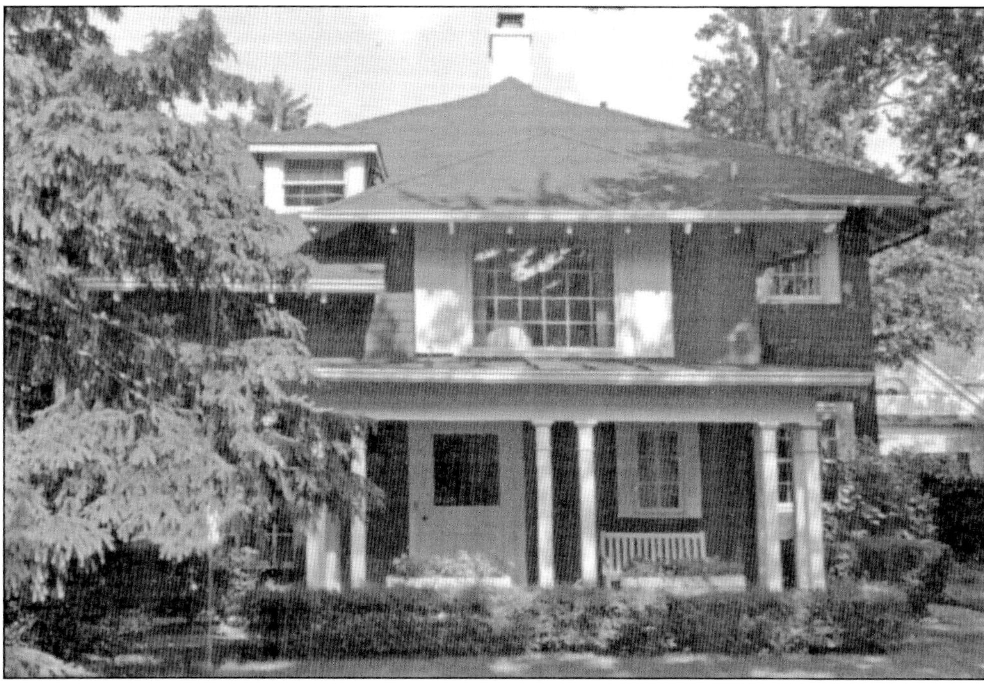

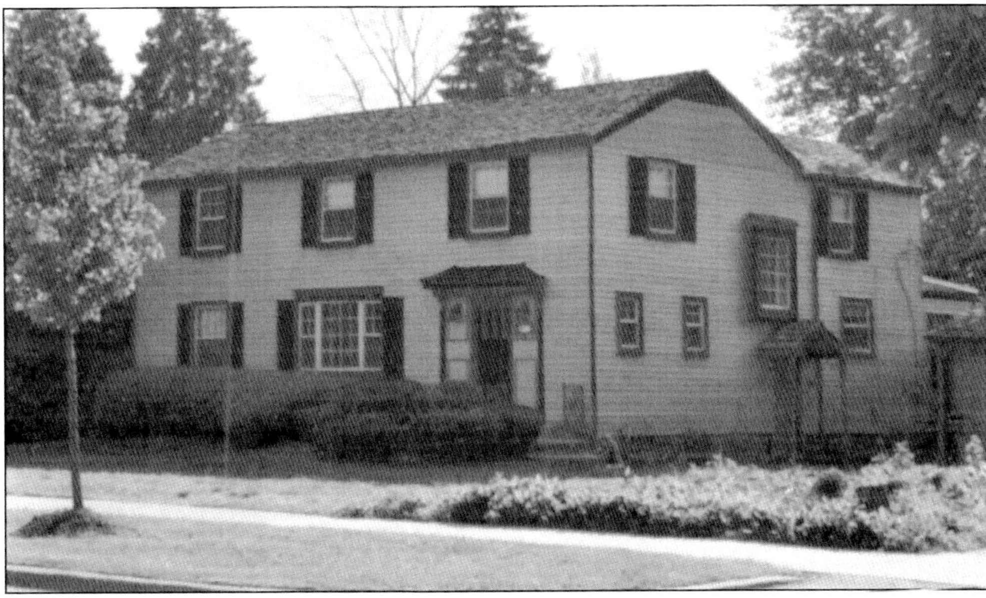

971 Lake Shore Road and 980 Lake Shore Road. In 1911, Chase S. Osborn was governor of Michigan and William B. Thompson was mayor of Detroit. The average annual income of a working man was $983. The median price of a new home was $2,625. The average price of a new automobile was $1,130. A quart of milk cost 8¢. A loaf of bread was 5¢. A first-class postage stamp cost 2¢. In Detroit, the Detroit College was reorganized as the University of Detroit, Chevrolet Motor Company was founded, the Detroit Zoological Society was formed, Herman Kiefer Hospital for Infectious Diseases opened, headlights and horns became standard equipment on the Model T, and Ty Cobb won his second American League batting title. Also in 1911, George Osius was elected the first president of the newly established Village of Grosse Pointe Shores. (Both, courtesy of the Village of Grosse Pointe Shores.)

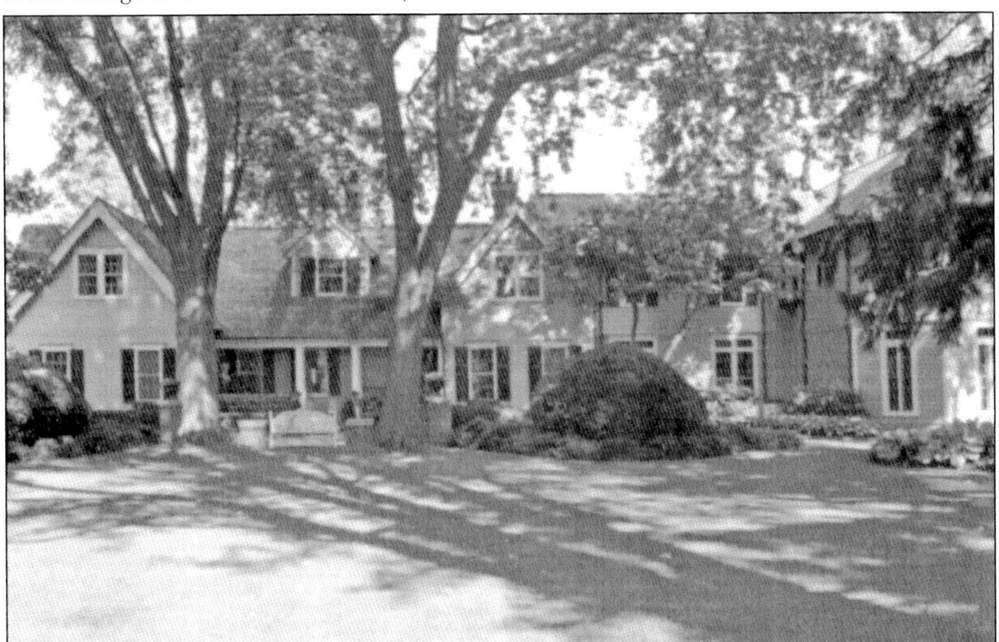

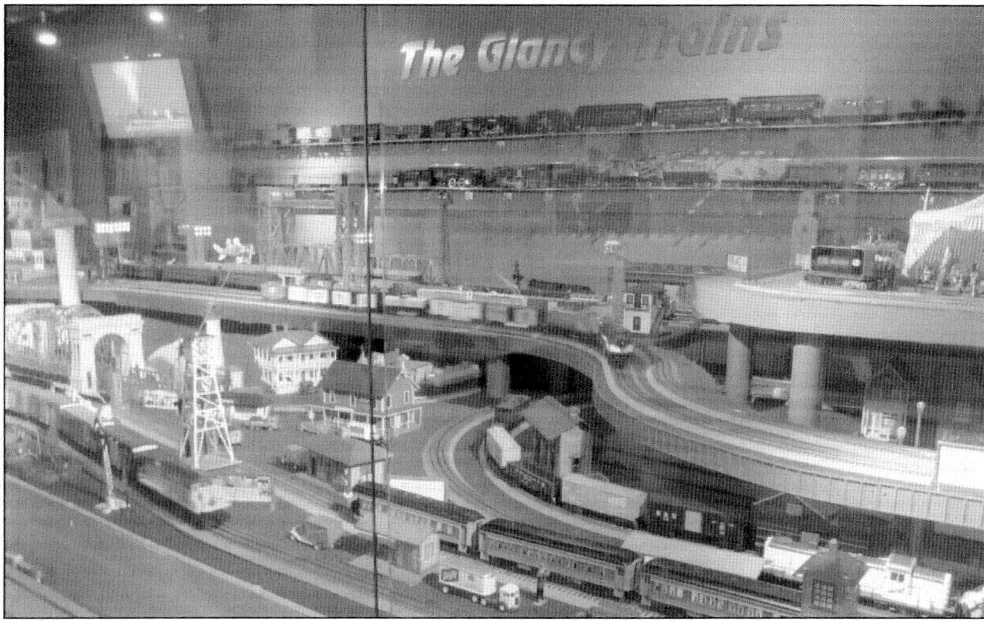

The Glancy Trains. These trains are from the collection of Alfred R. Glancy Jr., a real estate financier. During the 1950s and 1960s, Glancy enjoyed hosting train parties for friends, neighbors, schoolchildren, and scout groups each holiday season at his home in the Village of Grosse Pointe Shores. After his death in 1973, the Glancy family donated his collection to the Detroit Historical Museum, where it is now on permanent display. (Courtesy of the Detroit Historical Society.)

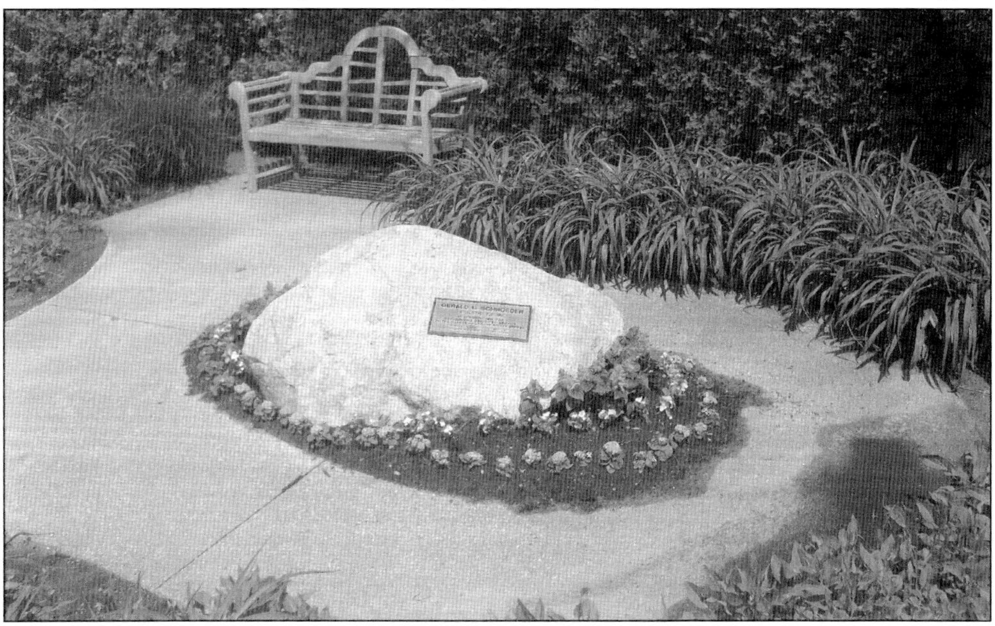

Schroeder Park. On October 21, 1990, the little league baseball diamond and youth soccer field at Ford Park, directly behind the village hall, were officially named the Gerald C. Schroeder Athletic Fields and dedicated to former mayor Schroeder for his more than 35 years of service to the village. In 2011, as part of the centennial celebration, the new Schroeder Field House at the park was formally dedicated. (Courtesy of the Village of Grosse Pointe Shores.)

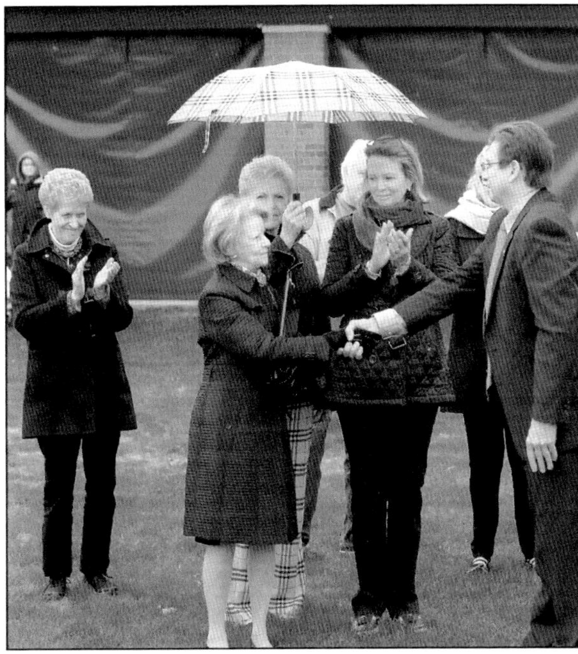

Two Residents Remembered. The Village of Grosse Pointe Shores is indeed a unique community. One of its special features is that it was home to not one, but two, National Football League team owners, William Clay Ford Sr. of the Detroit Lions, and Ralph C. Wilson Jr. of the Buffalo Bills. Both died in 2014, and in remembrance of these two fine gentlemen, memorial trees were planted in Osius Park. Seen here is village mayor Ted Kedzierski (right) recognizing Martha Ford (front center) and Mary Wilson (second from right). To the far left is Helen Bai, chair of the Village Beautification Committee. Holding the umbrella is Mary Matuja, Village Beautification Committee member. (Courtesy of the Village of Grosse Pointe Shores.)

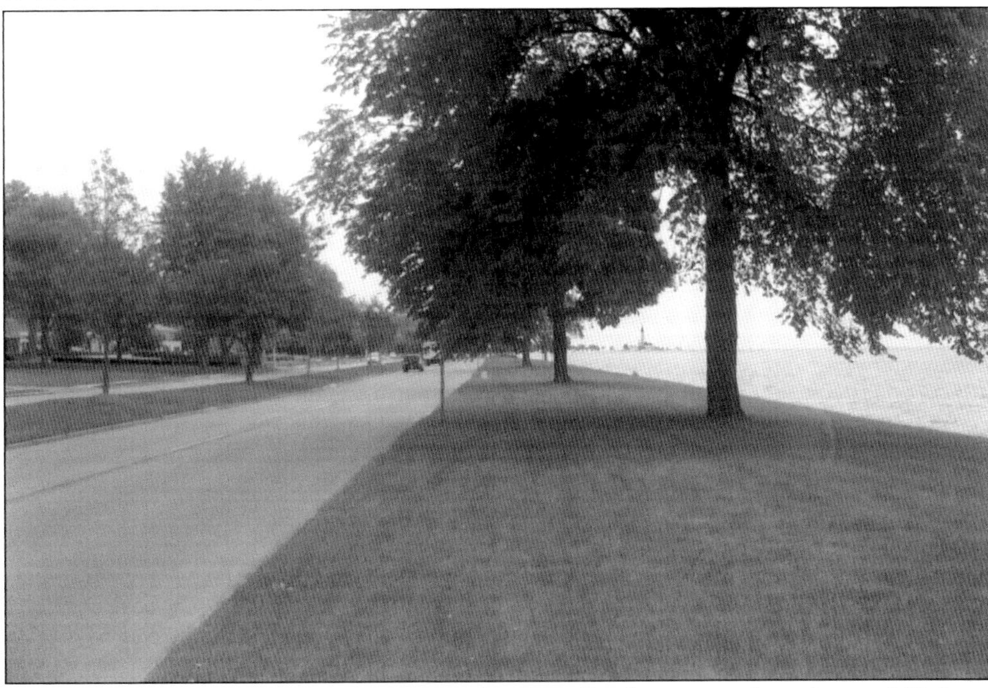

Picturesque Lake Shore Road. In 1911, Lake Shore Road was a two-lane dirt road. Today, it is a beautifully landscaped four-lane divided paved road. Several years ago, a survey of the most picturesque drives in Michigan included this stretch of Lake Shore Road. A view of this road, with the Grosse Pointe Yacht Club in the distance, was shown as a background to the rolling credits at the end of the movie *Gran Torino*. Lake Shore Road, with its wonderful view of Lake St. Clair, is the view that to many represents the Village of Grosse Pointe Shores. (Courtesy of the Village of Grosse Pointe Shores.)

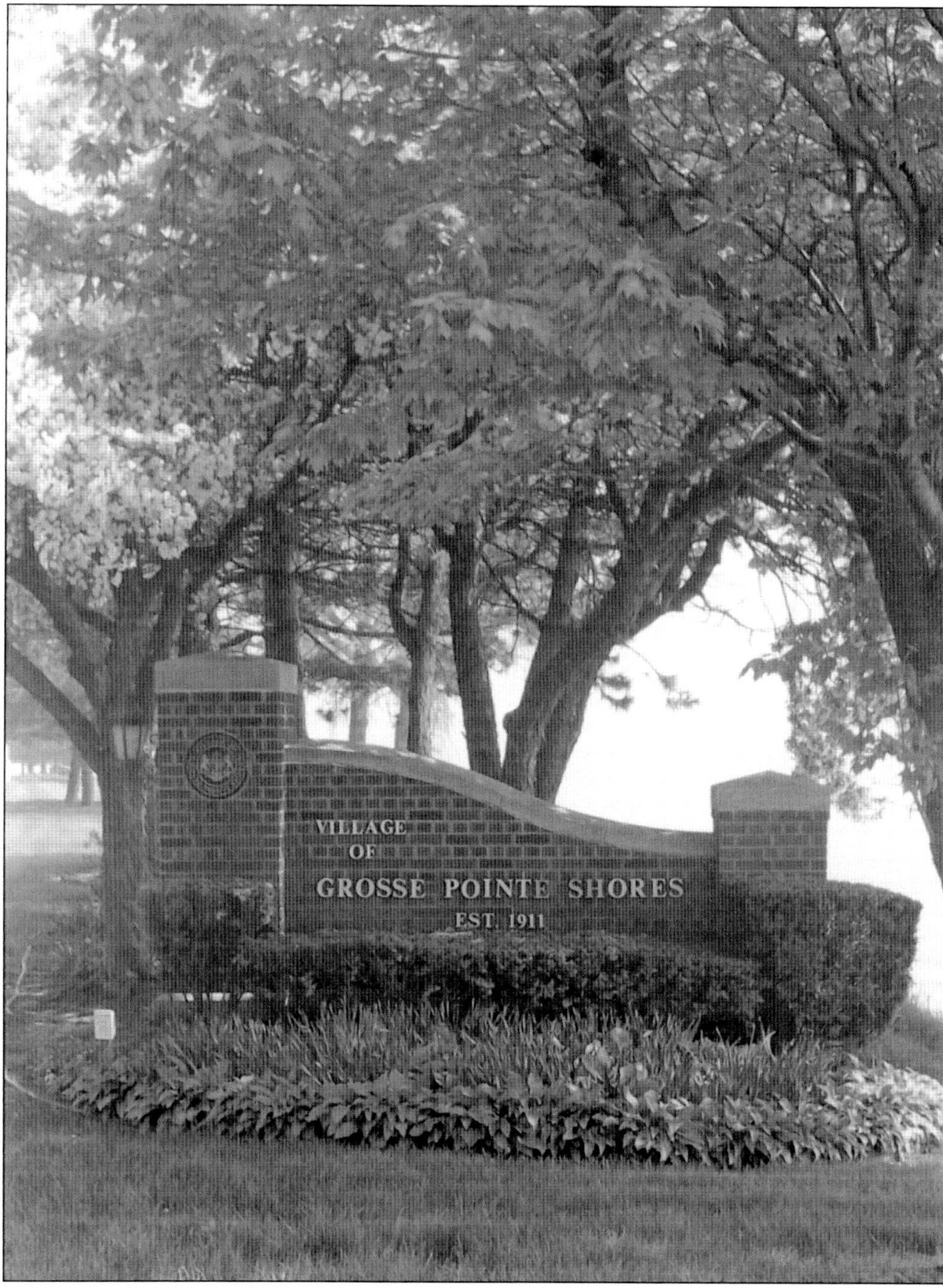

The Village Becomes A City. On February 24, 2009, village residents voted to incorporate as a city with a new name, the Village of Grosse Pointe Shores, A Michigan City. This incorporation brought a simplification of government structure and a streamlining of municipal operation. Grosse Pointe Shores was the last of the five Grosse Pointe communities to incorporate as a city, formally marking the end of Grosse Pointe Township in Wayne County, formed in 1848, and the end of Lake Township, formed in 1911. Although small in size, the village has a long and fascinating history. (Courtesy of the Village of Grosse Pointe Shores.)

Bibliography

Aliotta, Ann Marie, and Suzy Berschback. *Then & Now: Grosse Pointe*. Charleston, SC: Arcadia Publishing, 2007.

Bridenstine, James A. *Edsel & Eleanor Ford House*. Grosse Pointe Shores, MI: Edsel & Eleanor Ford House, 1988.

Ferry, W. Hawkins. *Buildings of Detroit: A History*. Rev. ed. Detroit: Wayne State University Press, 1980. Reissued with new introduction, 2012.

————. *The Mansions of Grosse Pointe: A Suburb in Good Taste*. Detroit: Michigan Society of Architects, 1956.

Hall, Theodore P., and Silas Farmer. *Grosse Pointe on Lake Sainte Claire*. Detroit: Gale Research Co., 1974. Reprint of 1886 edition.

Kahn, Albert. *The Legacy of Albert Kahn/edited by W. Hawkins Ferry*. Detroit: Wayne State University Press, 1987.

Morris, Robert R. *Gorsse Pointe Yacht Club: A Beacon of Tradition for 75 Years, 1929–2004*. Marengo, IL: Walsworth Publishing Co., 2004.

Socia, Madeline, and Suzy Berschback. *Grosse Pointe, 1880–1930*. Charleston, SC: Arcadia Publishing, 2001.

WPA Federal Writers' Project. *The Grosse Pointe Guide*. Detroit: Detroit Field Office, 1936.

Woodford, Arthur M. *This Is Detroit, 1701–2001*. Detroit: Wayne State University Press, 2001.

————. *Tonnancour; Life in Grosse Pointe and Along the Shores of Lake St. Clair*. Detroit: Omnigraphics Inc., vol. I, 1994, vol. II, 1997.